Integrating College Study Skills

Reasoning in Reading, Listening, and Writing

Integrating
College Study Skills
Reasoning
in Reading, Listening, and Writing
Third Edition

Peter Elias Sotiriou
Los Angeles City College

Wadsworth Publishing Company
A Division of Wadsworth, Inc.

Belmont, California

English Editor: Angela Gantner
Editorial Assistant: Tricia Schumacher
Production: Del Mar Associates
Print Buyer: Barbara Britton
Designer: Joe di Chiarro
Copy Editor: Rebecca Smith
Cover Design: John Odam
Cover Photograph: Renaud Granel/Index Stock Photography
Compositor: Thompson Type
Printer: R. R. Donnelley & Sons Company

This book is printed on acid-free paper that meets
Environmental Protection Agency standards for recycled
paper.

2 3 4 5 6 7 8 9 10 — 96 95 94 93

Library of Congress Cataloging-in-Publication Data

Sotiriou, Peter Elias.
    Integrating college study skills : reasoning in
reading, listening, and writing / Peter Elias
Sotiriou. — 3rd ed.
      p. cm.
    Includes index.
    ISBN 0-534-17892-8 (acid-free paper)
    1. Study, Method of.   I. Title.
LB2395.S597   1992
378.1'702812 — dc20   91-47685
                          CIP

Contents in Brief

Contents

Part Two: Basic Reading, Listening, and Writing Skills 25

Chapter 11   Mapping and the Cornell Note-taking System   203

Part Four: The Library, Study Skills Systems, and Test-Taking Strategies   215

Chapter 12   Library Basics   217

Chapter 13   The SQ3R Study System   225

Preface

In this third edition of *Integrating College Study Skills*, I have attempted to refine even further what I accomplished in the second edition and to listen to what the reviewers had to say about it. First and foremost, many users have asked for more exercises using material commonly taught in college. So you will see that I have rewritten all of the exercises in Chapters 3–7 and in Chapter 10. Students will be reading about environmental studies, economics, sociology, philosophy, music history, and consumer studies as they complete exercises reinforcing various study skills. They will also be asked to assess what they have learned in each chapter, apart from what they have learned about study skills. I have also expanded the use of the Cornell note-taking system in Parts Three, Four, and Five in answer to those reviewers who successfully use this system in their courses and want it incorporated into more of the exercises in the textbook. I have also included a chapter on the library (Chapter 12) for students and teachers who asked for an introduction to library research in college. Finally, I have included a complete textbook chapter in Part Five so students can read and study textbook material that is exactly like what they will be reading and studying in their content courses. Throughout the third edition, I have revised my introductions to reflect current reading and writing theory and have replaced dated exercises with material that is more recent. Well over half the exercises have been replaced.

What I have kept from the first and second editions is the textbook's careful sequencing and its challenging, college-level material. I still find the sequence of chapters from "Locating the Main Idea" to "Applying SQ3R to Textbooks" to be sound pedagogy. The only change I have made is to move "Summarizing and Paraphrasing" (Chapter 6), before "Reading and Listening for Inferences" (Chapter 7) and "Reading Graphs and Tables" (Chapter 8), which is now the last chapter in Part Two. Also, I have retained the sequenced progression of exercises in each chapter, so that each exercise is more challenging than the previous one. Almost every chapter ends with a longer textbook selection. The last selection in Part Five, in fact, asks students to respond entirely in short-essay and extended-essay answers to a complete textbook chapter.

I hope this third edition will even more effectively achieve what I set out to do in the first edition: to make students better readers, listeners, and writers of college material and to make them aware of how similar and interconnected reading, listening, and writing are. *Integrating College Study Skills*, 3rd edition, has become a more challenging textbook because students and teachers are asking more challenging questions about how best to prepare for college.

How to Use This Book

You have no doubt come to a study skills course for several reasons. For one, you probably need to upgrade your textbook reading skills. Two, you may want to improve your note-taking skills to capture the key points your instructors make. And three, you likely want to improve your test-taking skills. If you complete the exercises in this textbook, you will become a more successful college student — more efficient in reading, note-taking, and taking exams.

How This Book Is Organized

Before you begin to do the exercises in this textbook, you need to know how it is put together. The first part is called "Skills for Beginning Your College Career." Here, you will learn about the basic survival skills that college students need to know: how to use your college's counseling services, when and what to study, how much time to devote to your studies, and other equally important skills. This first part will head your college career in the right direction.

The next part of the textbook is the longest, dealing with the essential reading, listening, and writing skills you will need to master. In this part, "Basic Reading, Listening, and Writing Skills," you will learn several key reasoning skills. You will be shown how to locate the main idea, how to identify and use details, and how to summarize and paraphrase. You will also learn how to read and listen for inferences and how to read graphs and tables. Throughout this part, you will see how these skills apply to reading, listening, and writing. This is a unique feature of *Integrating College Study Skills*. As the title suggests, you will learn to integrate each study skill into the three activities of reading, listening, and writing. Also, in this part you will be introduced to material from college subjects. In Chapters 3–7 and in Chapter 10, the exercises for each chapter focus on one college subject.

In Part Three, "Lecture and Study Notes," you will be using the skills learned in the previous part to improve your note-taking skills. You will learn how to condense information and use abbreviations. You will also be introduced to the Cornell note-taking system, which will help you remember your notes, and to mapping, which is a visual way of taking notes that is especially helpful when you want to tie lots of material together.

In Part Four, "The Library, Study Skills Systems, and Test-Taking Strategies," you will be given guidelines for using your college library and for taking various kinds of tests: objective, essay, and math or science. Most importantly, in this part you will learn about the SQ3R study system, a successful method for learning and remembering what you read from textbooks.

Finally, in Part Five, "Practice in Applying SQ3R," you will use the SQ3R method and all the previous skills you have learned to read and understand three textbook excerpts and one entire textbook chapter.

How to Use This Textbook

Integrating College Study Skills follows a similar format throughout. Each chapter is divided into two parts: an explanation of skills and exercises that allow you to apply these skills. Follow these steps as you work through each chapter:

1. Read the introductory section carefully. The information presented in this section will give you the skills necessary to complete the exercises.

2. Before you begin an exercise, read the directions carefully. Know what you have to do before you begin.

3. Record your answers in the answer box that accompanies most exercises.

4. After you complete the exercise, check your answers. You will find the answers to most odd-numbered exercises at the end of the book. Your instructor will provide the answers to the even-numbered exercises. You will also need to consult your instructor for the correct answers to all exercises involving paragraph writing and to many short-answer essay questions. Finally, your instructor will provide all of the answers for the examinations that follow the study readings in Part Five.

5. Follow the directions for scoring each exercise. Compare your score with that printed directly underneath the directions. This percentage is the acceptable score, the one that shows mastery of the material. If your score is lower, check your errors to see what went wrong. You may want to ask your instructor for help.

6. For Chapters 3–7 and Chapter 10, complete the preview questions before you begin the exercises, and complete the follow-up questions after you have completed all the exercises. These questions will help you evaluate what you have learned about various college subjects.

When You Finish the Textbook

When you have finished *Integrating College Study Skills*, you will likely be ready for the demands of college work. You will be able to read many types of textbooks, take accurate lecture and study notes, use test-taking strategies, and write organized paragraphs and essays explaining what you have learned. Most importantly, when you have completed this textbook, you will be able to use the identical reasoning skills in all your reading, listening, and writing. Rather than completing each assignment in isolation, you will be able to see your work in college as an integrated activity.

Acknowledgments

Many thanks go to Angie Gantner whose careful preproduction work and thoughtful suggestions helped shape this third edition; to Nancy Sjoberg who, once again, made this production a smooth and enjoyable experience; and finally to my patient wife Vasi and sons Elia and Dimitri who gave me the many hours I needed to complete this third edition.

I am thankful for the comments made by my reviewers of the first edition: Nancy C. Cook, University of Arkansas; Pat John, Lane Community College; Denise McGinty, University of Texas at Austin; Penney Miller, Clayton Junior College; Linda Pounds, Georgia State University; and Margaret Rauch, St. Cloud State University. I would like to thank the reviewers of the second edition: Nancy Hoover, Bellarmine College; Allan Jacobson, Los Angeles Harbor College; Lorita Manning, Baylor University; and Melaine Evans Summey, Abraham Baldwin Agricultural College. And I would like to thank the reviewers of this third edition: Beverly Burch, Vincennes University; Muriel Davis, San Diego Mesa College; Karen Fenske, Kishwaukee College; Richard D. Grossman, Tompkins-Cortland Community College; Kathryn S. Hawes, Memphis State University; Cathy Leist, University of Louisville; Virda K. Lester, Tuskegee University; Thomas Minderman, Vincennes University; and Josef Raab, University of Southern California.

Skills for Beginning Your College Career

In this part of the book, you will become acquainted with the services that your college provides, you will complete schedules for your short- and long-term projects, and you will learn how to manage your study area. This information and these skills provide a necessary foundation for your college career.

1 Getting to Know Your School

The first week at a new college is frequently the most hectic. You have to pay tuition and fees, buy books, enroll in your classes, and organize a study and work schedule. Many students find colleges, particularly large ones, impersonal. Yet most colleges provide students with materials and services that can make their first semester a bit less trying.

College Catalog and Schedule of Classes

Weeks before you enroll in your classes, you can become familiar with your school by obtaining a college catalog and a schedule of classes. The catalog is usually published every year. It outlines college policies, gives a short history of the school, lists the services provided to students, names the departments and the courses offered, and names the faculty of each department. Reading the catalog is a smart way to begin your college career. Look for services that the college provides: scholarships, financial aid, tutoring, and so on. Read through the course offerings in those departments in which you plan to take classes. You will find out how many courses are offered, what kinds of courses are offered, and when during the calendar year courses are taught.

After most course titles, the catalog lists the prerequisites and the unit value of each course. Prerequisites are the courses that you must have taken or the exams that you must have passed in order to enroll. Knowing whether you fulfill the prerequisites is important. An introductory chemistry course, for example, may give as one of its prerequisites "appropriate score on placement test." If you do not take and pass this test before the first meeting, you may not be allowed to enroll. Some students enroll in courses without being aware of the prerequisites and are turned away the first day of class.

The catalog also lists next to the course title its unit value. A unit is usually equal to one hour per week of lecture or discussion. Many courses are three units, so you attend class three hours a week. Some foreign language and science courses are five units and usually require daily attendance or the equivalent of five hours a week. In most cases, if you are enrolled in fifteen units, you will be attending class fifteen hours a week.

The schedule of classes lists each course that will be offered for that semester, the time it is offered, its unit value, and the instructor of the course. This schedule is an important tool for you because it provides all the information that you will need to set up your study list for the semester.

Counseling Services

Most colleges and universities offer some sort of counseling service to all their students. If you are new to the college, you need to make an appointment to see a counselor. At this meeting, discuss your educational and career goals with your counselor. If you have transcripts of course work completed in high school or at other colleges, bring them to this appointment. Ask your counselor what exactly is required to complete a degree or certificate in your chosen major and what your job opportunities are once you graduate.

Your counselor may advise you to take a battery of tests. The results of these tests will often show you which courses you are qualified to take in English, math, and science. Many colleges also have career centers where you can go any time during the semester to get information about your intended career or any career you may be interested in.

Financial Aid

Well before you begin the semester, start planning your finances. Many students must drop out of college because they cannot pay all of their school bills. Almost all colleges and universities have a financial aids office. Go to this office before the semester begins to learn of benefits available to you. If you have already been awarded a scholarship or grant, find out when you will be given the allowance and what grade-point average and unit load you need to maintain to keep your funding. Also find out from the financial aids people what the cost of your education will be each semester or quarter. Then determine whether you can afford your education without having to work.

Job Placement Office

Most colleges and universities provide job placement services. Many students cannot afford to attend college without having to work. If you don't have a job and need extra money, see what jobs are available at the job placement office.

For most students who are serious about their college studies, being a student is a full-time job. Working full time and going to school full time is simply too much for them. School, work, or your health will suffer if you try to do too much. Part-time work of less than twenty hours per week is a reasonable work load for a college student. If you need to work full time, you may want to delay your full-time education until you have adequate savings. Many full-time workers go to school part time, often taking one or two courses at night. Taking twelve units is considered a full load, and you are advised not to work full time if you are also carrying a full load.

Orientation Activities

Many colleges and universities set aside a day or several days before the semester begins for orientation. At this time, new students are given a tour of the campus and are introduced to the various social and cultural activities the college provides. Take part in orientation activities, particularly if the college you have chosen is large. At the very least, on your first day of class you will know your way around the campus. You may also find out about a club or group that interests you.

First Class Meeting

The first class meeting for any course is an important one. The instructor officially enrolls you and usually gives you the course requirements: topics you will study, reading materials, exam dates, due dates for essays or projects, and the grading policy. Your instructor will also post office hours—hours when he or she will be able to meet with you outside of class. All of this information is usually presented in a syllabus, a calendar of course topics and a statement of class requirements. Save your syllabus, because you will be referring to it all semester.

Class Materials

You should take both pens and pencils to class. Take most of your notes in ink, but use pencil in math and science courses, where you will often be recalculating and erasing. You should have a separate notebook for each class, or at least a separate divider in a three-ring binder. Three-ring notebooks are particularly useful because you can add material for each course at any time during the semester, and you can keep your lecture notes in chronological order.

Buy your books during the first week of the semester or even before the semester begins. Be sure you know which books are required and which are recommended. Your syllabus will carry this information, and the bookstore will probably post "required" or "recommended" after each book title. After the first week of class, the bookstore may run out of some titles, and you may have to wait several weeks for the new order to arrive.

If you can afford it, buy new books. But if you buy used books, try to find those that have few or no markings. If you buy a heavily underlined book, you will be reading someone else's comments, which may not agree with yours.

Take only those books to class that you will use during lecture or lab or that you will want to study from during the day. Instructors often read from the textbook or refer to specific pages while lecturing. You will want to read along with the instructor or mark those important pages during the lecture. To carry those books that you will need for the day, you will need a briefcase, an attaché case, a large purse or satchel, or a backpack.

Class Contacts

During the first week of class, you should get to know at least one reliable classmate in each class. You should get this student's phone number and give yours to him or her. Whenever you cannot attend lectures, you can call this student to find out what you missed. You may also want to read over this student's notes whenever your notes are incomplete.

Most students enjoy studying with a classmate and find that they learn more than when studying alone. Often four or five students form a study group to prepare for a major exam. These groups are especially helpful if your instructor assigns several review questions before an exam. Students in the study group can divide up these questions, then meet to share their answers.

Try working in a study group to see whether you learn more easily this way. If you don't find study groups helpful, you may be one of those students who learn best alone.

Summary

Preparing for the first day of class takes work. By talking with a counselor, taking placement tests, and attending orientation meetings, you will get a clearer picture of your abilities and of the college you have chosen. The first day of class is also important, because you will find out what your instructors expect you to do during the semester or quarter. Finally, getting to know a few fellow classmates early in the semester will help you, so if you cannot attend class, you can call them to find out what you missed.

Summary Box   *Getting Started in School*

What do you need to do?	Why are these activities important?
Read the catalog and schedule of classes	To learn something about your school
Meet with a counselor	To plan your career goals
Attend orientation meetings	To familiarize yourself with the campus
Get the phone number of at least one student in each class	To find out what happened in class when you were absent

Skills Practice

Exercise 1.1
Completing
Important Activities

The following is a list of activities that you need to complete before the semester begins or soon after. When you complete each activity, enter the date. Check the "Does Not Apply" space for those activities that do not concern you.

Does Not Apply	*Date Completed*	*Activity*
1. _____	_____	Buy and read through the college catalog.
2. _____	_____	Buy and read through the schedule of classes.
3. _____	_____	Make an appointment to see a counselor.
4. _____	_____	Take placement tests.
5. _____	_____	Go to the financial aids office.
6. _____	_____	Go to the job placement office.
7. _____	_____	Go to orientation activities.
8. _____	_____	Buy paper, pens, and pencils for classes.
9. _____	_____	Buy textbooks.
10. _____	_____	Get the phone numbers of classmates.
11. _____	_____	Additional activities: _____

Exercise 1.2
Setting Goals for the
Semester

Answer the following questions pertaining to your plans for the current semester. Your answers should help you set reasonable goals for this and later semesters. Write "does not apply" if the question does not pertain to you.

1. What, according to your placement tests, are your strengths and weaknesses?

2. What, according to your career tests, are your vocational interests?

3. What courses have you decided to take this semester as a result of talking to a counselor?

4. What is your intended major?

5. How many units are required for you to complete your major? How many semesters do you need to complete your major?

6. Do you plan to complete all of your course work at your present college, or do you intend to transfer? If you plan to transfer, what school do you intend to transfer to?

7. Did you find, after meeting with people in the financial aids office, that you are eligible for aid, or do you need to work? If you need to work, how many hours a week do you plan to work?

2 Managing Your Time and Your Study Area

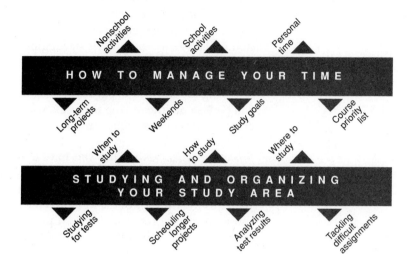

Being a student carries many responsibilities. In carrying out the job of being a student, you would be wise to prepare a schedule that indicates what you will be doing each day. A successful executive would be lost without a calendar of business and social appointments. So will you. As a student, you need to keep track of every hour that you spend in and out of school. Students who schedule their time find that there are many wasted hours during the day. Students also need to analyze their study areas to see whether these places are most conducive to concentration.

Setting Up a Study Schedule

Incoming freshmen will find they have many more free hours during the day than they had in high school, where they were often in classes five or six hours each day. Some days a college student may have only two hours of class, and the rest of the day will be free. For this reason, it is especially important for freshmen coming directly from high school to set up schedules that they plan to follow.

Nonschool Activities. Your first job in establishing a study schedule is to determine which hours during the day you cannot study. Be detailed.

Include the time it takes for you to get ready for class in the morning and get ready for bed at night, to eat your meals, and to take care of family matters. List all of these activities and the time allotted to each on a 3 × 5 card, as shown in Figure 2-1.

If you do not already follow a routine of getting up at a certain time, eating at set hours, and exercising regularly, start now. You will not be productive if you do not eat, sleep, and exercise well. Students who don't eat breakfast often become exhausted by midday. Similarly, students who do not exercise feel lethargic as the day wears on. Recent studies have shown that exercise gives your body more energy and fights depression. A half-hour to an hour of jogging, swimming, or brisk walking each day is time well spent. Finally, sleeping at least seven hours a night is important. Staying up late catches up with you. Even though it is tempting to stay up late, particularly if you live on campus, try not to. If you have slept little during the week, you will find yourself dozing off in class or sleeping through your morning classes.

School Activities.   Now that you have established regular times to eat, sleep, and exercise, you are ready to identify those hours you can devote to school. First, enter your hours of nonschool activities on a sheet of paper listing the days of the week and the hours in each day. Also include those hours that you must work, if part-time work is part of your daily schedule. Your schedule should look something like the one in Figure 2-2. In this schedule, the nonschool activities have been listed in the appropriate hours; for the moment, Saturday and Sunday have been left open.

This sample schedule has nine blank spaces in each day. Those represent nine hours that you can devote to school. Nine hours well spent can make you an excellent student.

You now need to include in this schedule the hours that you spend in class. The schedule in Figure 2-3 includes sixteen hours of class time. Notice that the student has spaced the classes. If you do not have to work, spacing your classes is wise. The more hours you are on campus during the day, the more time you will have to study. You will also have time to review your lecture notes right after class. If you check the schedule for Monday, you find that this student has the following hours to study: 9–10 a.m., 11–12 a.m., and 2–6 p.m.—a total of six hours.

Many instructors will tell you that for every hour of lecture you should spend two hours outside of class studying for that course. This

| 6–7 A.M.: Shower, get ready for school, eat breakfast. |
| 7–7:30 A.M.: Drive to campus. |
| noon–12:45 P.M.: Eat lunch on campus. |
| 10–11 P.M.: Exercise and get ready for bed. |

Figure 2-1   *Activity card.*

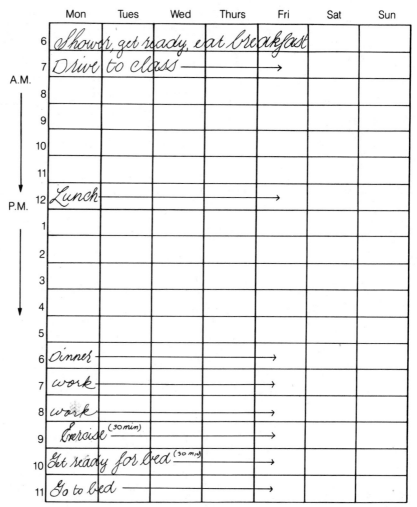

	Mon	Tues	Wed	Thurs	Fri	Sat	Sun
6	*Shower, get ready, eat breakfast*						
7	*Drive to class* ———————→						
8							
9							
10							
11							
12	*Lunch* ————————→						
1							
2							
3							
4							
5							
6	*Dinner* ————————→						
7	*work* ————————→						
8	*work* ————————→						
9	*Exercise* (30 min) ————→						
10	*Get ready for bed* (30 min) →						
11	*Go to bed* ————————→						

A.M. P.M.

Figure 2-2 *Weekly schedule with nonschool activities.*

may be true, but you will have to make a more realistic estimate. For each course, assess your background knowledge; if your background is limited in a particular course, you may have to devote more time to studying for that course than for your other courses. If you are carrying fifteen units, you may need to study fifteen, thirty, or even more hours during the week to be prepared.

It is best to write out a study schedule for each day. Figure 2-4 shows that this same student plans three hours of study on campus each Monday. In Exercise 2.2 you will determine your own study hours.

Daily Assignments.   Each day you will have different school tasks to do. The night before, jot down the work you need to complete for the next

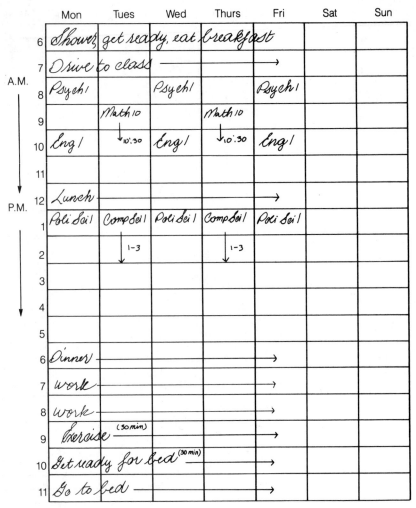

Figure 2-3   *Weekly schedule with school activities.*

Mon				
8	Psych 1			
9	Study	///		
10	Eng 1			
11	Study	///		
12	Lunch			
1	Poli Sci 1			
2	Study	///		

Figure 2-4   *Schedule showing study hours.*

9/27
1. Read carefully pp. 12–22 in Psych.
2. Complete 10 homework problems in Math.
3. Make an outline for Poli Sci paper.

Figure 2-5   *Assignment schedule.*

day. Figure 2-5 is a sample list of goals; note that the activities are specific and that each one can likely be completed in one hour.

When you look at a class syllabus at the beginning of the semester, you may feel overwhelmed, thinking that you can never get through all of the assignments. But breaking up large assignments into smaller tasks of no more than one hour each is an effective way of getting things done. Psychologists call the breaking up of larger activities into smaller tasks *successive approximations.*

Long-Term Projects.   During the semester, you will likely be assigned large projects—term papers, critical papers, lab reports, and so on. You will also have to prepare for midterms and finals—exams that require more than just a night or two of study. It is best to place the due dates of these larger tasks on a monthly calendar. You may want to buy a large calendar that you can place on the wall or desk where you normally study. On this calendar, enter the dates of the major projects and tests for each month. With this calendar, you can calculate the number of days you have to finish each assignment.

Look at how the month of May is marked in Figure 2-6. On May 1, this student has no more than eight days to finish a research paper and all month to study for a computer final.

Weekends.   If you keep up during the week, your weekends should not end up as study marathons; on weekends you should relax as well as study. You should use them to complete any late work, get a jump on assignments for the following week, and work on larger projects. It is best to set aside three or four hours on a Saturday or Sunday to work on an essay assignment. Writing requires concentrated, uninterrupted time.

If you have to work, weekends are best. Without having to attend classes on the weekend, you will be able to work and not feel rushed.

Time for Yourself.   The average student has ample time to study each day. You can therefore set aside some part of each day for fun. Psychologists have shown that students who vary their activities during the day actually retain more than those who study nonstop. So do not feel that you are wasting your time when you are not doing schoolwork. Give yourself some time each day to relax. On weekends, take advantage of the movies, plays, and concerts available to you on or off campus. If you come back

	Sun	Mon	Tues	Wed	Thurs	Fri	Sat
May							1
	2	3	4	5	6	7	8
	9	10 *Eng!* *paper due*	11	12	13	14	15
	16	17	18 *critical paper in poli sci due*	19	20	21	22
	23 / 30	24 *Math final* / 31	25	26	27	28 *Computer final*	29

Figure 2-6   *Deadlines marked on the calendar.*

to your studies refreshed, you will have a more positive attitude toward the new material.

What has been said so far about scheduling your time and making lists and calendar deadlines may seem tedious to you, and some of it is. But being organized is one of the most important characteristics of a successful student. If you stick to your schedules and continue to meet your deadlines, you will begin to enjoy the pleasures of being a successful student. Once being organized becomes a habit for you, you may want to dispense with written lists and goals entirely.

You are now ready to consider specific suggestions about managing your time and setting up your study area. With these suggestions, you will be able to make even better use of each study hour.

Setting Up a Course Priority List

At the beginning of each semester, you should look at all your courses and select the one or two that you think are most important. These courses may be the ones in your major or prerequisites to your major. You should list your courses in order of importance and then anticipate the grade you will earn in each. Then you can better predict the time you should devote to each course.

Study the following course priority list, designed by a student majoring in computer science:

	Course	*Predicted Grade*
1.	Computer Science 1	A
2.	Mathematics 10	A
3.	English 1	B
4.	Political Science 1	B
5.	Psychology 1	C

It is clear that this student will be exerting more effort in the computer science and math courses. Because she realizes the need to do very well in the computer science and math courses, the anticipated grade of "C" in psychology is realistic. She is not pressuring herself to do exceptionally well in all courses.

If you set up a priority list, you should be able to set some realistic goals early in the semester. During the semester, if you are not doing as well as you had predicted, you need to determine what is going wrong. Do you need to study more? Do other activities conflict with your studies? Or have you chosen a major that is ill suited for you?

In Exercise 2.5 you will be able to determine your own priority list.

Making the Best Use of Your Study Time

When should you study for each course? You should study for your priority courses when your mind is freshest. Each student's most productive hours vary. Some find the mornings best, others the evenings or late nights. Find out when you work best, and study for your most important courses then.

How to Study. In this book you will be introduced to several study techniques and learn a successful study system called SQ3R. But first, consider the following general study hints:

1. Never study with distractions. Music, although soothing, is often distracting. When you are doing concentrated studying, avoid listening to music.

2. Do not begin studying if you are more concerned about something else. Your study hours need to be concentrated ones. A brisk walk, run, or swim before you study can often clear your mind of daily problems.

3. Try to divide your studying into one-hour blocks. You can take a ten-minute break either at the end or in the middle of each hour. Gauge your breaks according to the difficulty of the material. The key to a successful study hour, though, is to put in fifty concentrated minutes of study.

4. After your hour is up, do something different. Either study for a course unrelated to what you have just studied or do something not related to school. Studying during spaced intervals is more productive than cramming your studying into a few days.

5. Devote some time during your school hours to reviewing what you have learned for that day. You need to review your lecture notes or the study notes you have taken from your textbooks. You tend to forget more of what you have learned during the first twenty-four hours, so it is important to review soon after you have learned something new. More will be said about how you remember in Chapter 14, "Mnemonic Strategies."

6. Be sure to complete your reading assignments soon after they are assigned. Listening to a lecture on completely new material can confuse and frustrate you. So make your reading assignments a study priority.

How to Tackle Difficult Assignments.　Sometimes your study material is difficult, and studying for a concentrated hour may be exhausting. If this happens, break your studying into shorter activities. Write out your goals before you begin studying. For example, if you have five difficult math problems to do, you can write out a list of shorter tasks, something like the following:

1. Complete problem 1.
2. Read and think about problem 2.
3. Take a four-minute break.
4. Come back to problem 2.

You will find that you will achieve your goals if you make them short and realistic. Instead of focusing on five difficult problems, reward yourself for completing one problem at a time.

How to Study for Tests.　Much will be said in this book on how to study for tests, including objective tests (Chapter 15) as well as essay and math or science tests (Chapter 16). For now, read the following time-management hints, which apply to preparing for any test:

1. Before you begin studying for a test, you should have completed all of your reading assignments. In addition, you should have reviewed your notes each day.

2. For a weekly quiz, take two days to study, one day to do your reviewing, and a second to let the material settle. If the course is difficult, you may need more days to learn the material.

3. For a midterm test, study for three or four days. On the last night, do not cram; review only the general concepts.

4. For a final examination, reserve about a week to study. As with the midterm, review only the general points the night before.

How to Schedule Longer Projects.   Do not wait until the last few days of the semester to complete a project such as a term paper. You need to divide up these larger assignments into smaller tasks and assign yourself deadlines to complete them.

If, for example, you are assigned a 500-page novel to read in ten days, you need to divide up the number of pages by the days you have to complete the reading. With this novel, you need to read fifty pages a day. For a research paper, you can divide your work into the following smaller tasks: finding library material, taking notes on this material, writing an outline for the paper, writing a rough draft, and writing a final draft. Look at this sample schedule for completing a research paper on the Hopi Indians:

Hopi Indians (30-Day Project)

1.	Go to the library, make up a bibliography	5 days
2.	Take notes from the book	8 days
3.	Write an outline	2 days
4.	Write a rough draft	7 days
5.	Type a final draft	4 days
		Total = 26 days

You may have noticed in this schedule that, although it is for a thirty-day project, the student has estimated twenty-six days for completing the project. The extra four days give him some breathing room in case one task takes longer to complete. Often these projects take longer to finish than you had originally planned. Generally it takes three to four weeks to complete a research paper. But once you have completed your first research paper, you will be able to estimate more accurately the time required to complete the next one.

Analyzing Your Test Results

You can learn much about your progress as a student by studying your test results, particularly your first test scores of the semester. Study your errors; try to determine why you made them. You may find that you need to study more or study in a quieter area.

By studying your results, you can also determine the kinds of tests your instructor gives and what study materials he or she emphasizes: lecture notes, textbook material, class discussion, and so on. Does the test emphasize details or concepts? Are any of the questions tricky? If the test is an essay, what does the instructor seem to be looking for? An organized essay? Accurate details? New ideas? The instructor's ideas? By answering these questions, you will likely do better on the next exam.

If you receive a low or failing score, try to figure out what went wrong. Did you study enough? Is this course too difficult for you? Do you need tutoring, or should you drop the class? Make an appointment to see your instructor. See what he or she has to say. Take these suggestions seriously.

Remember, a test score is more than a grade. By analyzing it, you become a more serious student.

**Setting Up Your
Study Area**

A successful student needs an organized study area. Ideally, you should have your own desk in a quiet place. On your desk you need a dictionary, and all the textbooks and notes that you need to use for that hour should be at arm's reach. Your desk should also have scratch paper, lined paper, and typing paper, as well as several pens and pencils. If possible, you should have a typewriter or word processor on your desk. Finally, your chair should not be too comfortable, because you want to stay alert while you study. A chair with an upright back support is effective. With these materials, you will be able to stay in one place during your study hour.

If these ideal conditions are not possible, you should still be able to create an organized study area. You may be living at home with younger brothers and sisters disturbing you. Or you may be living in a small apartment with several roommates. So it may be impossible for you to have your own desk in a quiet place. But you still can find a large box for all your books and notes for the semester. Keeping all of your material in one area is a must. Students waste precious time looking for books or notes.

If you cannot study without interruption where you live, you need to find a quiet study area in either a local library or your college library. If you go to the library with friends, sit away from them when you study so you will not be distracted.

Summary

Setting up schedules is a key to success in and out of school. To organize your time, you must first list those activities not related to school. Once you have listed nonschool activities, you can then include those hours when you attend school. Try to space your classes throughout the day. On this same schedule, you can mark those hours that you reserve for study. You must plan your hours of study the night before and stick to your plan. Finally, you need to place long-term projects on a monthly calendar so you know how much time you have to complete them.

To become a successful student, you also need to devise successful study strategies. Set up class priorities to determine which courses you need to concentrate on; then project the grade that you intend to receive in each of these courses. During your study hours, you should concentrate only on your school assignments. When you are working on large projects, you should break them up into smaller tasks, then set up a deadline for completing each one. Finally, you need to create a quiet study area for yourself, one that has all the materials you will need for that study hour.

In the rest of this book, you will be working on improving specific reading, listening, and writing skills. You may already be familiar with some of these skills; others may be new to you. Regardless, all of them are necessary for you to do well in college.

Summary Box   *Managing Your Time and Your Study Area*

What is time and study area management?	Why should you manage your time and your study area?
A way of analyzing how you spend your day so you can set aside certain quiet hours to study	To develop order in your life as a student
Some ways to manage your time and study area:	To provide time to complete reading assignments, study for tests, and complete term projects
1. Making nonschool schedules	To assess your progress in school
2. Making on-campus schedules	To get the most out of college
3. Making daily activity schedules	
4. Making time schedules for longer projects	
5. Making course priority lists	
6. Analyzing test results	
7. Designing a study area	

Skills Practice

Exercise 2.1
Setting Up a
Schedule of
Nonschool Activities

Answer the following questions. Then transfer the answers to these questions to the weekly activity schedule shown in Figure 2-7.

1. When do you get up each morning for school?

2. When do you eat breakfast, lunch, and dinner during the week (excluding Saturday and Sunday)?

3. When do you exercise?

4. When do you go to bed during the week (excluding Saturday and Sunday)?

5. If you work, what are your hours?

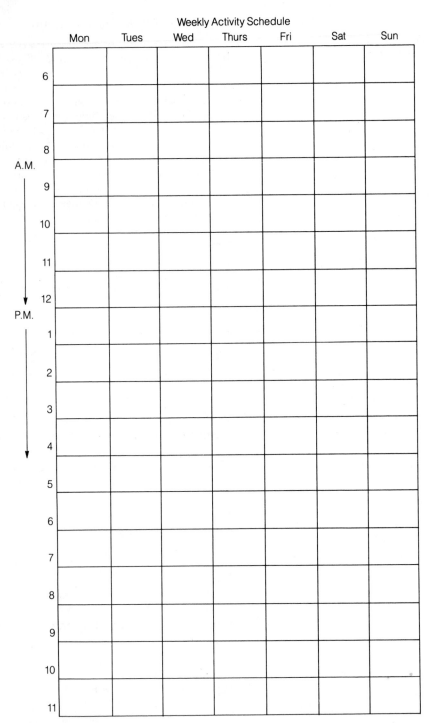

Figure 2-7 *Weekly activity schedule.*

**Exercise 2.2
Setting Up a
Schedule of School
Activities**

Answer the following questions concerning your school activities. Then transfer the answers to these questions to Figure 2-7.

1. How many units are you carrying this semester?

2. List your classes and the time they meet.

Class Name	*Time Class Meets*

a.

b.

c.

d.

e.

f.

g.

3. When do you study? In Figure 2-7, shade in the boxes of those hours you regularly reserve for study.

4. How many hours have you reserved for study? Do these hours equal or exceed the number of units that you are carrying? Have you reserved enough hours each week for study?

**Exercise 2.3
Making a Calendar
for Long-Term
Projects**

In Figure 2-8, you will find a calendar for a typical month. Fill in the name of the current month and the appropriate dates. Then enter the due dates for longer projects and major exams for this month.

   Use this calendar to remind yourself of important due dates for this month. At the end of the month, ask yourself whether this calendar was a useful reminder for you. If you found it helpful, continue using it.

**Exercise 2.4
Setting Up Daily
Schedules**

Use the activity reminders in Figure 2-9 for the next three days. Remember to list tasks that you can complete in an hour. At the day's end, see if you have completed each task. If you haven't, try to figure out why.

	Sun	Mon	Tues	Wed	Thurs	Fri	Sat
Month: ___							

Figure 2-8   *Typical month's calendar.*

```
1. First Day    Date: _____
To Do:
1. _____
2. _____
3. _____
4. _____
```

```
2. Second Day    Date: _____
To Do:
1. _____
2. _____
3. _____
4. _____
```

```
3. Third Day    Date: _____
To Do:
1. _____
2. _____
3. _____
4. _____
```

Figure 2-9   *Activity reminders for three days.*

***Exercise 2.5
Setting Up Course
Priorities***

In this exercise, set up a priority list of your courses. List them in their order of importance. Then predict the grade that you will receive in each.

Course	*Predicted Grade*

1.

2.

3.

4.

5.

6.

7.

Save this exercise; then, at the end of the semester, compare your predicted grade with the one you actually receive. If they are different, try to figure out why.

***Exercise 2.6
Assessing Your Time
Management and
Your Study Area***

The following ten questions concern your ability to manage time and your study area. Read each question carefully; then answer it by writing yes or no after the question. After you have answered all ten questions, you will be asked to use these results in determining where you need to improve your time management and study area.

1. Does your mind wander when you study? _____

2. Do you often take study breaks that are too long? _____

3. Do you often study for the same kinds of courses back to back? _____

4. Do you fail to review your reading and study notes frequently? _____

5. Do you often go to lectures without having completed the reading assignment? _____

6. Do you get frustrated when you read difficult material? _____

7. Do you wait until the last day to study for your exams? _____

8. Do you wait until the last days to complete longer projects? _____

9. Do you look only at your test score when you get an exam back? _____

10. Is your study area disorganized? _____

If you answered yes to any of these questions, you need to go back and reread the section that applies to the skill in question. Now make a list of those skills that you intend to improve during this semester.

Skills Needing Improvement

1. _____

2. _____

3. _____

4. _____

5. _____

6. _____

7. _____

8. _____

This semester, make it your goal to sharpen the skills you listed.

Basic Reading, Listening, and Writing Skills

In Part Two, you will learn skills that will help you read, listen, and write better in college. These are very important skills for you to acquire in order to succeed. So read each chapter carefully, and do as many of the exercises as you can. By the time you finish Part Two, you will have some very useful study skills at your disposal.

3 Locating Main Ideas

HOW TO DETERMINE THE MAIN IDEA

Find topic | Look at beginning | Look at end | Main idea in longer selections | No stated main idea

Determining main ideas in textbooks and lectures is perhaps the single most important study skill that you will learn. Without knowing what the main ideas are, you will be unable to follow the writer's or lecturer's train of thought. Details will seem confusing and meaningless. On the other hand, if you have the main ideas in mind, the textbook chapter or lecture will seem organized and informative. Furthermore, the main ideas will usually stay with you long after you have forgotten many of the details.

Understanding the Role of Main Ideas

Every well-planned lecture and textbook has a series of main ideas. But finding them is not always a simple matter. You often have to know what main ideas do and how they're used in order to find them.

In Relationship to the Topic. The first step in locating any main idea is to determine the *topic* of your reading or lecture material. If you determine the topic early in your reading or listening, you will be on your way to identifying main ideas.

The topic is generally easy to find in a reading selection because it is the title of the material. Most titles clearly tell you what the selection is about. An article with the title "Pollution: Research in the Nineties" is almost sure to tell you what scientists have found out about pollution in this decade. "Pollution: A Hopeless Problem?" will no doubt try to explain why pollution is not yet under control and may never be controlled. It is best to lock the title in your mind before you start reading, to begin examining what the material will cover.

In some articles, the title may be more indirect. For instance, the writer may use a quotation as a title. In this case, you may understand the meaning of the title only while reading or after reading the selection.

Let's say an article on pollution uses a question from Henry David Thoreau as its title: "What Is the Use of a House if You Don't Have a Decent Planet to Put It On?" You may not at first understand what this question has to do with pollution. But as you read this article, you may find that the article is not about building houses but about the uselessness of technology if the earth is too polluted to use the technology. With indirect titles, you may want to begin by jotting down a few notes about what you think the title means.

Locating the topic of a lecture is usually quite easy, because most instructors list the subject for that class meeting in the syllabus, next to the class date. For example, an environmental studies instructor might write "Monday, June 7 — Water Pollution." Write this title on the first line of your page of lecture notes for that day. You should then try to figure out how this topic fits into what your instructor said in the previous meeting. Did she discuss air pollution on Friday, June 4? As you start seeing connections among lectures, you will derive more meaning from each lecture.

What if your instructor does not provide a syllabus or does not begin the lecture with a stated topic? Then you are responsible for determining the topic. Give yourself no more than five minutes of listening to the lecture to determine the topic. Then write your own title on the first line of your lecture notes.

In Outlines.   With the topic in mind, you are now ready to read or listen for main ideas. Consider main ideas as umbrellas under which all significant details are included. Perhaps you can best see the main ideas as Roman numerals in an outline, where roman numerals like I represent the main idea and capital letters like A and B represent the supporting details. If you are already familiar with the traditional outline form, you know that the main ideas, preceded by roman numerals, are placed farthest to the left on your page of notes. You may also have learned that the farther to the right you go, the more details you get. A main idea, then, is more general than its details but more specific than the topic. See how a main idea is sandwiched between the topic and the details of support in the following outline of a lecture on air pollution:

Types of Pollution

I. Air pollution

    A. Types of pollution in the atmosphere
    B. Effects of air pollution on the rivers, lakes, and oceans
    C. Effects of air pollution on vegetation

Notice that "I. Air Pollution" is one issue under the topic "Types of Pollution" and that A, B, and C call out specifics of that main idea.

Whether you are reading or listening, see the main idea as the level of information between the topic and the details. Let this "I, A, B, and

C" organization be in your mind when you are locating main ideas in writing or in lectures. When you are comfortable with the traditional outline structure, you will be able to identify main ideas effortlessly.

Seeing and Hearing Main Ideas

Almost every paragraph or group of paragraphs and list of statements in a lecture must contain one main idea and one or more details. Here are some hints for finding main ideas.

At the Beginning. In many of the paragraphs you read, you will find the main idea in the first sentence. In the sentences that follow the first sentence, you will usually read details that support this main idea. Study the following paragraph on air pollution to see how the first sentence expresses the main idea and the sentences that follow present details:

> Most air pollution is made up of a combination of gaseous substances. Some of the air pollution is caused by automobile exhaust fumes in the form of carbon monoxide. Other types of air pollution, often found in smog, are made up of chemical oxides. The two most common oxides found in air pollution are nitrogen oxide and sulfur oxide.

Did you notice that the first sentence is the most general, the umbrella under which the other three sentences fall? Did you also notice that in each detail sentence specific types of air pollution are cited? In main-idea sentences you do not usually read a specific fact or figure. In this sense main-idea sentences are more general. Thus in the main-idea sentence of the sample paragraph, gaseous substances are introduced, not specific gaseous substances.

Similarly, instructors usually present main-idea sentences at the beginning of their lectures or parts of lectures. So you need to listen carefully when they begin a presentation or when they introduce new ideas during the lecture. These introductory remarks will usually be the I, II, and III of your notes.

At the End. In a smaller number of paragraphs, the main idea is presented at the end. In these cases, the detail sentences are presented first. The process of presenting specific information that leads to a general statement is called *induction*. Information is collected, and from this a main idea emerges. Study this paragraph on the sources of air pollution:

> Forest fires occur throughout the world. Wherever there are insects, they disperse pollen. The wind erodes the soil, and it ends up in the atmosphere. Volcanoes erupt and spew their material into the air. All of these are examples of natural events that create air pollution.

Did you notice the specific details in the first three sentences? Did you also notice how these sentences lead to a main-idea sentence at the end?

This statement about natural air pollution, like an umbrella, covers all the information about volcanoes, wind, insects, and fires.

This same pattern occurs in lectures. The speaker presents several details at the beginning of the lecture, and the main idea, or induction, is presented last. In your outline, you need to leave the blank next to item I temporarily empty while you jot down the details (A, B, C) of the lecture. Then, when the speaker presents the main idea, you can go back to fill in the space next to I.

In Longer Selections.   You can also look for the main idea of an entire essay or lecture. In these longer pieces, the main idea can usually be found in the first paragraph of an essay or the first section of a lecture, called the *introduction*. In these longer works, the main idea may be stated in more than one sentence.

In the paragraphs or sections that follow the introduction, often called the *body*, details are usually presented to support this main idea. The last paragraph or section — the *conclusion* — is usually as general as the introduction. It either summarizes the main idea of the essay or presents new conclusions that logically follow from the details. So when looking for the main idea in most essays, it is wise to read through the first and last paragraphs and then write out the main idea in your own words.

This outline should help you better understand the relationship between main idea and details in longer works:

I. Introduction: expresses main idea; introduces details

A. ⎫
B. ⎬ Body: explains the details more thoroughly in a series of
C. ⎭ paragraphs or sections

II. Conclusion: either summarizes the main idea or presents a new main idea that follows from the details in A, B, and C.

Through Signal Words.   Several *signal words* may introduce a main idea. You will find signal words most often in the introduction or conclusion of an essay or lecture. Become familiar with these words and phrases: "in general," "generally," "above all," "of great importance," "the main idea is," "the main point is," "the main feature is," "the key feature is," "the truth is." Look at how the following paragraph incorporates signal words into its sentences:

> *Generally,* the most significant cause of pollution in big cities is the emissions that come from automobiles and factories. *The main feature* of pollutants from both these sources is that they do not easily decompose or decay on their own. *Of great importance* is how these pollutants return to the earth in the form of acid rain. It is acid rain that we need to study more carefully next.

Do you see how these signal words introduce the key points that this author intends to cover?

The following words and phrases signal main ideas in conclusions: "in conclusion," "to conclude," "to summarize," "therefore," "thus," "consequently," "as a consequence," "as a result," "so," "it can be seen that," "it is suggested that," "it follows that," "from the above reasons," "it is safe to say." Let these words be signals for you to locate concluding main-idea sentences in your reading and in lectures. Authors frequently use these words and phrases to introduce a general statement that you may want to remember. Also, you need to use these signal words when writing conclusions of your own.

Inferring Main Ideas

The preceding suggestions about finding main ideas in first and last sentences cover most of what you will read and hear. In some material, though, you will not find a main idea explicitly stated. In these cases, you need to infer a main idea from the details. You will frequently find paragraphs with implied main ideas in descriptive writing, especially in short stories and novels where the author is creating a mood or re-creating an experience. Descriptive writing, therefore, does not follow the "main idea followed by details" pattern.

Read the following description and infer a main idea:

> The leaves on the trees seemed to have been burned by a harmful chemical. The water in the pond was stagnant, and strangely, it did not seem to have any living things swimming in it—no fish, no algae, no insects teeming above the water. All I could see was the stifling, brown air that seemed to hover around everything—the trees, the pond, and me.

Nowhere does the author state that he is describing a dangerously polluted environment, but do you see that all the details lead you to infer that he is? The leaves on the trees are brown, the pond has no living organisms in it, and the air is brown and stifling. The author wants the reader to be disgusted by the details in order to come upon the main idea: how ugly and life-threatening a polluted environment can be.

Applying Main-Idea Rules to Writing

Learning to spot signal words and knowing how essays and lectures are organized will help you locate main ideas. They will also help you write organized essays. You will frequently be asked to write essays as a test of your understanding of reading and lecture material.

Consider these suggestions when beginning a writing assignment. First, use the traditional outline form to jot down notes before you begin writing. Second, use some signal words to introduce your main idea in introductions and conclusions. Finally, fortify your essays with several well-developed paragraphs: an introduction, paragraphs introducing and explaining details, and a conclusion summarizing or synthesizing what you have said. (You will learn more about the extended essay in Chapter 16.)

Are you beginning to see that reading, listening, and writing involve similar processes? The same organizational rules seem to apply to all three activities. The major difference is that when you read and listen, you take in information and consider what it means; when you write, you write down more carefully what you think this new material means to you. Good readers and listeners are often good writers. You will learn more about this reading-listening-writing interconnection throughout this book.

Summary

Determining the main idea of a paragraph and locating the main ideas in a longer passage or in lectures are very important skills for students to learn. About half the main ideas that one reads or hears are found in the first sentence of a paragraph. In fewer cases, the main idea is in the last sentence. Implied main ideas are not stated at all but may be inferred from the details.

Whether the material is spoken or written, the relationship between a main idea and its supporting details can be represented in the outline pattern:

I.

A.
B.
C.

Dividing information into general and specific categories is a mental exercise you constantly perform when you read, listen, or write. In Chapter 4 you will study the A, B, and C of the outline form—the details.

Summary Box   *Main Ideas*

What are they?	Why do you need to use them?
Key statements made in writing or lecturing, usually found at the beginning and end of material, and implied in most descriptions	To understand the important points in what you read, hear, or write
More specific than topics, less specific than details	To serve as umbrellas for the details that support them

Topic: Environmental Studies

The exercises in this chapter all deal with the issue of environmental pollution, a topic of concern to us all and one that you will examine carefully if you enroll in environmental studies courses in college.

Before you begin these exercises, answer the following questions either individually or in small groups to get some sense for what you already know about the environment:

1. What does the term *environment* mean?
2. What are the most common environmental problems that we face today?
3. How have human beings contributed to environmental problems?
4. How are environmental problems being dealt with in the world today?

Exercise 3.1
Determining Stated
or Implied Main
Ideas

The following paragraphs discuss the ways humans affected the planet in ancient times. The main idea may be found in the first sentence or the last sentence, or it may be implied. Locate the letter of the main-idea sentence, and place it next to the appropriate number in the answer box. If there is no main-idea sentence, write *imp* for "implied" next to the number in the answer box.

Ancient Hunters and Gatherers

1. (a) For the vast majority of their time on earth, human beings have been hunters and gatherers. (b) They found that some wild plants could be eaten, so they began to gather them to share them with their family. (c) When they found that fish and game were edible, they became hunters. (d) The hunting was generally done by men, and the gathering was performed by women and children.

2. (a) These early hunters and gatherers formed groups of approximately fifty members. (b) As a group, they worked together to hunt game and gather food in order to feed their people. (c) Once the group grew beyond fifty, it often split up and began forming a second group, which hunted and gathered food on its own. (d) These groups, known as tribes, seemed to be the fundamental social group for hunters and gatherers.

3. (a) Often these tribes were forced to move from one place to another to find new game and edible plants. (b) The people in the tribes often could not tell how long their supply of game in a particular area would last, which was a source of frustration for them. (c) They also had a difficult time gauging when a particular type of edible plant would no longer be plentiful enough to feed the entire tribe. (d) As nomads, they were also subject to the changes of seasons and were forced to move when the weather proved intolerable.

1. _____

2. _____

3. _____

4. _____

5. _____

6. _____

7. _____

8. _____

9. _____

10. _____

_____

70%

(score = # correct × 10)

Find answers on p. 333.

4. (a) These tribes soon learned much about coping with weather changes. (b) They also found reliable water sources, even in dry areas. (c) These people eventually became shrewd enough to know which plants were edible and which could serve as medicine. (d) Each tribe also learned to use sticks and stones in preparing their plant and animal foods.

5. (a) Our current picture of these ancient hunting and gathering tribes calls our modern lifestyle into question. (b) In these tribes of fifty, women and children spent only fifteen hours per week gathering food. (c) The men tended to hunt only one week each month. (d) Furthermore, our ancient ancestors ate a healthy and varied diet, and the notion of stress was foreign to them.

6. (a) A negative aspect of the hunter-gatherer lifestyle was their high mortality rate. (b) Many infants died of infectious diseases. (c) For adults, the average life expectancy was about thirty years. (d) Because of this high death rate, the population increased slowly.

7. (a) The impact of the hunter-gatherer lifestyle on the environment was very slight. (b) Because their population did not grow quickly, they did not deplete the resources in the environment. (c) Also, because these people were nomads, they did not exploit any one area. (d) Finally, these people relied on their own energy rather than on energy resources in the environment to get most of their work done.

8. (a) About 12,000 years ago, hunters and gatherers began to change some of their behavior. (b) Most importantly, they improved their tools; cutting tools became sharper, and the bow and arrow were invented. (c) Also, hunters from various tribes began to work together to hunt herds of animals like bison and mammoths. (d) These people also began to burn some of their inedible vegetation to give the edible vegetation room to grow.

9. (a) As these hunters developed more advanced skills, some of the forested hunting areas began to turn to grassland. (b) As they became more proficient, these hunters were able to kill off a few more game. (c) The gatherers also changed some of the vegetation patterns by allowing more of the edible vegetation to grow. (d) All in all, though, both hunters and gatherers tended to live in harmony with their neighbors and with nature.

10. (a) Today people living in industrial areas rarely consider where the piece of meat they eat for dinner comes from. (b) They also tend not to reflect on where or how the vegetables they buy for their salads are grown. (c) They also rarely ask what resources are needed to make the plastics and metal items they use each day. (d) Moreover, people in modern industrial cities often tend to consume more food and purchase more manufactured items than they really need.

**Exercise 3.2
Determining Topics
and Main Ideas**

The following exercise is a series of paragraphs on the history of agricultural societies, continuing the discussion on hunters and gatherers begun in Exercise 3.1. Read the following ten paragraphs carefully; you may choose to reread them. As you read each one, ask the following questions: What is the topic? What is the main idea? Remember that the topic — the subject of the paragraph, usually phrased in two or three words — tends to be more general. The main idea is the point of the paragraph, what all the sentences in the paragraph are about. Choose the correct letter of the topic and main idea for each paragraph and put them in the answer box next to the appropriate number.

Ancient Agricultural Societies

The use of agriculture began about 10,000 years ago. That is when people began to plant crops in one area and began to tame animals so they didn't have to migrate to hunt. What is interesting is that the use of agricultural methods occurred in several parts of the world at about the same time. These methods ultimately made hunting and nomadic living less attractive. Agriculture had some profound effects on how human beings lived.

1. The topic is

   a. the dangers of agriculture
   b. the birth of agriculture 10,000 years ago
   c. hunting and nomadic living
   d. where agriculture was first introduced

2. The main idea concerns

   a. the importance of taming animals
   b. the lack of interest in hunting
   c. the difficulty of introducing agriculture into tribal life
   d. the effect of agricultural methods on social behavior

It is believed that the first cultivation of plants occurred in the tropical areas of Burma, Thailand, and eastern India. The women of the tribes in these areas began to cultivate small vegetable gardens. Anthropologists believe these women realized that their staple food, yams, could be planted and harvested successfully in one area. These pioneering farmers realized that they could clear an area by cutting down the vegetation and then burning it. The ash from the burned vegetation provided rich fertilizer for the yams they planted on this cleared area of land. Food could now be grown and cared for in one area.

3. The topic is

   a. the invention of cultivation
   b. the use of yams in the diet
   c. the value of using rich fertilizer
   d. the ancient people of Burma, Thailand, and eastern India

4. The main idea concerns

    a. new farming methods
    b. the use of ash in cultivating yams
    c. how cultivation changed farming methods
    d. how cultivation kept farming methods the same

These pioneer women farmers invented the notion of *shifting cultivation*. That is, they realized that planting their crops in one area would yield rich harvests for no more than five years. Then they had to clear a new agricultural area. The old agricultural plot needed to remain un-planted, or fallow, for ten to thirty years. During this fallow time, the soil replenished itself; then it was ready for a new round of planting and harvesting. Shifting cultivation is still used by farmers throughout the world.

5. The topic is

    a. the invention of shifting cultivation
    b. rich harvests
    c. keeping land fallow
    d. where shifting cultivation is used today

6. The main idea concerns

    a. the difficulty of shifting cultivation
    b. ways of clearing new agricultural areas
    c. the value of shifting cultivation
    d. how soil replenishes itself

Where the climate was less warm and humid, farmers devised different agricultural techniques. In such areas as East Africa and China, farm-ers had to clear forested areas; chopping down trees was often quite difficult. Once the area was cleared, the women often planted grains like rice or wheat instead of yams. The farmers in these temperate climates learned the same thing as those in tropical climates: that the area they cleared could yield a successful harvest for only a certain number of years. Shifting cultivation was the most profitable way to get consistently rich harvests.

7. The topic is

    a. temperate climates
    b. the farmers of East Africa and China
    c. the agricultural techniques of farmers in East Africa and China
    d. the planting of rice and grain

8. The main idea concerns

    a. the difficulty of clearing forested areas
    b. the similar agricultural techniques of farmers in tropical and temperate areas

    c. the success of harvesting in temperate climates

    d. the differences between the farmers of temperate and tropical areas

What pioneering farmers in both tropical and temperate climates learned was the value of *subsistence farming*. That is, they learned to harvest enough food to feed their tribe and no more. These farmers did not want to make a profit from any harvest that remained. Subsistence farming proved to be an environmentally sensible type of agriculture, because it used relatively small areas of land. Also, the people did not deplete their area's resources in an attempt to make the farms productive. They used their own strength to clear the farm areas, and they fertilized their farms with burning vegetation grown in the same area. For these reasons and many more, subsistence farming had little negative impact on the environment.

9. The topic is

    a. the depletion of the environment

    b. the negative effect of subsistence farming on the environment

    c. the nature of subsistence farming

    d. burning vegetation as fertilizer

10. The main idea concerns

    a. the use of land in subsistence farming

    b. subsistence farming as environmentally wise

    c. the profit resulting from subsistence farming

    d. the difficulty of feeding family and tribe

To this day, farmers throughout the world continue to use shifting cultivation and subsistence farming techniques. In Latin America, Southeast Asia, and parts of Africa, up to 200 million people still use these agricultural procedures. Environmentalists call them very sound because they do not deplete the environment. With shifting cultivation, the soil is never wasted; with subsistence farming, no area's resources are ever overused. When these two techniques are not used effectively, then the soil becomes depleted, which leads to erosion and sometimes permanent damage to the soil and the surrounding environment.

11. The topic is

    a. farming techniques in Latin America and Southeast Asia

    b. the use of subsistence farming today

    c. the use of subsistence farming and shifting cultivation today

    d. the cause of erosion

12. The main idea concerns

    a. the dangers of soil erosion

    b. the hazards of depleting the environment

   c. soil cultivation and subsistence farming as environmentally sensible today

   d. how poor people farm

Plows were invented about 5000 B.C. These early plows, made of metal, were pulled by tamed animals and steered by the farmer. With a plow, farmers could plant more crops and therefore harvest more food. The plow also allowed farmers to plant in areas that, before introduction of the plow, could not be cleared because the roots in the soil were too deep. Plows also allowed farmers to dig ditches and bring water to dry areas. By helping the farmer harvest more, the plow gave him more food than his family could eat, and he could then sell some of the excess to families with less food.

13. The topic is

   a. the invention of the plow
   b. the use of water in agriculture
   c. the profit resulting from farming
   d. how farmers fed their families

14. The main idea concerns

   a. the origin of the plow
   b. why the farmer dislikes the plow
   c. how plows clear roots that are deep in the soil
   d. how the plow changed farming in fundamental ways

Farmers' ability to save and sell their product had several effects on society. Because more food was harvested, more people could settle in an area. Because food products could now be bought, not everyone had to be a farmer. Some people began to work in other occupations and use their earnings to purchase food from farmers. After introduction of the plow, jobs began to be specialized. Finally, in part because of the plow, cities emerged, and farming towns grew on the outskirts of these cities. The plow, therefore, had a profound effect on the structure of society.

15. The topic is

   a. why farmers lost their power
   b. why farming became a popular occupation
   c. the emergence of cities
   d. the plow's effect on society

16. The main idea concerns

   a. the plow's important role in changing occupations and altering city and town life
   b. the plow's dangerous effect on society

c. the importance of profit in society

d. why farmers moved out of the city

The separation of cities from farm areas had additional effects on human society. Most importantly, wealth became a reality. That is, some people had more food and more manufactured products than others had. So there emerged a need for a class of people who could manage the city's wealth. Also, problems emerged between those who had more and those who had less — or the *haves* and the *have nots*. Conflict between these groups and wars between cities were some of the unwanted results of the development of wealth.

17. The topic is

    a. the development of city managers

    b. the problems caused by war

    c. how wealth was given to the people

    d. how wealth came to be

18. The main idea concerns

    a. how wealth restructured society and caused conflict and war

    b. the greed of city managers

    c. why the farmers became wealthy

    d. the occasional need for wars

With increased and more intensive farming came environmental concerns that the hunters and gatherers had never known. City people were no longer living in harmony with the environment. When more land was cleared for larger harvests and bigger cities, certain plants and animals were forced out of their natural habitat. Some plants and animals even died out completely. Overuse of the land led to a depletion of the soil's riches. What was once fertile territory sometimes became a desert because of overfarming. Urban or city life generally had a negative effect on the environment.

19. The topic is

    a. urban life

    b. the death of certain plants and animals

    c. overuse of the land

    d. city life and its effect on the environment

20. The main idea concerns

    a. how cities create deserts

    b. how city dwellers moved the farmers out

    c. how the hunter-gatherer is similar to the city dweller

    d. how city dwellers did not live in harmony with their environment

Exercise 3.3
Determining More
Topics and Main
Ideas

The following ten paragraphs treat the issue of industrialization and continue the discussion begun in the previous two exercises. After reading each paragraph, write a topic and a main idea for each. Remember that the topic is normally expressed in a phrase that can serve as the title of the passage. The main idea, often stated in the first or last sentence of the paragraph, expresses the passage's intent. For example, "industrialized countries" can serve as the topic of a paragraph with the main idea "the pollution caused by industrialized countries." Writing out your own topics and main ideas is a big part of what you do when you take lecture and study notes.

How Industrialized Societies Developed

The next big change in human society occurred during the mid-1700s in England. It was called the Industrial Revolution. Industry seemed to take over because there were so many inventions in such a short time. These inventions included the steam engine (1765), the steam locomotive (1829), and the steamship (1807). They made England and most of Europe less farm-based and more urbanized, or city-centered.

1. *Topic:* _____

2. *Main idea:* _____

All of these new inventions had one thing in common: They were driven by natural resources. Coal was the first fuel used to run these machines. Then oil and natural gas were discovered as energy sources to replace human energy. The results were far-reaching, extending the plow's effects on society thousands of years before. Fewer people were needed to do most work, because machines replaced them. Farmers found themselves out of work, and they began to move from the outlying farms to the large cities to find jobs. They often found jobs in large factories.

3. *Topic:* _____

4. *Main idea:* _____

By World War I (1914–1918), machines were becoming more and more sophisticated. These machines helped society in several ways. Because products could be produced in larger quantities, they were often cheaper to buy. Also, the average wage of each working individual went up. Furthermore, farming was more productive, so food was more plentiful. Industrialization also improved practices in medicine, sanitation, and nutrition. Consequently, people tended to live longer. So along with its negative effects on the environment, industrialization had some positive effects on human beings.

5. *Topic:* _____

6. *Main idea:* _____

Industrialization had a negative effect on the environment. Industry tended to create pollutants. The quality of the air, water, and soil was damaged by the waste materials expelled from smokestacks and drain-pipes. People soon found that air, water, and soil pollution affected not only their own city but also cities and countries beyond their border. Environmental pollution was no longer a local concern, but a *global* one. That is, people soon began to realize that the actions of a factory in London could affect the entire country and even the world.

7. *Topic:* _____

8. *Main idea:* _____

Industrialization has caused additional social problems. When farmers moved to the cities to find work, the population density of urban areas increased. If the migrants could not find work, the city government had to provide them with some sort of welfare. By increasing the city's pop-ulation density, these migrants also made the transmission of diseases easier. Furthermore, unemployment and poverty made crime a more serious problem in large cities.

9. *Topic:* _____

10. *Main idea:* _____

How did industrialization affect the city's environment? Like developing cities throughout human history, industrialized cities destroyed topsoil and ate up forests and grasslands. Urban sprawl into the farmlands forced farmers to move farther out. Wildlife was either pushed out of the city or made extinct. What was a city's problem then became a global problem—one that affected all of nature.

11. *Topic:* _____

12. *Main idea:* _____

The Industrial Revolution also affected the economy of the city and the overall economy of the country. Solving each social and environmental problem required money. To cover increased welfare benefits, the city needed to collect taxes. Furthermore, taxpayers needed to address the pollution problems created by large factories. Cleaning up the air and the rivers and lakes took money. So, although the Industrial Revolution improved the average citizen's standard of living, it also made him pay for the social and environmental problems it caused.

13. *Topic:* _____

14. *Main idea:* _____

Today people in industrialized countries throughout the world are asking the same question. Is industrialization helping us or hurting us? Obviously, the Industrial Revolution has made humans more productive. It has increased our standard of living, lengthened human life, and made our life more comfortable. But the Industrial Revolution has also created an unhealthy environment. It has made much of our air unfit to breathe and our water unfit to drink. Environmental pollutants have also created many cancer-related diseases.

15. *Topic:* _____

16. *Main idea:* _____

The Industrial Revolution has also given us an attitude toward nature very different from the one our ancestors had. In ancient times, human beings saw themselves as living in harmony with nature. They never took too much from nature and respected the power nature had over them. As human inventions came to the fore, we started seeing ourselves in a much more powerful role. Nature no longer controlled human beings; we controlled nature. We now often see ourselves as *superior* to nature.

17. *Topic:* _____

18. *Main idea:* _____

It is this superior attitude toward nature that industrialized society needs to question. Yes, in many ways we can control parts of nature. We can build bridges and dams and send satellites outside of the earth's atmosphere. Yet nature still has some power over the organisms that live within it. Our challenge in the twenty-first century is to enjoy the benefits of industrialization but also to respect nature and live in harmony with it. We have to realize that our inventions can make life both better and worse.*

70%

(score = # correct × 5)
Find answers on p. 333.

---

19. *Topic:* _____

20. *Main idea:* _____

---

*Exercises 3.1–3.3 adapted from G. Tyler Miller, Jr., *Living in the Environment*, 5th ed. (Belmont, Calif.: Wadsworth, 1988), pp. 25–31.

Exercise 3.4
Determining the
Main Idea in a
Longer Passage

To determine the main idea of a passage, you can apply the same rules that you used to determine the main idea of a paragraph. Read the following extended essay on the greenhouse effect, another important environmental issue caused by technology, and follow these steps to determine the main idea:

1. Read the introductory paragraph to determine what the main idea of the entire passage is.

2. See how the four paragraphs that follow (the body) give details to support the main idea. Locate a main-idea sentence for each of these paragraphs.

After you have taken these steps, answer the five questions that follow. You may look back. Place all answers in the answer box.

The Greenhouse Effect

(1) Of the sun's rays that reach earth, 70 percent are absorbed by the land, sea, and air; 30 percent are reflected back into the atmosphere. When the earth's environment cools, the absorbed heat is released in the form of infrared rays, or heat. Some of the energy escapes into space, and some of it is absorbed by water vapor and carbon dioxide in the atmosphere. The carbon dioxide and water vapor then repeat the cycle, returning some of this energy into the atmosphere and giving some back to the earth. This returning to earth of heat originally absorbed by the carbon dioxide and water of the atmosphere is called the *greenhouse effect*. Because of the greenhouse effect, the earth's temperature has increased about 10 degrees centigrade, or 18 degrees Fahrenheit, from what it would be without water vapor and carbon dioxide in the atmosphere.

(2) This natural cycle is being altered by the burning of coal as a fuel. Coal burning increases the amount of carbon dioxide and water in the atmosphere. This increase then allows for more heat to be returned to the earth because of the greenhouse effect.

(3) What might happen if the greenhouse effect causes average temperatures to rise worldwide? Scientists speculate that an overall increase in temperature will cause rainfall patterns to shift and crop-growing patterns to change. For example, the wheat belt in the United States might shift upward to Canada, where the soil is not so rich. Ultimately, the greenhouse effect might be responsible for less food production.

(4) A second result of an increase in temperature would be melting of the polar ice caps. This melting would increase the water level in the oceans of the world. Scientists now speculate that the sea-level increase would be gradual, probably taking place over hundreds of years.

(5) Despite its potential to flood the land, the greenhouse effect seems to pose greater potential danger to the earth's food-producing capacity. If less food is produced in the next fifty years, the worldwide

hunger problem might increase, because in the same fifty-year period the world's population is expected to double.*

<table>
<tr><td>1. _____</td></tr>
<tr><td>2. _____</td></tr>
<tr><td>3. _____</td></tr>
<tr><td>4. _____</td></tr>
<tr><td>5. _____</td></tr>
<tr><td>_____
80%</td></tr>
</table>

Ask instructor for answers.

1. The main idea of paragraph 1 concerns

    a. how the sun reaches the earth
    b. how the earth cools
    c. how carbon dioxide is created
    d. how the greenhouse effect returns heat to the earth

2. The main idea of paragraph 2 concerns

    a. how coal burns
    b. the value of burning coal
    c. how coal burning increases the vapor and carbon dioxide level
    d. how coal burning decreases the vapor and carbon dioxide level

3. The main idea of paragraph 3 concerns

    a. the difficulty of producing food
    b. how the greenhouse effect might cause less food to be produced
    c. where the wheat belt is in the United States
    d. why wheat can be grown effectively in Canada

4. The main idea of paragraph 4 concerns

    a. how ice caps are created
    b. the greenhouse effect and its relationship to water level
    c. how fast the polar ice caps are melting
    d. how carbon dioxide affects polar ice caps

5. The main idea of paragraph 5 concerns

    a. the greenhouse effect and food production
    b. food production
    c. world hunger
    d. world hunger and the increase in population

Exercise 3.5
Writing Your Own
Paragraph from
Main Ideas

The excerpt on the greenhouse effect in Exercise 3.4 can easily be outlined in the following way:

I. Main Idea of the Passage (expressed in paragraph 1)

    A. ⎫
    B. ⎪ Supporting details for the main idea of the passage
    C. ⎬ (consisting of the main ideas of paragraphs 2–5)
    D. ⎭

_____

*Adapted from Miller, *Living in the Environment*, pp. E20–24.

If you are still unclear about what the main idea of each paragraph is, review the correct answers to questions 1–4 in Exercise 3.4.

Now use the following outline to state, in a phrase, the main idea of each of the five paragraphs in Exercise 3.4.

I. _____

   A. _____

   B. _____

   C. _____

   D. _____

With this outline to guide you, answer the following essay question in a paragraph of five sentences (one main-idea sentence and four supporting sentences).

Essay question: In one paragraph, define the greenhouse effect and discuss its four possible effects on the environment.

70%

Ask instructor for answers.

**Exercise 3.6
Determining the
Main Ideas in a
Textbook Excerpt**

The following excerpt is from a textbook chapter on world hunger. It ties in to the previous excerpts you have read on farming techniques and the Industrial Revolution. Read through it quickly to get a sense for the topic. Then go back and read it slowly.

When you finish rereading, answer the following five questions. You may return to the excerpt in deciding on your answers. Only two terms are not defined in the excerpt: *LDC*, which means "less developed country," and *MDC*, which is defined as "more developed country."

(1) Poor people living mostly on one or more plants such as wheat, rice, or corn often suffer from *undernutrition*, or insufficient caloric intake or food quantity. Survival and good health require that people must consume not only enough food but food containing the proper amounts of protein, carbohydrates, fats, vitamins, and minerals. People whose diets are insufficient in these nutrients suffer from *malnutrition*.

(2) Severe undernutrition and malnutrition lead to premature death, especially for children under age 5. Most severely undernourished and malnourished children, however, do not starve to death. Instead, about three-fourths of them die because their weakened condition makes them vulnerable to normally minor, nonfatal infections and diseases such as diarrhea, measles, and flu. The World Health Organization estimates that diarrhea kills at least 5 million children under age 5 a year.

(3) *Famine* occurs when people in a particular area suffer from widespread lack of access to food as a result of catastrophic events such as drought, flood, earthquake, or war. Because it is so visible and dra-

matic, famine receives most of the media attention. Yet the overwhelming majority of hunger-related deaths are caused not by famine but by chronic undernutrition and malnutrition among many people in LDCs. Because this condition is "normal" and spread out over much of the world, it is undramatic, often goes unnoticed, and is not widely reported by the media.

(4) Adults suffering from chronic undernutrition and malnutrition are vulnerable to infection and other diseases and are too weak to work productively or think clearly. As a result, their children also tend to be underfed and malnourished. If these children survive to adulthood, they are locked in a tragic malnutrition-poverty cycle that perpetuates these conditions in each succeeding family generation.

(5) Most world hunger is protein hunger, because poor people are forced to live on a low-protein, high-starch diet of grain. The two most widespread nutritional-deficiency diseases are marasmus and kwashiorkor. *Marasmus* (from the Greek "to waste away") occurs when a diet is low in both total energy (calories) and protein. Most victims of marasmus are infants in poor families where children are not breast-fed or where there is insufficient food after the children are weaned. A child suffering from marasmus typically has a bloated belly, thin body, shriveled skin, wide eyes, and an old-looking face. Diarrhea, dehydration, anemia, muscle deterioration, a ravenous appetite, and possible brain damage are also part of marasmus. If treated in time with a balanced diet, however, most of these effects can be reversed. *Kwashiorkor* (meaning "displaced child" in a West African dialect) occurs in infants and in children 1 to 3 years old when, often because their mothers have a younger child to nurse, they are changed from highly nutritious breast milk to a high-starch grain or sweet potato diet, which is sufficient in calories but deficient in protein. Children with kwashiorkor have swollen tissues because fluids collect under the skin, liver degeneration, permanent stunting of growth, hair loss, diarrhea, skin rash and discoloration, mental apathy, possible mental retardation, and irritability. But if malnutrition is not prolonged, most of the effects can be cured with a balanced diet.

(6) Without a daily intake of small amounts of vitamins that cannot be synthesized in the human body, various vitamin deficiency effects occur. Although a combination of balanced diets, vitamin-fortified foods, and vitamin supplements have greatly reduced the incidence of vitamin deficiency diseases in MDCs, millions of cases occur each year in LDCs. In many parts of Asia people survive primarily on a diet of polished rice, made by removing the outer hulls. These individuals lack sufficient vitamin B_1, or thiamine (found in rice hulls), and often develop beriberi, which leads to stiffness of the limbs, enlargement of the heart, paralysis, pain, loss of appetite, and eventual deterioration of the nervous system. People who exist primarily on a corn diet have an insufficient intake of vitamin B_5, or niacin, and suffer from pellagra. Their skin becomes scaly when exposed to sunlight, and they also suffer from diarrhea, inflammation of the mouth, inability to digest food, and severe disturbance of the central nervous system. Each year at least 250,000 children are partially or totally blinded as a result of severe vitamin A deficiency.

(7) Other nutritional-deficiency diseases are caused by the lack of certain minerals, such as iron and iodine. Too little iron can cause anemia, which saps one's energy, makes infection more likely, and increases a woman's chance of dying in childbirth. Iron deficiency anemia affects about 10% of all adult men, a third of all adult women, and more than one-half of the children in tropical regions of Asia, Africa, and Latin America. Too little iodine can cause goiter, an abnormal enlargement of the thyroid gland in the neck. It affects as much as 80% of the population in the mountainous areas of Latin America, Asia, and Africa, where soils are deficient in iodine. Every year iodine insufficiency also causes deafness or muteness in an estimated 200 million people in these areas.

(8) This tragic loss of human life and life quality, especially in the world's children, could be prevented at relatively little cost. UNICEF officials estimate that between half and two-thirds of the annual childhood deaths from undernutrition, malnutrition, and associated diseases could be prevented at an average overall cost of only $5 to $10 per child. This program would involve a combination of the following simple measures:

- Immunizing against childhood diseases such as measles
- Encouraging breast-feeding
- Counteracting diarrhea with low-cost rehydration therapy in which infants drink a solution of a fistful of sugar and a pinch of salt in water
- Preventing blindness by administering large doses of vitamin A twice a year (35 cents per dose)
- Providing family planning services to help mothers space births at least two years apart
- Increasing female education with emphasis on nutrition, sterilization of drinking water, and improved child care

(9) While 15% of the people in LDCs suffer from undernutrition and malnutrition, about 15% of the people in MDCs suffer from *overnutrition*, which leads to obesity, or excess body fat. Although the causes of obesity are complex and not well understood, experts agree that a major cause is overeating—taking in food containing more energy than the body consumes. In the United States, 10% to 15% of children and 35% to 50% of middle-aged adults are obese, weighing at least 20% more than their normal, desirable weight. These overnourished people exist on diets high in calories, cholesterol-containing saturated fats, salt, sugar, and processed foods and low in unprocessed fresh vegetables, fruits, and fiber. Partly as a result of these dietary choices, overweight people are at significantly higher than normal risk of diabetes, high blood pressure, stroke, and heart disease. Some elements of this diet are also associated with intestinal cancer, tooth decay, and other health problems.*

*Miller, *Living in the Environment*, pp. 243–244.

1. _____

2. _____

3. _____

4. _____

5. _____

1. The topic of the excerpt is

 a. a definition of undernutrition
 b. a contrast between malnutrition and undernutrition
 c. a definition of overnutrition
 d. a definition of undernutrition, malnutrition, overnutrition, and famine

2. The main idea of paragraph 1 concerns

 a. a definition of undernutrition
 b. how malnutrition concerns the intake of insufficient nutrients
 c. ways that undernutrition is different from malnutrition
 d. what is meant by caloric intake

3. The main idea of paragraph 3 concerns

 a. the fact that hunger kills more people than famine
 b. the fact that famine kills more people than hunger
 c. the media coverage of famine
 d. the pain caused by hunger and famine

4. The main idea of paragraph 4 concerns

 a. what undernutrition and malnutrition are
 b. the tragic life cycle of hungry adults and their children
 c. the kinds of diseases hungry people experience
 d. how hunger negatively affects the mind and body

5. The main idea of paragraph 9 concerns

 a. a definition of overnutrition
 b. where overnutrition occurs
 c. how obesity causes diabetes and heart disease
 d. the nature of overnutrition and the several diseases caused by it

   Now go back to reread the excerpt. Then answer the following three questions in a short phrase or sentence without looking back at the excerpt.

6. Define one of the following two diseases: marasmus or kwashiorkor. (1 point)

_____
70%
Ask instructor for answers.

7. Briefly discuss two diseases caused by lack of vitamin intake. (2 points)

8. Name two measures that could help stop the diseases caused by famine. (2 points)

Follow-up on the Environmental Studies Exercises

Now that you have completed these exercises, it may be helpful to see how your reading on this topic has changed some of your ideas about the environment. You may want to go back to Exercises 3.1–3.6 and reread them just for their content, or for what they have to say about the environment. Then answer the following questions either individually or in small groups:

1. How would you now define the terms *environment* and *environmental studies*?
2. In history, how have human beings contributed to the environmental problem? How have they helped solve some of the problems in the environment?
3. What one environmental problem that you read about in these exercises is of most concern to you? Why?
4. What other issues related to the environment do you now want to study further?

4 Locating Major and Minor Details

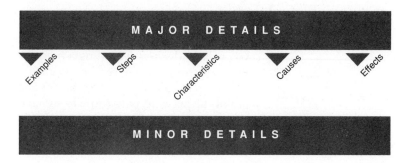

Now that you have practiced locating and writing main-idea sentences, you are ready to learn about the detail sentences in reading and lecture material. You can also use them in your own writing. Details may be either major or minor.

Major Details

Major details are the A, B, C, and so on of outline format. They support the main idea by giving examples, steps, characteristics, causes, or effects. Major details often answer the who, what, where, when, why, which one(s), or what kind(s) of a sentence or passage. Major details are usually found in the body of a paragraph, essay, or lecture.

Major Details That Give Examples. Main-idea sentences often express a point of view, as in the following: "America is experiencing a series of economic problems." In the major-detail sentences supporting a point of view like this one, you would be looking for examples. In general, examples should answer the question "What kinds?" For the sample main-idea sentence, you would likely be looking for sentences discussing such economic problems as unemployment, inflation, and poverty.

Note how a writer uses examples in the following paragraph:

> Economics is the study of how money is used on the personal and social level. On the more local level, it studies personal and business questions.

ex Economics also concerns itself with a nation's economy—how money is spent and used on a larger scale. Finally, economics also examines international economic questions—how nations throughout the world address economic issues.

Do you see how economic questions related to a person or group, a nation, and several nations become the examples that support the main idea—that economics is the study of how money is used on a personal and social level?

When you come across the names of persons, places, and things, you probably have found details. The details become the support that you will need when defending a point of view. Start using the abbreviation *ex* in the margin to remind yourself that you are reading or listening to examples. Did you notice that this abbreviation was used in the margin of the previous paragraph to signal the three examples?

Major Details That Give Steps.   Details are sometimes laid out in sequence. For example, your instructor may be discussing the steps involved in reading a graph in an economics textbook, or you may be reading about the steps that the federal government used to close down a savings and loan association that was going bankrupt. The main-idea sentence that comes before the steps usually alerts you to the number of steps involved. In general, steps often answer the question "Which ones?"

Consider this main-idea sentence: "There are three steps to remember in reading a graph in economics." The details that follow this sentence should include these three steps. Be alert to the following signal words when you read or listen for steps: "first," "second," "third," and so on; "last" and "finally."

Notice how the details in the following excerpt spell out steps:

steps There are four basic steps to follow in reading an economics graph. *First*, look to see what the horizontal axis represents. *Second*, see what the vertical axis measures. *Third*, study how these two variables relate to each other. *Finally*, study what the graph shows about this relationship.

In this paragraph, the main-idea sentence introduces the number of steps necessary in reading a graph in economics. This sentence is general, but it is followed by specific directions for reading a graph. Did you notice the signal words that led you through the four steps? Like examples, steps provide specific information. Unlike examples, steps are more closely interrelated. A writer cannot present the second step before the first one. A writer presenting examples is usually not concerned with correctly sequencing them. You will learn more about steps as details in Chapter 5, "Identifying Organizational Patterns."

Finally, did you notice the marginal note *steps* in the previous paragraph? It is there to remind you of the steps in the excerpt. Marginal notes like *steps* or *ex* help direct your reading or listening.

Major Details That Present Characteristics.   Some major details are neither examples nor steps. Rather they are descriptive. Major details that present characteristics frequently include adjectives or adverbs. Such details may sketch a character, review a film or book, or define a word. Look at how the characteristics are used in the following main-idea sentences to support a point of view: "Japan has developed an *amazing* economic system" or "Adam Smith was a *superb* economist." Saying that Japan successfully sells automobiles to the United States would not fully describe the characteristics of Japan's economy, nor would mentioning that Adam Smith developed the idea of a laissez-faire economy necessarily describe the kind of economic thinker he was. Each of these main-idea statements needs details expressing qualities or feelings that answer the "why" of the main-idea statement.

Note how the following paragraph effectively uses characteristics:

characteristics Economics is a peculiar study in several ways. It is not a pure science like physics, because it studies how people behave in financial matters. Yet it is scientific in that it attempts to derive economic principles that apply to all economic matters. Much economic work is *mathematical* and *formulaic*. On the one hand, economics is *descriptive* of how people act in financial matters; on the other, it is *prescriptive*, in that it tries to show what people will do in certain economic situations.

In this paragraph, the author does not refer to specific economic studies or works. Rather, this passage emphasizes the qualities that make economics a unique field of study. Note how the author uses the adjectives "mathematical," "formulaic," "descriptive," and "prescriptive" to describe what economics is. By placing the comment *characteristics* in the margin, you remind yourself that you are emphasizing the qualities that explain economics.

Major Details That Present Causes and Effects.   Many major-detail sentences are closely related to the main-idea sentence. They do not give examples or qualities to support the main idea, nor do they list steps that follow from the main-idea sentence. Instead, these sentences are the reasons for, the causes of, or the results or effects of what the main idea suggests. They usually answer the "what" questions suggested in the main-idea sentence. Words that signal causes include "cause," "reason," "factor," "source," and "influence"; those suggesting effects are "effect," "consequence," "result," and "outcome."

Read the following paragraph and note how all the major-detail sentences provide some suggested causes for poverty:

causes Some economists believe that poverty is *caused* by society, not by the individual. They contend that a major *source* of poverty is a society that does not care for its poor. They often show that these types of government help the rich through loans and tax exemptions but do not give the poor a decent wage, federal health coverage for their families, or a quality education for their children. They contend that a major *reason* for poverty is little or no federal money going to those who need it the most.

Do you see how the words "caused," "source," and "reason" signal causes? Do you also see that these major-detail sentences provide specific information to support the main-idea sentence's point of view that society, not the individual, is the cause of poverty? Finally, note how the word *causes* in the margin reminds you of the kind of information found in this paragraph.

Now look at this paragraph, which deals with the effects of poverty:

> *effects* Poverty has numerous dangerous *results* for children. A poor child often has poor nutrition. *Consequently*, she does not attain her full physical and mental potential. This in turn *results* in generally low school achievement. The *outcome* is often a young adult who stays within the circle of poverty, perpetuating it.

Do you see how the signal words "results," "consequently," and "outcome" suggest a paragraph of effect? Again, notice that the major-detail sentences give specific information about the results of poverty. And the word *effects* in the margin is the signal that this paragraph is treating poverty's results.

Major-detail sentences of cause and effect often provide important information. Like steps and examples, they are specific; but unlike examples, causes and effects require you to see time relationships — how one occurrence may lead to another. You will learn much more about how cause-and-effect details are used in lectures and textbooks in Chapter 5, "Identifying Organizational Patterns."

Remember that in your lecture and reading notes you should mark major details as examples, steps, characteristics, causes, or effects, as done in the previous examples. Actively identifying details gives direction to your reading or listening and helps you organize and connect information. By identifying details as you read or listen, you will also make it easier to review this study material for exams.

Signal Words in Major-Detail Sentences.   A number of words and phrases can be used to introduce any type of major detail. Once you become familiar with the following words, you will have another way of locating major details in reading materials and lectures.

for example	furthermore	again	last
for instance	moreover	another	of course
in addition	besides	specifically	
also	next	finally	

You should also begin using these words and phrases when you write essays. These signal words alert your reader to details that you consider important.

Minor Details

By now, you should be able to recognize the four types of major details. Thus it will be easier for you to locate minor details. You will find minor-detail sentences right after major-detail sentences; minor details provide you with more information about the major detail. When you come upon a minor detail, ask yourself whether or not you want to include it in your notes. Often all you need to learn are the main ideas and the major details.

However, you will need to use minor details when you write paragraphs or essays. Adding a minor detail on an essay exam, for example, shows your instructor that you are well prepared. Often a minor-detail sentence picks up a word or phrase that was used in the preceding major-detail sentence.

Look at the following paragraph on inflation, and note that the last sentence further explains the preceding sentences. It is therefore a minor-detail sentence.

> Inflation is defined as a general rise in prices for a long time, usually for at least a year. Inflation generally means that what you buy costs more each month, yet your salary does not seem to increase to pay for these higher prices. Therefore, your money does not go as far. *That is, you cannot buy as many items or at the same quality as you did in the previous year.*

Do you see how this last sentence further explains inflation's influence on your purchasing power?

You can see more clearly what minor detail sentences are by studying an outline of the previous paragraph. The minor detail is the material farthest to the right in the outline, the 1 under B.

I. Inflation — A General Rise in Prices

    A. Items cost more each month
    B. Money does not stretch as far as it once did

        1. You buy fewer items, or the quality is not as good as it once was

Remember that it is often only the I (main idea) and the A and B (major details) that you need to write as lecture notes and remember on exams. You may use the 1 (minor detail) more effectively in your essays.

The following words and phrases are frequently used to introduce minor-detail sentences. Use them when you introduce minor details in your essays, and look for them as signal words for minor details in lectures and in textbooks.

a minor point to be made	another way of saying
incidentally	restated
that is to say	namely
in other words	as an aside
of less importance	related to this issue
this is further clarified by	a corollary to this issue
as further clarification	subordinate to this issue

Summary

Major details provide the information necessary to support main ideas. Major details may be examples, steps, characteristics, causes, or effects. They answer questions of who, what, where, when, why, which one(s), or what kind(s). When you can identify the types of major details in your reading or listening, you tend to understand the material better.

Minor-detail sentences further explain a major-detail sentence that comes before them. Minor details are often not necessary in your reading and lecture notes, but you should use them in essays.

The following summary box should help you see how main ideas, major details, and minor details interrelate.

Summary Box   *Main Ideas, Major Details, and Minor Details*

What are they?	*Why do you use them?*
Main ideas (I): general statements in a paragraph or longer passage	To read and listen more effectively for major and minor details
Major Details (A, B, C): support for the main ideas, presented as examples, steps, characteristics, causes, or effects	To understand the main idea better; to see whether the main idea is based on sound evidence
Minor Details (1, 2, 3): further support for the major-detail sentence that comes before it	To further explain a major detail; used in essays, but often not necessary in reading or lecture notes

Topic: Economics

The exercises in this chapter all deal with the issue of economics, a topic that you may study in college and one that you face every day as you make purchases.

Before you begin these exercises, answer the following questions either individually or in small groups to get some sense for what you already know about economic matters:

1. How would you define *economics?*
2. What are the most common economic problems that our country is facing today?
3. How do you think our government is dealing with these problems?
4. How do you think we should deal with these problems?

*Exercise 4.1
Locating Major
Details*

Under each of the following ten main-idea sentences are five sentences, three of which support the main-idea sentence. The other two sentences are either minor details or main-idea sentences that would themselves introduce a new paragraph. Place the letters of the three major-detail sentences in the answer box.

All of the sentences in this exercise deal with the issue of scarcity, an important introductory concept for students studying economics.

Scarcity and Theories of Thomas Malthus

1. *Main-idea sentence:* Because we have only a limited amount of money and time to spend at any one moment in our life, we constantly face the economic issue of *scarcity*, or determining what we can and cannot have.

   a. Because of the reality of scarcity, we must constantly decide what we want to do with our money.
   b. Some economists focus on the cost element involved in scarcity.
   c. That is, some economists focus on how prices and price changes affect the issue of scarcity.
   d. Psychology deals with scarcity but from the perspective of how people are affected by what they do not have.
   e. Other economists focus on the benefits that occur because of our decisions regarding scarcity.

2. *Main idea sentence:* Thomas Malthus was one of the first economists to study the issue of scarcity.

   a. His book treating the issue of scarcity was titled *An Essay on the Principle of Population as It Affects the Future Improvement of Society* (1799).
   b. Malthus focused on the population explosion that he anticipated.

    c. A population explosion would result in the birth of too many humans for the earth to sustain.

    d. Malthus concluded that the earth's population would double every twenty-five years.

    e. Malthus's work is also studied in history and sociology, but it is interpreted a bit differently.

3. *Main-idea sentence:* Malthus predicted dire consequences as a result of a population explosion.

    a. First, he concluded that we would soon not have enough land to provide the food for these increased numbers of people.

    b. Thus there would be too little food produced to meet the demand.

    c. Finally, this scarcity of food would result in worldwide hunger.

    d. Environmentalists have also treated the issue of global hunger.

    e. That is, they have studied hunger on a worldwide basis.

4. *Main-idea sentence:* Most economists agree that Malthus's predictions were wrong.

    a. Although he was right in saying that population would increase, he was wrong about how fast it would increase.

    b. Incidentally, some people still believe that Malthus's predictions will come true.

    c. It has been shown that population growth is not consistent but very uneven.

    d. By uneven, most economists mean that population growth is not the same throughout the world.

    e. Finally, Malthus's prediction of world hunger has not come to pass as yet, and some rich countries like the United States even have food surpluses.

5. *Main-idea sentence:* The major flaw in Malthus's argument is that he did not consider the use of birth control to keep the population down.

    a. He did not anticipate that people in cities would not have an economic need for large families.

    b. Farm families in agricultural societies used the children to do much of the labor on the farm.

    c. Countries like China also realized that large families were a drain on the economy of the entire country.

    d. Currently, birth control measures worldwide have kept the population increase to no more than 1.7 percent each year.

    e. Many consider abortion to be an unsafe and immoral form of birth control.

6. *Main-idea sentence:* Yet some economists do not think that Malthus's idea of scarcity was totally wrong, particularly as it relates to the issue of pollution.

   a. Population and technology have created serious pollution problems.
   b. Nuclear accidents like the one at Chernobyl in Russia in 1986 have affected the entire world's population.
   c. Acid rain in the atmosphere has also destroyed vegetation and wildlife that people need in order to exist.
   d. Personal annual income is also a problem in some underdeveloped countries.
   e. Some people in Ethiopia and India, for example, earn less than $400 a year.

7. *Main-idea sentence:* Although some of Malthus's predictions are wrong, economists have learned the importance of the concept of scarcity.

   a. Many economists have realized that people must take greater care of the environment.
   b. Many biologists also believe in the value of environmental protection.
   c. Marine biologists, who see how many fish have been killed off, have spoken for greater protection of the world's waters.
   d. Economists have also discussed the need to analyze carefully which products should be produced and which should not.
   e. Economists have also realized that scarcity applies to both the rich and poor classes of the world.

8. *Main-idea sentence:* Economists continue to emphasize that scarcity is the fundamental issue faced by people all over the world.

   a. People must always exert a certain amount of effort to get what they want.
   b. People must also constantly choose what they want among a series of options.
   c. Restated, economic options are central to what humans do each day.
   d. The amount of effort and the nature of the choices, then, determine the kind of economic scarcity that people face at each moment.
   e. Related to this issue of scarcity is the concept of supply.

9. *Main-idea sentence:* Scarcity is also closely related to the concept of demand.

   a. If an item is scarce, then it is in greater demand.
   b. That is to say, scarcity influences demand.
   c. Also, a scarce item is more difficult to purchase.

1. _____ _____ _____
2. _____ _____ _____
3. _____ _____ _____
4. _____ _____ _____
5. _____ _____ _____
6. _____ _____ _____
7. _____ _____ _____
8. _____ _____ _____
9. _____ _____ _____
10. _____ _____ _____

70%

(score = # correct × 10, + 10 bonus points)
Find answers on p. 333.

    d. Finally, a scarce item generally is more expensive.

    e. Taxation laws also influence the overall price of an item.

10. *Main-idea sentence:* Scarcity is also related to the issue of supply.

    a. The law of supply and demand is a fundamental economic concept.

    b. If an item like gold, for example, is scarce, it is in short supply.

    c. The scarcity of a particular product, like gold, often brings out the most ingenious shoppers for it.

    d. Finally, a desired product like gold that is in short supply is more expensive.

    e. Gold is used most often in the manufacturing of jewelry.*

Exercise 4.2
Identifying Types
of Major Details

The following paragraphs present different kinds of details to support the main-idea sentences. Your job is to read each paragraph and identify the kind of detail that is used. Write in the answer box *EX* if the details are examples, *ST* if the details are steps, *CH* if the details are characteristics, *CS* if the details are causes, and *EF* if the details are effects. The signal words used in some of the paragraphs should help you recognize the kinds of details that are used.

All of the paragraphs deal with the great economist Adam Smith, who like Malthus greatly influenced the newly emerging study of economics.

Adam Smith's Contribution to Economics

1. Adam Smith wrote a very important book, titled *An Inquiry into the Nature and Causes of the Wealth of Nations* (1776). Many economists have found it to be a ground-breaking book. It was considered a brilliant interpretation of markets and prices. Others have praised its logic and power in explaining just what economists should study.

2. In this work, Smith insisted that self-interest guides people's economic decisions. Butchers sell meat because they want to make money, not because they want to feed society. Doctors see patients so they can make a profit. Only beggars, Smith notes, look to people's kindness rather than to their self-interest.

3. What are the effects of self-interest, according to Smith? Because of self-interest, the economy of any society is able to function. It makes producers earn a profit. And it brings satisfaction to buyers. Another effect of self-interest is the jobs people choose: People generally choose jobs that bring them pleasure.

---

*Adapted from Philip C. Starr, *Economics: Principles in Action*, 5th ed. (Belmont, Calif.: Wadsworth, 1988), pp. 5–6.

4. According to Smith, what are the economic results of allowing people to pursue their self-interest? He maintained that the economy would flourish if the government left people alone. By leaving government out of buyers' decisions, Smith believed, the system would produce many products for its people to enjoy. By allowing people the right to follow their own interests, an economy would continue to improve.

5. Smith referred to an economy in which government is not involved as a *laissez-faire* economic system. He provided several examples of how this system works. Producers who are left alone will produce what the buyers want, he contended. Buyers will shop for the best deal. If there is a demand for an item, then there will be many different types and prices of this item for buyers to choose from. Buyers and producers will not be living in a society of scarcity.

6. Economists who direct laissez-faire systems are advised to use the following procedures. First, they are asked to let buyers and sellers work out their own problems. Furthermore, they are advised to refer any problem between buyer and seller back to the buyer and seller themselves. Finally, they are told to discourage the government from helping either buyer or seller with tax breaks or loans.

7. How does Smith's laissez-faire system account for economic bad times, namely recessions and depressions? Many economists have insisted that a hands-off policy is the major cause of depression. Self-interest, they argue, encourages a few people to make much money and forces many people to live in poverty. A government that does not help the poor and needy only makes their economic condition worse.

8. Economists who question Smith's ideas suggest that a government should help a society's economy in several ways. For example, government should protect society from large, greedy companies. The government should also provide goods and services that private companies do not want to provide, like inexpensive housing and transportation. These economists also argue that the government should get involved when the economy is very weak.

9. Over the issue of laissez-faire economics, a liberal position and a conservative position have emerged. A conservative economist would encourage people to be competitive, aggressive, and self-supporting. In contrast, a liberal economist would ask citizens to be concerned about both themselves and society. A liberal economist would encourage them to be cooperative as well as competitive. The liberal and conservative economic positions are very different indeed.

1. _____

2. _____

3. _____

4. _____

5. _____

6. _____

7. _____

8. _____

9. _____

10. _____

80%

Ask instructor for answers.

10. Smith's economic ideas speak to our current economic conditions. People are still asking the same questions. How much should government help the poor and needy? Should the government get involved during times of recession? Does a hands-off policy always mean that the economy will be strong? One finds people on both sides of the argument, the liberal and the conservative economic points of view.*

*Exercise 4.3
Identifying Main
Ideas, Major Details,
and Minor Details*

The following paragraphs contain main-idea sentences, major-detail sentences, and minor-detail sentences. Read each paragraph carefully. Then, next to the appropriate number in the answer box, write *MN* for main-idea sentence, *MA* for major-detail sentence, and *MI* for minor-detail sentence. Look for transition words that signal the kind of sentence each one is.

The following ten paragraphs define the key economic terms involving payments. You will learn how concepts like rent, interest, wages, and profit are related. They should help you understand some of Adam Smith's ideas about self-interest.

Payments and Related Issues

(1) Payments are made to owners of property or business for a variety of reasons. (2) Landowners receive rent. (3) This rent is often paid monthly but may be paid weekly. (4) Owners of businesses receive payments in the form of interest on their investments.

(5) Rent is defined in economics as the money one pays for the use of land. (6) Rent is determined by how profitable the land is to the owner and how much the renter is willing to pay. (7) Clearly owners want to make a profit on their property. (8) Equally clearly, renters want the rent to be less than what the property earns or what they make as wages.

(9) Wages work similarly to rent. (10) In this case, employers buy the labor of their employees. (11) Employers want to know that their employees are making a profit for the business. (12) That is to say, owners want what the workers do for the company to bring in more money than the cost of their salary.

(13) But wages do not always work out so neatly. (14) Some people earn more than they are really worth, and others earn less. (15) Some people criticize movie stars' and athletes' high salaries, arguing that they would gladly work for less if others in their field earned less as well. (16) A corollary to this issue is that some athletes are earning as much as $4 million a year.

(17) Some people are blocked from advancing to another job because of racial discrimination. (18) Others are kept in the same unsatisfying position because of their age. (19) Still others do not have the extra money to be trained in a field they are particularly interested in pursu-

1.	_____
2.	_____
3.	_____
4.	_____
5.	_____
6.	_____
7.	_____
8.	_____
9.	_____
10.	_____
11.	_____
12.	_____
13.	_____
14.	_____
15.	_____
16.	_____
17.	_____
18.	_____

*Adapted from Starr, *Economics*, pp. 20–21.

19. _____

20. _____

21. _____

22. _____

23. _____

24. _____

25. _____

26. _____

27. _____

28. _____

29. _____

30. _____

31. _____

32. _____

33. _____

34. _____

35. _____

36. _____

37. _____

38. _____

39. _____

40. _____

_____
75%

(score = # correct × 2.5)
Find answers on p. 334.

ing. (20) All of these job factors are known in economics as *barriers to entry*.

(21) A term related to wages is *capital*. (22) Capital includes products such as tools, equipment, and buildings. (23) Tools and equipment, incidentally, include items used by workers in their particular job. (24) A word processor would thus be part of the equipment for a secretary of today.

(25) What constitutes the capital of fishermen in a primitive tribe? (26) The nets used to catch the fish would, of course, be part of their capital. (27) The value of a fishnet in economic terms is how much profit it can create. (28) That is to say, if a fishnet can allow the fisherman to catch more fish than before, then it is capital that provides for profit.

(29) Profit is different for an independent businessperson than it is for a wage earner. (30) If a concession stand can make you $500 a week but you can earn $510 a week working for a larger fast-food business, then your stand is not making you a profit. (31) To make a profit in your own business, you must be able to earn more than what you would earn as a wage earner. (32) Economists believe that independent businesspeople should earn more than wage earners because they are taking greater risks.

(33) How much profit is considered good enough for an independent businessperson? (34) There is no fixed percentage. (35) That is, there is no number that will tell a businessperson that the business is profitable. (36) Psychological factors are involved, such as how much you value working for yourself.

(37) Clearly rent, wages, profit, and capital are closely related. (38) When people consider the profit of a particular investment, they must factor in issues like rent and wages. (39) They must also determine how much capital they must purchase initially and must replace in time. (40) As an aside, note that it is often the initial cost of capital investments that discourages businesspeople from going into a particular venture.*

_____

*Adapted from Starr, *Economics*, pp. 22–24.

Exercise 4.4
Writing Effective
Topic Sentences

In composition textbooks, main-idea sentences are often called topic sentences. *Topic sentences* are general statements, usually found at the beginning of a paragraph. Like main-idea statements, topic sentences indicate what the paragraph will say.

Effective topic sentences are neither too specific nor too general. They direct readers to the details of support and do not become details of support themselves.

Look at the following ineffective topic sentences and their revisions:

1. Adam Smith was an economist. (too general)
   Adam Smith was an economist who introduced the concept of laissez-faire economics. (acceptable)

Notice that the first sentence does not introduce the contribution that Smith made to the study of economics. Effective topic sentences clearly identify the "what" of an issue.

2. Thomas Malthus studied population. (too general)
   Thomas Malthus was an economist who studied how population growth could affect the economy. (acceptable)

Note how the revised sentence introduces Malthus's profession (economist) and shows how population is related to the economy. In this case, the revised sentence clarifies both the "who" and the "what" of the general topic sentence.

3. An ax is an example of capital. (too specific)
   Capital is defined in economics as tools, equipment, or buildings. (acceptable)

Do you see that the example of the ax would be better as a supporting detail after the acceptable topic sentence is introduced?

Your task in this exercise is to determine whether the following ten topic sentences are too general or too specific. Write in the answer box "general" or "specific." Then revise the topic sentences, making them more effective. These sentences are based on the material you studied in Exercises 4.1–4.3. Review these exercises before or while you complete this assignment.

1. *Scarcity* is an important economic term.

   Revision: _____

2. The population increase is now only 1.7 percent each year.

   Revision: _____

3. According to Smith, doctors see patients in order to make a profit.

Revision: _____

4. Smith studies self-interest.

Revision: _____

5. A word processor is an example of equipment a secretary uses.

Revision: _____

6. In economics, *rent* is defined in a certain way.

Revision: _____

7. There are many barriers to entry.

Revision: _____

8. *Profit* is another important economic term.

Revision: _____

9. Some economists question Smith's ideas.

Revision: _____

10. Some economists believe in a hands-off policy.

Revision: _____

1. _____

2. _____

3. _____

4. _____

5. _____

6. _____

7. _____

8. _____

9. _____

10. _____

_____
80%
Ask instructor for answers.

Exercise 4.5
Locating Major and
Minor Details in a
Longer Passage

In this exercise, you will be reading a longer passage that explains the three major economic systems in our world. It should help explain further some of Adam Smith's ideas and show you how economic terms like *capital, wages,* and *profit* are used in studying a country's economic system.

Your job is to read for main ideas, major details, and minor details. After you have read the passage, answer the ten questions. If necessary, you may return to the passage while you answer the questions. Answer the first five questions in the answer box.

Socialism, Communism, and Capitalism

(1) Today the world seems to be divided into three forms of economy: socialism, communism, and capitalism. Communism and socialism seem to be more closely related to each other than they are to capitalism. But even socialism and communism have important differences when one studies them carefully.

(2) What are the major features of socialism? In socialism, the government plays an important role, controlling all of the major industries. There are many different kinds of socialism. For example, in France and Italy the government controls many of the major industries. In the People's Republic of China, the government owns and operates all of the country's industry.

(3) One must keep in mind that socialism is not dictatorship. That is, in most socialist countries the people can still vote in free elections. In many socialist countries, the government is trying to control some or many industries in order to provide more jobs for its people and prevent serious economic declines.

(4) Communism can be seen as an extreme form of socialism. In theory, communists believe that the people, not the government, run the country. All of its people work together and take from the country only what they need. Theoretically, no one would want to earn a huge salary. No country has as yet reached this communist ideal. Countries like the People's Republic of China, which is seen by others as a communist country, exert a tremendous amount of government control over their people.

(5) Like communism, capitalism is also an economic system in theory only. In a capitalistic society, people, not government, own property. Also, people are free to choose their own occupation and earn the amount of money they want. That is, capitalism emphasizes self-interest. Competition is encouraged, not discouraged as it would be in communism.

(6) No capitalistic country follows these ideals to the letter. In capitalistic countries like the United States, the government does control some industries, like transportation and utilities, and wholesale competition is sometimes discouraged if people or industries are treating other people unfairly. Some economists have called this more realistic type of capitalism *mixed capitalism.**

1. The topic of the passage is

   a. a definition of socialism
   b. a description of communism
   c. a definition of capitalism
   d. all of these

2. The main idea of paragraph 2 concerns

   a. socialism in France and Italy

---

*Adapted from Starr, *Economics*, pp. 29–30.

    b. how socialism as an economic system differs from country to country

    c. reasons why the People's Republic of China controls all of its industry

    d. how socialism differs from communism

3. A major detail presented in paragraph 3 is

    a. most citizens in socialist countries can vote

    b. socialism is not dictatorship

    c. socialism provides fewer jobs to its people than dictatorships do

    d. there are never economic declines in socialist countries

4. The major details in paragraph 4 include all *but*

    a. communists believe that the people run the country

    b. the citizens from a communist country take only what they need

    c. in theory, there would be no rich people in a communist country

    d. the People's Republic of China comes closest to being a true communist state

5. The last sentence in paragraph 5 is a

    a. major-detail sentence

    b. minor-detail sentence

    c. main-idea sentence

    d. topic sentence

6. What is the main idea of paragraph 3? _____

_____

7. What is the main idea of paragraph 4? _____

_____

8. List one major detail from paragraph 5. _____

_____

9. What is the main idea of paragraph 6? _____

_____

10. List a major detail from paragraph 6. _____

_____

1. _____

2. _____

3. _____

4. _____

5. _____

_____
80%
(score = # correct × 10)
Find answers on p. 334.

Exercise 4.6
Writing Your Own
Paragraph from
Main Ideas, Major
Details, and Minor
Details

Now go back to the passage on economic systems in Exercise 4.5 and locate its main idea (found in paragraph 1); the five major details (found in paragraphs 2, 4, 5, and 6); and the minor detail (found in paragraph 3). Jot down this information in the following outline:

I. _____

   A. _____

      1. _____

   B. _____

   C. _____

   D. _____

From this outline, answer the following essay question. Use only the outline to answer this question.

Essay question: Identify the three major economic systems in the world today, and briefly describe each.

70%

Ask instructor for answers.

Exercise 4.7
Determining Main
Ideas and Major
Details in a Textbook
Excerpt

The following is an excerpt from a textbook chapter on economic systems. It further explains how the notion of scarcity is important to the study of economics. Read through it quickly to get a sense of the topic. Then go back and read it slowly.

When you finish rereading, answer the five questions that follow it. You may return to the excerpt in deciding on your answers. Place the answers to the first five questions in the answer box.

An Introduction to Economic Systems

(1) Scarcity forces us to measure the inevitable costs and hoped-for benefits of every decision. This chapter describes the different routes societies take in making those decisions. After some preliminaries, most of the chapter is devoted to describing our kind of economic system, its history, and some of its successes and failures. The chapter is divided into four sections: (1) the three questions every economic system must answer, (2) three different ways of answering those questions, (3) a brief history of our market-price system, and (4) an evaluation of our market-price system.

The Three Questions Every Economic System Must Answer

(2) First, what do we mean by *economic system*? An economic system is the particular body of laws, habits, ethics, and customs (religious or otherwise) that a group of people observe to satisfy their material wants.

' (3) All systems, from primitive to advanced, face three fundamental questions: (1) What goods and services should be produced (and in what quantities)? (2) How should they be produced? (3) For whom should they be produced? Let's now examine each of these questions.

What Goods and Services Should Be Produced?

˅ (4) Every economic system must decide, consciously or not, what goods (TV sets or stereos or bicycles) and services (medical care or legal advice or plumbing) are to be produced and in what quantities. These decisions require, of course, an evaluation of opportunity cost. If we decide to devote more of our resources to making cars, we will have fewer resources for building rapid transit systems. The opportunity cost of each new car is measured by the amount of rapid transit we could have provided but did not.

(5) This observation must be qualified. For example, if people are unemployed, we might be able to use some of them to build cars without having to divert people already employed in rapid transit. Also, if new technology (new machines, tools, or production methods) makes it easier to produce cars, that will release some people from automobile production to work on rapid transit. A surplus of workers and/or new technology enables us to have more of both products.

How Should the Goods and Services Be Produced?

' (6) Every society must decide not only what products and services it wants (and in what quantities) but also *how* it should produce them. The question of how involves choosing some combination of machines and people. For example, should we use large numbers of people working with garden tools to cultivate potatoes or a much smaller number of people working with tractors?

(7) Either way, we have to consider the opportunity costs of employing the machines and people in growing potatoes. We have to measure this cost in terms of the lost production of something else.

(8) But the problem is more complex than that. Let's take a very simple example. A potato farmer is understandably tired of cultivating his fields by hand. He wants to purchase a "machine"—in his case, a horse and plow. To buy the horse and plow, he will have to sell some of his potatoes. Consequently, the opportunity cost of the horse and plow is measured by the sacrifice the farmer and his family have to make in not consuming some of their potatoes. In some cases, this opportunity cost may be severe—the family may not get enough to eat. Of course, the decision to buy the horse and plow is made with the expectation that future benefits will make up for these present costs.

(9) In poor countries, this kind of trade-off is an excruciating problem. If the government in one of these countries decides to build a hydroelectric dam, many hundreds of people may have to be taken away from food-producing activities. The opportunity cost of the dam may be further starvation of the people. Thus, the question of *how* may involve some very difficult decisions.

For Whom Should the Goods and Services Be Produced?

, (10) Every society must decide who receives the products and services produced, which is another way of saying that a society must decide how income will be distributed among its people. Needless to say, whether by design or circumstance, the world's production and income are very unequally distributed. About 60 percent of the world's population receives only about 10 percent of total income, whereas 10 percent of the people receive about 50 percent of total world income.

(11) In the United States, the lowest 20 percent of families receive only 5 percent of total income, while the highest 20 percent of families receive over 40 percent of the total. And roughly 25 million people in the U.S. are classified as poverty-stricken.

(12) Part of the "for whom?" question involves deciding which generation, present or future, should receive the goods and services produced. Decisions to use resources for long-term projects like the Tennessee Valley Authority or cancer research often mean a sacrifice for today's generation in favor of some expected benefit for tomorrow's. Most of the working population pays Social Security taxes for the benefit of older people. Research expenditures on power from hydrogen fusion are expected to be $1 billion per year for twenty years; commercial use of hydrogen fusion is not expected until the year 2015. Again, we must measure opportunity cost.*

1. The topic of this excerpt is

   a. what one should buy
   b. what one should sell
   c. from whom one should buy
   d. what, how, and for whom goods and services should be produced

2. The main idea of paragraph 5 is

   a. the unemployed should be allowed to work
   b. technology makes production easier
   c. both additional workers and better technology are needed to produce more of the desired product
   d. new technology equals new machines

3. A major detail *not* mentioned in paragraph 9 is

   a. a hydroelectric dam does not require many economic decisions
   b. opportunity costs are generally not involved in the production of a dam
   c. poor countries do not produce hydroelectric dams
   d. producing a dam in a poor country may require the additional starvation of its people

*Philip C. Starr, *Economics: Principles in Action*, 4th ed. (Belmont, Calif.: Wadsworth, 1984), pp. 18–19.

4. A major detail *not* mentioned in paragraph 11 is

    a. in the United States, 5 percent of the poorest people receive 20 percent of the income

    b. there are 20 million poverty-stricken people in the United States

    c. wealthy people in the United States seem to control most of the country's money

    d. 25 million people in the United States are in the poverty category

5. A major detail mentioned in paragraph 12 is

    a. the central question is which generation deserves the goods and services

    b. one generation must sacrifice in order for the other to receive

    c. the people will not use the energy from hydrogen fusion until the year 2015

    d. opportunity cost is involved in making decisions about who receives goods and services

1. _____
2. _____
3. _____
4. _____
5. _____

Now read the following three questions. With them in mind, go back and reread the selection. Then answer each question in a short phrase or sentence without looking back at the excerpt.

6. Why does a country that produces more cars often get involved in fewer transportation projects? (1 point)

7. Why is it that the potato farmer who buys a horse and plow will have fewer potatoes for his family to eat? (2 points)

8. Why does cancer research require sacrifices of a society that is involved in it? (2 points)

_____
70%
Ask instructor for answers.

Follow-up on the Economics Exercises

Now that you have completed Exercises 4.1–4.7, it may be interesting to see how your reading of this topic has changed some of your ideas about economics. You may go back to reread the exercises just for their content, or for what they have to say about economics, before you answer the following questions. Answer these questions either individually or in small groups:

1. How would you now define the term *economics*?

2. Discuss three economic issues that you were introduced to in these exercises.

3. What do you now feel is the role of government in solving economic problems?

4. What issues in economics would you now like to study more?

5 Identifying Organizational Patterns

Information is frequently organized in one of a few standard patterns: cause-effect, definition, sequence of events, spatial-geographic, thesis-support, comparison-contrast, and description. If you know what those standard organizational patterns are, you can look for one as you read or listen to lectures and thereby have one more insight into the author's or lecturer's meaning. Then you will likely understand the material better. Main ideas and important details will also be clearer if you understand which organizational pattern is being used.

The Cause-Effect Pattern

Cause-effect is perhaps the most common organizational pattern that you will come across. You will find it in almost every subject that you study, but it is most evident in the sciences and social sciences. You learned something about cause and effect in Chapter 4, which discussed major details. You will now study cause and effect as a pattern that can organize an entire chapter or lecture. Cause-effect sentences, paragraphs, or essays have two parts: the cause, or the source of the change, and the effect, or the result of the change.

In addition, cause-effect relationships can be either direct or indirect. If cause-effect statements are *direct*, they are always true. Look at the following cause-effect statement from chemistry: "When water is lowered to 32 degrees Fahrenheit, it freezes." Do you see that lowering the water's temperature to 32 degrees is the cause and that the water freezing at this temperature is the effect? This relationship is direct because water always freezes at this temperature (at least under normal physical conditions). In your notes, you can show this relationship by using an arrow. "Lowering temperature of water to 32 degrees F. → water freezing."

An *indirect* cause-effect relationship is one whose effect is caused by several factors. Indirect causes are also called *contributory* causes. Indirect cause-effect relationships are often found in the social sciences and the humanities. Consider the following statement from sociology: "Criminal behavior seems to be caused by a deprived social environment." The term of qualification "seems" suggests that this relationship is indirect. A deprived social environment may be one of several influences on criminal behavior. One frequently finds contributory causes in relationships dealing with people and events, and often these relationships are worded with qualifying terms.

The following terms of qualification are often associated with indirect cause-effect relationships:

it appears	perhaps	one can safely say
it seems	probably	one can say with reservation
apparently	likely	there seems to be a link
one can assume	contributing to	there seems to be a relationship

For a more thorough list of terms of qualification, see the lists in Chapter 7 titled "Words and Phrases That Express a Little Doubt" and "Words and Phrases That Express Some Doubt," p. 127. Certain transitional phrases also suggest results, like "consequently," "therefore," "so," "as a result," and "as a consequence."

How should you note cause-effect relationships? If you find them in your reading, you may want to separate cause from effect in the margin. From the previous example dealing with crime, you could write:

cause: crime
effect:
bad environment

Criminal behavior seems to be caused by a deprived social environment.

You should also note whether the cause is direct or indirect. You can write the same kinds of comments when you take or review your lecture notes.

The Definition Pattern

You will find definitions in the lecture and textbook material of every course you take. Definitions make up a large part of what you will be asked on examination questions, so you should listen and read carefully when you come upon a definition. Definitions are often expressed concisely, so you should also write down every word of a definition.

In your lecture and reading notes, use the abbreviation *def* as your signal that a definition follows. Look at the following example from sociology:

def: social class   A social class is a particular category of a social system. Working, lower, middle, and upper are the most common classes.

Another successful technique to use when you are learning definitions is to list the general category of the term first, then to give examples or features of the term. See how the above definition of "social class" can be effectively divided up into these categories:

Term	*General Category*	*Specific Features*
social class	social system	divided into working, lower, middle, and upper

This method of categorizing is similar to classifying information into main ideas and details. Also, the chart helps you visualize each part of the definition.

When you come upon a definition, you should listen or read more actively. At first you may have trouble remembering all the parts of a definition, because each part tends to be written concisely. But learn to remember definitions, because they are the foundations for any course that you take. They are especially important in your understanding of introductory courses. More will be said about how to remember definitions in Chapter 13, "The SQ3R Study System," and Chapters 15 and 16, which are about examination strategies.

The Sequence-of-Events Pattern

You will find the sequence-of-events pattern in all subjects, but you will often see it in history material, in which dates are presented chronologically. You will also find the sequence-of-events pattern in vocational material, in which you must follow procedures to make or repair an object or to work a machine like a computer. You were introduced to this pattern in the previous chapter, where it was presented as a type of major detail. Now you will see it as a structure that can organize a textbook chapter or a lecture.

The following signal words often introduce a sequence-of-events pattern: "first, second, third," and so on; "last," "now," "later," "before," "often," "soon," "finally," "next."

When you listen to or read material arranged in a sequence-of-events pattern, you should number the events or steps. Make the number stand out so that, in reviewing your notes, you can make a picture of the sequence in your mind. Look at how information is sequenced in the list that follows this paragraph on a juvenile offender:

James's history follows a particular pattern that many juvenile offenders seem to fall into. First, he was born to a single parent, a mother who did not work. Second, he did most of his own child rearing, feeding and clothing himself from the age of four. Third, when he began school, he returned home to an empty house. Finally, as a teenager he found himself spending more time on the streets with dropouts than at home.

James's Childhood History

1. Born to a single mother who did not work
2. Began caring for himself at age four
3. Returned from school to an unattended home
4. As a teenager, his friends were dropouts

By arranging the sequence of events vertically, you get a clearer picture of the significant moments in James's life.

The Spatial-Geographic Pattern

The spatial-geographic pattern is frequently used in biology and geography courses. In this pattern, you must visualize the various parts of an organism or the relative location of countries, states, or cities on a map.

In biology courses, the following signal words are used to direct you to various parts of an organism:

above	between	inward	anterior	distal
below	upper	external	posterior	
next to	lower	dorsal	medial	
behind	outward	ventral	lateral	

In a biology lecture, your instructor will use these terms along with a slide or diagram. Start associating these terms with what you see. If you can sketch, make a rough picture of the organism during the lecture. In biology textbooks, organs and organ parts are often mentioned in conjunction with a diagram. As you read, refer to the diagram. After you have read the material and studied the diagram, close your book and draw the organ or organism from memory. Your biology instructor may well ask you to label an organism on an exam. On such exams, your spatial-geographic skills will assist you.

The same skills are necessary in geography courses. Your geography instructor may present maps in a lecture and ask you to remember the correct location of various parts. If you can, copy any maps that you see in lectures and important maps that you find in your reading. If you cannot draw well, be sure to use accurate signal words as you take notes. Here are some signal words found in geography readings and lectures:

north	bordering	up
south	adjacent	down
east	next to	opposite to
west		

Let signal words like these help you visualize parts of a city, state, county, or continent. "Southwestern," for example, should be the key word that you hear in the statement "The southwestern border of the city is the area with the most affluent homeowners — the city's upper class."

The Thesis-Support Pattern

The thesis-support pattern is used in all disciplines; its organization is similar to that of the multiple-paragraph essay, which is discussed in Chapter 16. A *thesis* is a point of view expressed by a speaker or writer. Usually the thesis is in the first paragraph of an essay or at the beginning of a lecture.

When you locate a statement that seems to be the thesis, write *thesis* in the margin; then summarize it. For example, if your sociology instructor begins a lecture with a statement like "Power is a fundamental drive that seems to organize all types of society," you could write something like this:

Thesis: power — a basic drive organizing societies

Underline the term "thesis" so that, in reviewing your notes, you will remember to reread this statement. On exams, you are expected to know well the thesis of a lecture or an article.

Be sure that you can distinguish between a thesis and a fact. Like a main idea, a thesis expresses an opinion that needs support. Like a detail, a *fact* may support a thesis. Unlike a thesis, a fact does not ask you to question it. Which of the following two statements is the thesis and which is the fact that supports it? (1) "Power is expressed in the amount of money and capital an individual possesses." (2) "Members of the upper class always possess more money than the classes below them do." Do you see that in the second statement the writer is not presenting an argument, merely a fact? But in the first statement, you may question whether money is the only indicator of power.

Once you have located the thesis, you need to analyze its details. Remember that a thesis is only as good as its details. Some details are well chosen; others are not. Start training yourself to look for the well-chosen detail. Make marginal comments in your textbook or when taking lecture notes, stating whether the details support the thesis well. If a sociology instructor said that social power is expressed in several ways, you would be correct in wanting to know what is meant by "several." Are there three ways or thirteen? In your notes, you should identify important details with the abbreviation *det*.

Here are some signal words that introduce a thesis-support pattern:

the thesis is	for example	especially
it is theorized that	for instance	one example is
the hypothesis is	specifically	the idea is supported by
it is my belief that	in particular	proof is found in

You can use these same signal words in writing your own thesis-support essay.

The details used to support a thesis may be causes, effects, spatial or geographic words, or descriptions. The thesis-support pattern is the most general of the seven and may include other organizational patterns.

The Comparison-Contrast Pattern

The comparison-contrast pattern is used in all disciplines. Like the thesis-support pattern, it may be made up of several paragraphs, and it may include other organizational patterns. The comparison-contrast pattern asks you to find similarities and differences in what you read or hear.

Here are some of the most common signal words for the comparison-contrast pattern:

Contrast

but	on the one hand	although	opposed
however	on the other hand	while	opposing
yet	contrary	different from	conversely
nevertheless	on the contrary	differently	whereas
at variance	in contrast	oppositely	
otherwise	rather	opposite	

Comparison

and	similar	as	parallel to	exactly like
also	similarly	just as	much the same	analogous
like	as if	resembling	comparable	analogously

Use these signal words not only to recognize comparison-contrast patterns but also to write essays that show comparison or contrast. Use them to highlight the similarities and differences that you present in your writing.

When you take reading and lecture notes that show comparison or contrast, you can best show these similarities or differences in a chart like this one:

Similarity or Difference

Topic	*Topic*
1.	1.
2.	2.
3.	3.

This chart lets you neatly place similarities and differences side by side and thus more easily see how pieces of information relate.

Look at the following information taken from a sociology lecture; then see how a chart can be used to explain it.

Capitalism and socialism begin with different ideologies. Capitalism believes in private ownership, but socialism assumes state ownership of certain property. Capitalism allows its people to pursue economic gain; socialism controls the economic gains of its people.

Differences

Capitalism	*Socialism*
1. Private ownership of property	1. State ownership of most property
2. Economic freedom for its people	2. Economic control of its people

Do you see how this chart highlights the differences between socialism and capitalism?

A lecturer or an author of a textbook may present similarities and differences by using such a chart. If you come upon comparison-contrast patterns presented in paragraph form, you may want to create your own chart. These charts often allow you to remember compare-contrast information more easily.

The Descriptive Pattern

The descriptive pattern is different from the other organizational patterns. You will find it most often in literature: short stories, novels, poems, plays. Descriptive patterns re-create experiences through the suggestiveness of language and often use characteristics as details. Your job is to see how description awakens your senses. In your notes, comment on how well the description re-creates an experience.

Read this excerpt about a young man fleeing from the law, from John Edgar Wideman's *Brothers and Keepers*:

visual images

Johnny-Boy wasn't from Pittsburgh. *Small, dark, greasy,* he was an outsider who knew he didn't fit, ill at ease in a middle-class house, the meandering conversations that had nothing to do with anyplace he'd been, anything he understood or cared to learn. Johnny-Boy had trouble talking, trouble staying awake. When he spoke at all, he *stuttered* riffs of barely comprehensible ghetto slang. When the rest of us were talking, he'd *nod off.* I didn't like the way his *heavy-lidded, bubble eyes* blinked open and searched the room when he thought no one was watching him.

Do you see how the descriptions "small, dark, greasy" and "heavy-lidded, bubble eyes" present a clear picture of this young fugitive? Also, "stuttering" and "nodding off" are vivid actions that describe him. If you were reading this novel, a marginal comment like "vivid picture" would be helpful as you reread the work.

In any literature course you take, you will come upon the descriptive pattern. Your literature instructor will probably give you reading strategies to use in analyzing descriptions. When you read any descriptive passage, remember to study the words and what they suggest rather than analyzing the thesis and details of support.

Summary

Organizational patterns are used by speakers and writers to present their ideas more clearly and to show the structure of their arguments. Recognizing which organizational pattern is being used and knowing how that pattern works will help you better understand the material. Organizational patterns often overlap; that is, several structures may be used by a lecturer or writer. Don't expect each paragraph you read or each lecture you hear to use only one organizational pattern. The seven most common organizational patterns are cause-effect, definition, sequence of events, spatial-geographic, thesis-support, comparison-contrast, and descriptive. Each organizational pattern has its own logic and signal words that show you how the material is organized. Being familiar with these seven organizational patterns will make your reading and lecture notes clearer and will improve your writing.

Summary Box   *Organizational Patterns*

What are they?	*Why are they used?*
Structures used in writing and speaking to explain ideas, describe experiences, or show the logic of an argument	To help a reader or listener understand an argument better and take better reading and lecture notes
Seven common patterns: cause-effect, definition, sequence of events, spatial-geographic, thesis-support, comparison-contrast, descriptive	To help a writer compose logical and organized essays

Topic: Sociology

The exercises in Chapter 5 all deal with some issue from sociology, a subject you will probably study sometime during your college career.

Before you begin these exercises, answer the following questions either individually or in small groups to get some sense for what you already know about sociology:

1. What do you think sociology covers?
2. What are some of the problems that you currently see in society?
3. How do you think these problems should be addressed?
4. Why do people in society act the way they do? Are they born to act in a certain way? Or does society teach them?

Exercise 5.1
Identifying Thesis
Statements

Some of the following ten statements express a point of view and would qualify as thesis statements; others are statements of fact. All of the statements discuss what sociology is, so they should provide you with an introduction to this discipline. In the answer box, write "thesis" or "fact" on the appropriate lines.

Some Introductory Statements About Sociology

1. Sociology is the study of how people make agreements and how they organize, teach, break, and change them.
2. Sociology is a less difficult discipline than psychology.
3. Sociology also studies how people come to disagree.
4. People who study sociology usually become dissatisfied with society.
5. Sociology is a scientific study of how people agree and disagree.
6. Sociology tests what it knows by carefully measuring and analyzing how people behave.
7. Sociology is the most intelligent discipline to have emerged in the past fifty years.
8. Sociology focuses on action, or on what people do.
9. People tend to accomplish goals more by acting than by speaking.
10. Actions are shaped by what has come before, or previous actions.

The following five paragraphs on social activities each have only one thesis statement. Write in the answer box the letter of the sentence that is the thesis statement.

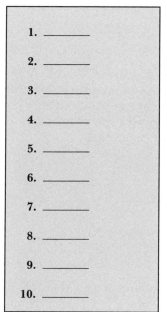

1. _____

2. _____

3. _____

4. _____

5. _____

6. _____

7. _____

8. _____

9. _____

10. _____

Social Activities

11. (a) A conversation is one of the most amazing examples of human social activity. (b) People meet, and they exchange glances. (c) They shake hands. (d) And they proceed to get to know one another by sharing experiences in their lives.

12. (a) A fistfight is an example of social interaction. (b) A mugging is also a type of social activity. (c) The mugger points a gun at you and demands your money. (d) Some social interactions are painfully inharmonious.

13. (a) Sociologists study many interesting aspects of social interaction. (b) They may focus on spoken communication. (c) They may specialize in aggressive behavior. (d) Still others may specialize in aggressive behavior manifested in speech.

14. (a) When two people interact, they establish a system of roles. (b) These roles may be learned before the interaction or as the interaction occurs. (c) During the interaction, the particular roles a person plays may even be challenged. (d) These roles form the basis of human relationships, which are the fundamental ways people express meaning to one another.

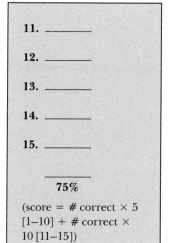

11. _____

12. _____

13. _____

14. _____

15. _____

_____
75%

(score = # correct × 5 [1–10] + # correct × 10 [11–15])
Find answers on p. 334.

15. (a) In the roles people play, status relationships are set up. (b) One person may feel more important than another and act accordingly. (c) One's status in a relationship determines the respect or lack of respect received from the other partner. (d) Status has proven to be a very important way of wielding power over others.

Exercise 5.2
Locating Steps in an
Argument

Read the following paragraphs on how sociologists conduct their research. Then reread them and list in correct sequence the steps presented in each paragraph.

Research Methods in Sociology

1. Some sociologists use deductive reasoning in their research. A deduction starts with a general idea—for example, "All people will eventually die." Then the deduction moves to a particular case: "John is a person." It then applies the general premise to the particular case and comes upon a new idea: "John will eventually die."

   Three Steps in a Deduction

   1.

   2.

   3.

2. Sociologists more often use inductive reasoning in their research. It involves three basic steps. The sociologist observes a particular human action. She then begins to record those actions that seem to follow a particular pattern. From a study of these observations, known as *data*, the sociologist comes upon a general statement or idea. Inductions move from the specific observation to the general conclusion, but deductions start at the general level and move to the specific conclusion.

   Three Steps in an Induction

   1.

   2.

   3.

3. The general ideas developed from inductions are also called *hypotheses*. To determine whether a hypothesis is accurate or valid, sociologists do what is called *hypothesis testing*. The first step in this procedure is to state clearly what the hypothesis is. Then the researcher studies the data he has collected and sees if they follow a

pattern. He usually sets up graphs to see what kind of pattern the data show. Finally he studies the graph to see if the hypothesis is supported by what the graph shows.

Steps in Hypothesis Testing

1.

2.

3.

4. Sociologists often study what large groups of people do. The first question they ask is which population they are studying. Once they have answered the "which" and have observed this group, they put their observations into categories. Finally, once the data have been put into categories, they are analyzed, and researchers then draw conclusions about the group in question.

Steps in Studying Large Groups

1.

2.

3.

Now read the following four paragraphs, and look for the proper sequence of events in each. Before you list the steps, write an appropriate title.

5. Random sampling is sociologists' way of determining what a large group of people will do, even though they study a small number. In studying attitudes toward abortion, for example, sociologists often select telephone area codes at random and numbers from all over the area that they are focusing on. They then check to see if these numbers are random by testing them with mathematical equations. Finally, they publish their conclusions, usually in the form of percentages and graphs, to say what most people in that area feel about abortion.

6. Some sociologists engage in field research. In field research, they both observe a particular action in society and participate in this activity in some way. During this activity, sociologists gather data. They use the data to write a report—which is often a case study, or an in-depth report on a particular social event.

7. Sociologists also conduct surveys to try to answer a particular sociological question—for example, "Are schoolteachers satisfied with their jobs?" Once the overall question has been formulated, researchers devise more specific survey questions. The people they question are asked to respond either over the telephone or in writing.

80%

Ask instructor for answers.

---

8. Most sociological studies, then, follow a set sequence. The researcher begins with an interest in a particular social activity—crime, for example. This interest then leads to an unsupported idea or intuition: "Society creates criminals." Finally, this intuition is then tested and made into a theory: the social theory of criminal behavior.*

*Exercise 5.3
Understanding
Definitions*

The following ten statements define sociological terms that you have read about in Exercises 5.1 and 5.2. After reading each statement, separate the definition into a general category and an example. Be brief. Place all of your information in the chart that follows the statements. Use the following definition of "survey research" as a model: "A sociological research method is one using questionnaires that people answer either on their own or with the help of an interviewer. Asking a large number of people what their attitudes are regarding tax increases is an example of a survey question."

Term	General Category	Examples
survey research	determining a group of people's attitude on a topic	tax increases

---

*Adapted from Thomas R. Dye, *Power and Society,* 5th ed. (Belmont, Calif.: Wadsworth, 1990), pp. 23–30.

Key Sociological Terms

1. Conflict theory is the aspect of sociology that studies why people disagree; sociologists who study crime often use conflict theory.

2. A deduction (as used in sociology) is a logical process that moves from a general idea to a theory about a specific person or group. A sociologist who contends that women are discriminated against on the job might deduce that female executives receive a smaller salary than male executives.

3. Demography is a careful sociological look at population — what it is and why it acts the way it does. A study of the movement of Mexicans into California in the nineties would be a demographic study.

4. An empirical study involves gathering data from what the researcher observes. A sociologist observing how American males greet each other would collect empirical, or observational, data.

5. In sociology, field research requires going into the natural setting to observe a particular activity. Carefully observing political rallies would qualify as field research in sociology.

6. A hypothesis in sociology is a conclusion that a researcher draws through either observation or intuition. Assuming that criminals are victims of society is a hypothesis.

7. An induction in sociology is a conclusion that a researcher draws based on the careful study of data, or observations. A sociologist who concludes after studying a statewide survey that New Yorkers are not in favor of increased state taxes is using inductive logic.

8. In sociology, a population is a group or category of people that merits careful study. Students in community colleges nationwide are an example of a sociological population.

9. Random selection is a sociological research tool designed to ensure that a large group of people are selected for a study by chance and not through a particular researcher's bias. Random selection can be achieved by asking a computer to select a group of people through the use of random numbering.

10. Social interaction is defined as the way one person directs the responses of another person or persons. A conversation is an excellent example of social interaction.*

---

*Adapted from Earl R. Babbie, *Sociology: An Introduction*, 2nd ed. (Belmont, Calif.: Wadsworth, 1980), pp. 574–584.

Term	General Category	Examples

1.

2.

3.

4.

5.

6.

7.

8.

9.

10.

80%

(score = # correct × 5)
Find answers on
pp. 334–335.

Exercise 5.4
Identifying
Comparisons and
Contrasts

The following ten statements compare various disciplines to sociology or compare pairs of terms used in sociology. In a one-sentence explanation of each statement, identify the issue that is compared or contrasted. Be sure that you use the word "compare" or "contrast" in your explanation. Here's an example:

> Although inductions and deductions are both ways by which sociologists explain their data, they begin with very different ways of looking at the data.
> *Explanation:* This statement contrasts inductions and deductions as ways sociologists interpret their data.

1. Sociology and psychology are different in that psychology generally studies what an individual does and sociology analyzes what occurs between people.

   Explanation: _____

2. The major difference between sociology and anthropology is that until recently anthropology studied preliterate peoples, those unable to read and write, and sociology generally studied literate people. The distinctions between these two studies have recently been blurred.

   Explanation: _____

3. Economics and sociology share a focus on how people relate and interact. Economics specifically focuses on financial interaction.

Explanation: _____

4. Political science differs from sociology in that it specifically addresses how people use power. In sociology, power is just one of many areas that is studied.

Explanation: _____

5. Social welfare and sociology are very similar disciplines, except that social welfare focuses on how to help people and sociology considers ways to study them.

Explanation: _____

6. Socialism is not sociology. Socialism is an economic system in which most industry is controlled by the government, but sociology studies how humans interact. Socialism could, therefore, be a topic studied in sociology.

Explanation: _____

7. Furthermore, sociology is not synonymous with social reform. Social reformists want to make the world better; that is not the goal of sociology, which merely studies social behavior.

Explanation: _____

8. Sociology differs from history in that history records, narrates, and interprets human experience. Sociology focuses exclusively on interpreting human interaction.

Explanation: _____

9. Racial inequality and sexual inequality can be considered similar in that both express how a group of people — a race or women — have been treated unfairly by the ruling class.

Explanation: _____

10. Urban life is characterized by large numbers of people living in a concentrated area, whereas rural life is characterized by fewer people and more space between groups of people.

Explanation: _____

The following five paragraphs present either comparisons or contrasts of terms used in sociology. Read over the paragraphs carefully. Then complete the comparison and contrast chart that follows each paragraph.

11. There are several similarities between the upper-class population and the middle-class population. For one, both are future-oriented; that is, they are constantly making plans for a better life. Both groups are self-confident, believing that they have reasonable control over the experiences in their lives. Finally, they are both also willing to make financial investments that will improve their future financial status.

Similar Beliefs

Upper Class	*Middle Class*
1.	1.
2.	2.
3.	3.

12. The differences between the working class and the lower class are minor. The working class generally works to pay the bills for themselves and their family; the lower class often does not work, and when they do they often move from one job to another. Working-class families are often married couples, but lower-class families are more often run by single women. Finally, a working-class person often belongs to and regularly attends church; the lower-class individual attends church infrequently.

Differences

Working Class	*Lower Class*
1.	1.
2.	2.
3.	3.

13. An issue that continues to surface in sociological studies is the difference between *nature* and *nurture*. Believers in the influence of nature contend that heredity, or one's genetic makeup, determines one's actions. Proponents of the influence of nurture assume that social forces—family, friends, environment—determine how one acts. Nurture theorists would say that one's mother is a dominant force in one's behavior. Nature theorists would say that some of a

mother's genetic makeup is given to her child and that is why the child behaves in a particular fashion. In studying twins that were separated at birth, a nature proponent would be looking for evidence of similar behavior. Oppositely, a nurture theorist would be looking for proof that their behavior is different because it is shaped by a different environment.

How Their Ideas Differ

Nature	Nurture
1.	1.
2.	2.
3.	3.

14. There are three differences between the liberal and the conservative positions in the United States today. Whereas liberals favor federal aid for education, health, and Social Security, conservatives work toward cutting funds in these areas. Conservatives believe in spending more on defense. Liberals see military spending as too great and want to cut it. Finally, conservatives favor aid to foreign countries. In contrast, liberals fear that aid to foreign countries will lessen the amount spent on the needs of American people.

Different Beliefs

Liberal	Conservative
1.	1.
2.	2.
3.	3.

15. Are urban and suburban lifestyles and environments different? Suburbs tend to be less densely populated than their urban counterparts. Homes in the suburbs tend to be built on larger parcels of land than urban dwellings, which are often built on smaller pieces of land and are several stories high. Violence is also an important factor for those who decide to move from a large city to a suburb. Suburban violence tends to be less common than that experienced in large cities.*

---

*Adapted from Dye, *Power and Society,* pp. 5–9, 76–77.

Differences in Lifestyle and Environment

Suburb	Large City
1.	1.
2.	2.
3.	3.

70%

Ask instructor for answers.

Exercise 5.5
Identifying
Organizational
Patterns

The following ten paragraphs discuss the sociological issues of heredity versus environment and the sense of self, expanding on the issue of nature and nurture that you read about in Exercise 5.4. Each paragraph is structured according to one of the organizational patterns described earlier. Read each paragraph; then identify the organizational pattern that describes it. Some paragraphs use more than one organizational pattern; in this case, choose the one that seems to dominate the paragraph. Place the appropriate code in the answer box: *C-E* = cause-effect, *DEF* = definition, *C-C* = comparison-contrast, and *SEQ* = sequence of events.

Heredity, Environment, and the Self

1. What is the nature-nurture controversy? Some sociologists believe that we are the product of our genes, or nature; our sex, our race, our physical characteristics are qualities we inherit at birth. Others believe that nurture, or our upbringing, is more important. Our ability to use language and our attitudes toward politics and religion, they argue, are shaped by our environment.

2. Identical twins have been studied carefully for answers to the nature-nurture question. Some studies have asked what causes intelligence. Identical twins, even if they are raised apart, seem to show very similar intelligence quotients (IQs). This result would suggest that heredity greatly influences intelligence.

3. What are the social forces that a typical child faces in the first seven years of life? During the first weeks, months, and sometimes years, a child is cared for by her mother. In our present society, this child is then often cared for by baby-sitters or day-care workers. Then, at the age of three, she is often enrolled in preschool, where she experiences the influence of teachers and a large group of peers. Finally, at five she moves to a formal schooling experience, interacting with a teacher and a large group of peers in a self-contained classroom.

4. Two studies have offered different views of how intelligence is shaped. One study, using evidence from identical twins who have been raised apart, suggests that intelligence is transmitted genetically. Another study of foster children suggests that environment

plays a key role in intelligence. This study shows that foster children, who are not related biologically to their parents, have an IQ similar to that of their foster parents.

5. Related to this issue of nature-nurture is the sense of self, which seems to develop in identifiable stages. A newborn has no sense of self apart from his attachment to his mother. Before the child begins to speak, at about the age of one, he begins to see himself as separate, often pointing to himself in the mirror. By the age of three, the child often is able to use language to explain who he is in relationship to others in his family.

6. What is the sociological meaning of the self? The self is one's sense of being, apart from one's occupation or social position. It is the continuous sense of who one is, in private, at work, and in social interaction. Some sociologists are finding that this continuous sense of oneself cannot be separated from the society feeding this self.

7. How does socialization affect the sense of self? As children mature, they learn to wear various masks — one at school, one at church, and so on. As they interact more with society, they learn that each occasion calls for a different side of themselves. Their notion of who they are thus becomes more and more complex.

8. Socialization, then, is a process in which the individual learns to use a variety of social selves. It is also a process by which these social selves become integrated with one another. Socialization thus gives to each individual both a personal and a social identity.

9. Sigmund Freud did much to help us understand the concept of self. He was interested in the effect of childhood experiences on adult behavior. He believed that people held many of their painful childhood experiences in what he called the *unconscious*. These unconscious memories often caused individuals to express themselves in strange, unexplained ways. These strange behavior patterns often led troubled individuals to seek help from psychoanalysts like Freud.

10. Both Sigmund Freud and Erik Erikson were psychologists interested in the development of the self, what they both termed the *ego*. Freud and Erikson differed slightly in their concept of how the ego developed. Freud believed that the ego resulted from a constant battle between the unconscious (the *id*) and the *superego* (society's values). In slight contrast, Erikson believed that the ego developed as a result of the individual's sense of sameness, or continuity, from one experience to the other. When there is a sharp contrast between who the individual thinks she is and who society thinks she is, the ego faces a crisis.*

1. _____
2. _____
3. _____
4. _____
5. _____
6. _____
7. _____
8. _____
9. _____
10. _____

_____
80%

(score = # correct × 10)

Find answers on p. 335.

*Adapted from Babbie, *Sociology,* pp. 127–132.

Exercise 5.6
Identifying More
Organizational
Patterns

The following ten paragraphs concern the sociological issue of groups—what they are and how they operate. This discussion ties in with the previous discussion of the self. Again, these paragraphs are structured around various organizational patterns. Your job is to identify the organizational pattern that best describes each paragraph. If more than one pattern seems to apply, choose the pattern that seems to dominate the paragraph. Place the appropriate code in the answer box: *S-G* = spatial-geographic, *T-S* = thesis-support, *DES* = descriptive, and *C-E* = cause-effect.

A Sociological Look at Groups

1. In general speech, the term *group* has several meanings. A teacher can refer to a group gathered outside the classroom door. A spokesperson for the manufacturer of a sports car can refer to a group that consistently buys that car. And a rock star can mention the "groupies" who follow her from concert to concert.

2. What is key to understanding groups in sociology is how each group fits into a particular category. Brown-eyed Americans constitute a category. So do college professors. And so do people who buy the same sports car. What is common among all these groups is that, although the people in them belong to a particular category, they do not necessarily know or interact with one another.

3. How do groups influence behavior? Sociologists would argue that your membership in a group determines to a large degree your sense of self, or who you think you are. The friends you had in school determine how you see yourself as a student. Whether you thought you were part of the "in-group" or the "out-group" also determines how successful a student you see yourself to be.

4. To be part of an in-group is meaningful only if you see that another group—an out-group—is not as successful as the group you identify with. The in-group often refers to the others in the group as "we" and to those in the out-group as "them." In schools, students are often categorized as athletes (the "jocks") and academic types (the "nerds"). Each one of these groups sees itself as part of a "we" that is unlike, and in conflict with, the "them."

5. What do in-groups provide people? By being in an in-group, you develop a sense of being wanted. Your group members support you and are loyal to you. Being part of an in-group gives you a sense of stability, and as Erik Erikson would argue, this stability lets your ego develop without conflict.

6. A *reference group*, or the group that one looks up to as a standard, gives individuals ways to improve. If you are a "B" student in sociology and your close and respected friend consistently receives "A" grades, she may provide you with a reference point for how well you

are doing and for how much better you may want to become. Her "A" may very well prod you to study more for the next sociology examination. Reference groups are important because people need to see themselves in a better light if they are ever to develop their abilities.

7. But comparing yourself to others can also lead to what sociologists call *relative deprivation*—or doing poorly because others are doing better. Instead of looking up to a successful person or group, an individual may develop feelings of inadequacy whenever she compares herself to the more successful peer or acquaintance. This feeling of inadequacy may prevent the individual from trying her hardest. In extreme circumstances, relative deprivation can lead to feelings of apathy or even depression.

8. In-groups and reference groups can be visualized as two or more floating platforms, with individuals on each. The people below can look up at the other individuals above them. They see them as happy and somehow more comfortable. In contrast, the people above—the in-group—can look down and feel better because the out-group seems to be more crowded and uncomfortable, wishing in vain that they could join the in-group. But if the in-group looks up from where they are, they will invariably see still another group—even less crowded and more comfortable, enjoying life even more than they do.

9. One sociology student described herself this way in a journal entry: "In college, I usually have not felt part of an in-group. I've always looked to others and envied who they were. I envied them for their grades and for how well they could speak up in class and get the teacher to listen. I see myself as a shy student who still has a long way to go before I can feel comfortable expressing myself in class and with other students outside of class. I want to be like these more successful students. They are becoming my models."

10. Another student had this to say about his first day in college: "I was born in Taiwan and went to school there until I was thirteen. This college is big. The buildings are large, and there is much land between buildings. I still have not gotten used to how much of everything there is here. There are three cafeterias in this school and five libraries. The parking lots are as large as the land that my elementary school was on in Taiwan. I still feel a little strange when I compare my college to the schools back home."*

1. _____
2. _____
3. _____
4. _____
5. _____
6. _____
7. _____
8. _____
9. _____
10. _____

80%

Ask instructor for answers.

*Adapted from Babbie, *Sociology*, pp. 201–204.

*Exercise 5.7
Recognizing
Organizational
Patterns in a Longer
Passage*

Read the following passage on *stratification* (a sociological term that treats a person's relative ranking in society). The discussion of stratification is a further elaboration of the discussion of in-groups and out-groups in the previous exercise. Make marginal comments on the major organizational patterns that you come across. Then answer the questions that follow the passage. You may go back to review it as you answer the questions. Place the first five answers in the answer box; then answer the rest of the questions in the spaces provided.

Various Views on Stratification

(1) Sociologists refer to inequalities in society with the term *social stratification*. Each stratum in society is made up of a group of people who have a similar social rank. Sociologists have found that social rank depends on factors that vary from one culture to another. Some of the most common criteria for assigning social rank are status within the family, possessions, occupation, education, and religion.

(2) In most cultures, newborns achieve a particular status because of the family they are born into. If a child is born into a rich family, that child is automatically part of the rich stratum of society. A child who is born into a royal family automatically becomes part of a royal stratum at birth. Some families are considered morally upright, and a child born into such a family will have high social standing as long as he continues to practice the values of his family and the community continues to share these respected values.

(3) In the United States, money seems to give an individual the greatest social status. Many types of wealth define a rich American: a high salary, expensive possessions, a lot of property. Alongside these physical manifestations of wealth are the people of equal wealth whom a rich American knows. High status is assured if the rich American belongs to exclusive clubs or is selected to be a member of an exclusive organization. The number of wealthy contacts one has in a society that values possessions automatically increases one's status as a wealthy person.

(4) One's occupation also plays an important role in status. Interestingly enough, the amount of money one makes is not always the only criterion for assigning rank. Some of the most prestigious occupations are Supreme Court justice, doctor, scientist, governor, and college professor. Although doctors and governors often earn a high salary, scientists and college professors sometimes do not. So clearly, in some cases, factors other than salary are often involved in assigning status to an individual's occupation.

(5) In many cultures, particularly developed ones, education is a consistently important way to improve one's social status. People in most cultures seem to assign value to an educated individual, even if that individual does not earn a lot of money. Something about education confers instant respect on an individual. And this has been true throughout history. In most cultures, the wise person has been awarded a special place in the community.

(6) The same value seems to be given to people who choose a religious vocation, like priests. Although religious people tend not to earn

a big salary, and some even live in poverty, society consistently seems to rank religious vocations high on their list of respected occupations. Society seems to believe that both educated and religious people possess valuable knowledge. In a sense, spiritual or intellectual possessions are as important as the physical possessions of the wealthy.

(7) The issue of social stratification is a difficult one to understand, because it seems that many factors are involved. Material wealth, education, religious knowledge — all seem to give certain individuals a privileged position in society. The reasons for assigning social status, like so many expressions of group behavior, are mysterious and the result of many different motivations.*

1. The bulk of the sentences in paragraph 1 fit into the organizational pattern of

　　a. sequence of events
　　b. description
　　c. cause-effect
　　d. definition

2. The last sentence in paragraph 1 is a

　　a. topic sentence
　　b. main-idea sentence
　　c. minor-detail sentence
　　d. major-detail sentence

3. The major organizational pattern of paragraph 2 is

　　a. description
　　b. sequence of events
　　c. definition
　　d. thesis-support

4. Paragraph 2 presents three

　　a. topic sentences
　　b. minor-detail sentences
　　c. major-detail sentences
　　d. none of these

5. The main idea of paragraph 3 concerns

　　a. the value of knowing rich people in the United States
　　b. the value of belonging to exclusive clubs in the United States
　　c. the value of wealth in achieving social status in the United States
　　d. the number of wealthy people one knows

1. _____

2. _____

3. _____

4. _____

5. _____

80%

(score **=** **#** correct × 10)
Find answers on p. 335.

---

*Adapted from Dye, *Power and Society*, pp. 66–69.

Answer each of the following five questions in a short phrase or sentence.

6. What is the main idea of paragraph 4?

7. Find a major detail in paragraph 4.

8. What organizational pattern does paragraph 4 seem to fit into?

9. What is the main idea of paragraph 6?

10. What organizational pattern does the entire excerpt seem to fit into?

Exercise 5.8
Writing an Effective
Paragraph Using
Organizational
Patterns

Now that you have read the selection on stratification in Exercise 5.7, go back to reread it. As you do, complete the following outline:

I. Main Idea of the Excerpt:

II. Factors That Influence Social Status

    A. Family:

    B. Wealth:

    C. Occupation:

    D. Religion and education:

70%

Ask instructor for answers.

Refer only to this outline in answering the following:

> *Essay question:* In an organized paragraph, define social stratification. Then show how it applies to one's family and one's occupation.

Exercise 5.9
Determining Main
Ideas, Major Details,
and Organizational
Patterns in a
Textbook Excerpt

The following is an excerpt from a sociology textbook on class and lifestyle, an issue related to social stratification. Read through the excerpt quickly to get a sense for its organization. Then go back and reread it slowly. When you finish, answer the five questions that follow. You may refer to the excerpt in deciding on your answers. Place your answers to the first five questions in the answer box.

Class and Lifestyle

The Upper Class

(1) The typical upper-class individual is future-oriented and cosmopolitan. Persons of this class expect a long life, look forward to their future and the future of their children and grandchildren, and are

concerned about what lies ahead for the community, the nation, and mankind. They are self-confident, believing that within limits they can shape their own destiny and that of the community. They are willing to invest in the future — that is, to sacrifice some present satisfaction in the expectation of enjoying greater satisfaction in time to come. They are self-respecting; they place great value on independence, creativity, and developing their potential to the fullest. In rearing their children, they teach them to be guided by abstract standards of social justice rather than by conformity to a given code ("Do things not because you're told to but because you take the other person into consideration"). Child rearing is permissive, and the only coercive measures taken against the child are verbal and emotional. Instructions to the child are always rationalized. Upper-class parents are not alarmed if their children remain in school or travel until the age of thirty. Sex life in upper classes is innovative and expressive, with great variety in sexual practices. Women enjoy nearly equal status with men in family relationships. The goals of life include individuality, self-expression, and personal happiness. Wealth permits a wide variety of entertainment and recreation: theater, concerts, and art; yachting, tennis, skiing; travel abroad; and so on.

(2) Upper-class individuals take a tolerant attitude toward unconventional behavior in sex, the arts, fashions, lifestyles, and so forth. They deplore bigotry and abhor violence. They feel they have a responsibility to "serve" the community and to "do good." They are active in "public service" and contribute time, money, and effort to worthy causes. They have an attachment to the community, the nation, and the world, and they believe they can help shape the future. This "public-regardingness" inclines them toward "liberal" politics; the upper classes provide the leadership for the liberal wings of both Republican and Democratic parties.

The Middle Class

(3) Middle-class individuals are also future-oriented; they plan ahead for themselves and their children. But they are not likely to be as cosmopolitan as the upper-class person, being more concerned with their immediate families than about "humanity" in the abstract. They are confident about their ability to influence their own futures and that of their children, but they do not really expect to have an effect on community, state, or national events. They show some independence and creativity, but their taste for self-expression is modified by their concern for "getting ahead."

(4) The middle-class individual is perhaps even more self-disciplined and willing to sacrifice present gratification for future advantage than the upper-class individual. In the lower-middle class, investing time, energy, and effort in self-improvement and getting ahead is a principal theme of life. Middle-class people strongly want their children to go to college and acquire the kind of formal training that will help them get ahead. Child rearing in the middle class is slightly less permissive than in the upper class; it is still based largely on verbal and emotional punishment. This can be quite severe, however, and the middle-class child may be more closely supervised and disciplined than

either upper- or lower-class children. Authority is rationalized for the child, but values and standards of behavior are drawn from surrounding middle-class society rather than from abstract concepts of social justice. In matters of sex the middle-class individual is outwardly conventional. The middle-class adolescent experiences first intercourse at a later age than the lower-class youth. However, in adult life, vis-á-vis lower-class individuals, the middle-class person enjoys greater variety in sexual activity, women have greater equality in the family, and the family has fewer children (though home activities are frequently child-centered). Recreation and entertainment include golf, swimming, movies, sports events, and travel in the United States. In general, the middle-class person is less able than the upper-class one to afford an interest in theater, art, symphonies, or travel abroad.

(5) As a rule, middle-class individuals deal with others according to established codes of conduct and behavior. They are likely to be middle-of-the-road or conservative in politics; they tend to vote Republican. They have regard for the rights of others and generally oppose bigotry and violence. However, they do not hold those attitudes as strongly as do members of the upper class, nor do they feel as much responsibility to the community as the upper-class individual does. Though they join voluntary organizations, many of which are formally committed to community service, they are less willing to give their time, money, and effort to public causes.

The Working Class

(6) Working-class individuals do not invest heavily in the future; they are much more oriented toward the present. They expect their children to make their own way in life. They have less confidence than the middle class in their ability to shape the future and a stronger sense of being at the mercy of fate and other uncontrollable forces. They attach more importance to "luck" in getting ahead than to education, hard work, or self-sacrifice. They are self-respecting and self-confident, but these feelings extend over a narrower range of matters than they do in middle-class individuals. The horizon of the working class is limited by job, family, immediate friends, and neighborhood. Self-improvement or getting ahead is not a major concern of life; there is more interest in having a "good time" with family and companions. The working-class family has more children than do middle-class or upper-class families.

(7) Working-class individuals work to maintain themselves and their families; they do not look upon their jobs as a means of getting ahead and certainly not as a means of self-expression. In rearing their children, they emphasize the virtues of neatness, cleanliness, honesty, obedience, and respect for authority. They seldom rationalize authority over their children ("Because I said so, that's why") and sometimes use physical punishment. They are not interested in stimulating their children to self-expression, but rather in controlling them — teaching them traditional family values. They would like their children to go to college, but if they do not, it is no great matter. The working-class youth experiences first sexual intercourse at an earlier age than do middle- and upper-class young people; young working-class men are more likely to

categorize women as "good" or "bad" depending on their sexual activity. There is very little variety in the adult sexual behavior of the working class, and the woman is relegated to a subordinate role in sexual and family affairs. Frequently a double standard allows promiscuity in the man, whereas extramarital sex by the woman can be the cause of family disruption.

(8) In relationships with others the working-class individual is often intolerant and sometimes aggressive. Open bigotry is more likely to be encountered in the working class than in the middle or upper classes. Violence is less shocking to the working class than to middle-class persons; indeed, sometimes it is regarded as a normal expression of a masculine style. To the working class, the upper class appears somewhat lacking in masculinity. The working-class individual's deepest attachment is to family. Most visiting is done with relatives rather than friends. Working-class persons do not belong to many organizations other than union and church. Whether Protestant or Catholic, their religious beliefs are fundamentalist in character; they believe in the literal meaning of the scriptures and respect the authority of the church. In their views toward others in the community, they are very "private-regarding"; they believe they work hard for a living and feel others should do the same. They are not interested in public service or "do-goodism"; they look down on people who accept welfare or charity unless those people are forced to do so by circumstances over which they have no control. When they vote, they generally vote Democratic, but they are often apathetic about politics. Their opinions on public matters are more likely to be clichés or slogans than anything else. They are liberal on economic issues (job security, fair labor standards, government guarantees of full employment, and so on) but conservative on social issues (civil rights, welfare, youth, and so forth). The working-class position in politics is motivated not by political ideology but by ethnic and party loyalties, by the appeal of personalities, or by the hope for occasional favors. For recreation the working-class individual turns to bowling, stock-car racing, circuses, fairs, carnivals, drive-in restaurants, and drive-in movies.

The Lower Class

(9) Lower-class individuals live from day to day, with little interest in the future. They have no confidence in their ability to influence what happens to them. Things happen *to* them; they do not *make* them happen. They do not discipline themselves to sacrifice for the future because they have no sense of future. They look for immediate gratification, and their behavior is governed largely by impulse. When they work, it is often from payday to payday, and they frequently drift from one unskilled job to another, taking scant interest in the work. Their self-confidence is low, and occasionally they even suffer from feelings of self-contempt. In relations with others, they are suspicious, hostile, and aggressive. They feel little attachment to community, neighbors, and friends and resent all authority (for example, that of policemen, social workers, teachers, landlords, and employers). Lower-class individuals are nonparticipants—they belong to no voluntary organizations, attend church infrequently, have no political interests, and seldom vote.

(10) The lower-class family is frequently headed by a woman. Lower-class women not only have more children than middle- or upper-class women but also have them earlier in life. A woman may have a succession of mates who contribute intermittently to the support of the family but who take almost no part in rearing children. In child rearing, the mother (or the grandmother) is impulsive; children may be alternately loved, disciplined, and neglected and often do not know what to expect next. The mother may receive welfare or work at a low-paying job, but in either case children are generally unsupervised once they have passed babyhood. Physical punishment is frequent. When these children enter school, they are already behind other children in verbal abilities and abstract reasoning. For the male offspring of a lower-class matriarchal family, the future is often depressing, with defeat and frustration repeating themselves throughout his life. He may drop out of school in the eighth or ninth grade because of lack of success. Without parental supervision, and having little to do, he may get into trouble with the police. The police record will further hurt his chances of getting a job. With limited job skills, little self-discipline, and low aspiration levels, the lower-class male is not likely to find a steady job that will pay enough to support a family. Yet he yearns for the material standard of living of higher classes—a car, a television set, and other conveniences. He may tie up much of his income in installment debts; because of his low credit rating he will be forced to pay excessive interest rates, and sooner or later his creditors will garnish his salary. If he marries, he and his family will have overcrowded, substandard housing. As pressures mount, he may decide to leave his family, either because his inability to support a wife and children is humiliating, or because he is psychologically unprepared for a stable family relationship, or because only in this way will his wife and children be eligible for welfare payments.

(11) Frequently, to compensate for defeat and frustration, the lower-class male will resort to risk taking, conquest, and fighting to assert his masculinity. Lower-class life is violent. The incidence of mental illness is greater in the lower class than in any other class. The lower-class youth may have engaged in sexual activities from a very early age, but they are stereotyped in a male-dominant–female-subordinate fashion. Entertainment may be limited to drinking and gambling. Many aspects of lower-class culture are unattractive to women.*

1. The main idea of the entire excerpt seems to be about

   a. what the upper class does
   b. the negative lifestyle of the lower class
   c. how the lower class is different from the middle class
   d. the differences and similarities among the upper, middle, and lower classes

---

*Dye, *Power and Society*, pp. 76–82.

2. The main idea of paragraph 2 concerns

a. the generally tolerant attitudes of the upper class
b. the political activity of the upper class
c. the liberal politics of the upper class
d. the desire of the upper class to serve the community and the nation

3. The major organizational pattern of paragraph 3 seems to be

a. definition
b. cause-effect
c. sequence of events
d. spatial-geographic

4. The major organizational pattern of paragraph 5 seems to be

a. spatial-geographic
b. definition
c. cause-effect
d. sequence of events

5. Two organizational patterns seem to structure the entire excerpt. They are

a. sequence of events and cause-effect
b. compare-contrast and cause-effect
c. definition and compare-contrast
d. definition and cause-effect

1. _____

2. _____

3. _____

4. _____

5. _____

Now read the following questions. Then go back and reread the excerpt. Answer these questions in a phrase or sentence without looking back.

6. What is the working class's attitude toward work? How is it different from the lower class's? (2 points)

7. How do the working class and lower class compare in the way they rear their children? (2 points)

8. How would you describe the lower-class male? (1 point)

70%
Ask instructor for answers.

***Follow-up on the
Sociology Exercises***

Now that you have completed these exercises, it may be helpful to see how your reading of this topic has changed some of your ideas about social issues. You may want to go back to these exercises to reread them just for their content or for what they have to say about sociology. Then answer the following questions either individually or in small groups:

1. How would you now define *sociology*?
2. What sociological issue that you read about interests you the most? Why?
3. Where do you stand on the issue of nature versus nurture?
4. What area of sociology do you now want to study further?

6 Summarizing and Paraphrasing

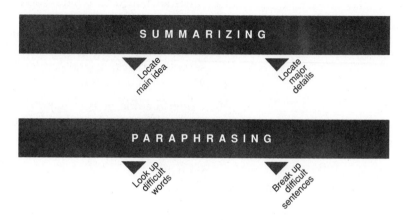

Being able to summarize information from textbooks, lectures, and lecture notes is one of the most important skills to master. A *summary* is an accurate restatement of material, presented in condensed form. The key words to remember are "accurate" and "condensed." Inaccurate summaries are useless. Lengthy summaries are only slightly more convenient than the original. However, organized summaries are helpful study sheets for exams.

Summarizing, like note taking and critical reading, is a complex skill that improves with practice. So do not expect to be an expert summarizer right away.

How to Summarize

To be able to summarize efficiently, you need to be able to identify main ideas and major details in both lectures and textbooks. As your summaries improve, you will focus on only the significant major details. You will rarely include minor details.

For now, follow these steps when you summarize textbooks and lectures. Most of these hints apply best to summarizing written material. You will learn more about summarizing lectures in Part Three.

1. In each paragraph of text or on each page of lecture notes, locate the main idea (which is often the first sentence). You must include this main idea in your summary. Underline the main idea twice or use a wavy line. And underline the important parts of the sentence. Look at this example:

   Philosophy is a study that examines the most compelling human questions, such as: What is good? What is knowledge? What is God?

2. Sometimes main ideas are implied, and often in textbooks two or three shorter paragraphs work like one big paragraph. If you read several paragraphs and cannot locate a main-idea sentence, write your own in the margin.

3. Underline one or two major details in each paragraph of text or section of lecture notes. Do not underline the entire sentence, just the important words. Underline these details once to differentiate them from main ideas. See how the major detail is highlighted in this sentence:

   Epistemology is a study in philosophy analyzing human knowledge — how one knows and what one knows.

   Which details should you include? This choice may be difficult at first; just keep asking yourself which are the important details and which most directly support the main idea. The layout of the textbook should help you. Main ideas and certain major details are often in boldface print or in italics. In lectures, listen for comments like "I want you to remember this," "It's important to remember," and "I repeat." Also, note what the instructor writes on the blackboard. These are the instructor's clues pointing toward key points.

4. When you have finished reading five or six paragraphs in a textbook and have underlined main ideas and major details, stop reading. Alternatively, when you have marked a page or two of lecture notes, put your pen down. Then write a summary of five or six sentences or phrases, either in outline form or in a short paragraph. It is often better to put your summaries in outline form, because it clearly separates main ideas from major details. Put summaries in your own words so they are easier to learn. When you are copying from a textbook or from your lecture notes, you are not actively thinking, and you will probably not remember what you have copied. Only when you read or hear a definition should you copy; in that case the exact wording is necessary for you to understand the term.

   You will learn more about summarizing textbook material in Chapter 13, which introduces the SQ3R study system.

Read the following five-paragraph excerpt on philosophy and wisdom. See if you can locate the main ideas and significant major details. Then write your summary in the outline skeleton that follows the excerpt. Use your own words wherever possible.

Philosophy as the Love of Wisdom

(1) If we took the time to trace the history of the physical, natural, and social sciences, we'd find their roots in philosophy as it was practiced about 2,700 years ago in Greece. In those times, people of infinite curiosity puzzled over certain aspects of the world and their experience of them. We saw that one of the questions that they asked concerned reality. But these profoundly curious people wondered about other things as well: Why does anything exist? Why is there something rather than nothing? How can things change? How do we come to know things? What's the nature of knowledge? What's the difference between right and wrong? What's goodness? How can we best achieve happiness? What's justice? What is the just state? On what basis, if any, can society compel us to obey its rules if we don't wish to obey them? Those who asked these questions clearly showed a marked curiosity in the things of experience, a curiosity that could be described as a vital concern for becoming wise about the phenomena of the world and the human experience. For this reason, such people were termed *philosophers* and their study *philosophy*, which literally means "the love of wisdom." Philosophers were originally lovers or seekers of wisdom; they still are.

(2) Wisdom, then, is not the expertise or technical skills of professional people. Indeed, as Socrates points out, such knowledge may impede the quest for wisdom by deluding people into thinking that they know what they don't. In contrast, the wisdom of Socrates consists of a critical habit, an eternal vigilance about all things and a reverence for truth, whatever its forms, wherever its place. His is a perspective that allows him to transcend the narrowness, the smugness, the arrogance, and the pettiness of mundane ego fulfillment.

(3) Others have viewed wisdom, and thus philosophy, differently. Some, like Aristotle (384–322 BC), have tried to gain an organized knowledge of the world and an understanding of the nature of things and the relationships among them. Part of this is an understanding of how we ought to live. By exposing all stated and implied assumptions, theories, and methods of all beliefs, philosophy seeks the wisdom that comes from systematically organizing, structuring, and relating all available data and experiences. Thus, the love of wisdom is all-encompassing; it is not bounded by the limitations of this subject or that discipline.

(4) Others view wisdom more actively. For them, philosophy consists of participation in life — to change things, to solve human problems, or to discover the meaning of existence. Still others feel that the wisdom of philosophy is in helping us to think more clearly and precisely.

(5) No philosopher has a monopoly on wisdom or its meaning. For us Socrates' critical perspective will do, for it suggests an attitude, a temperament, that underlies other views. But the other perspectives

have merit. On wisdom, as on other subjects, our knowledge is a drop, our ignorance an ocean.*

I. Philosophy as the Love of Wisdom

    A. Definition of philosophy: _____

    B. _____

    C. _____

    D. _____

    E. _____

Compare your underlining and your summary with the suggestions on p. 104. Now consider these points:

1. In paragraph 1, you should have studied the italic print, which directs you to the definition of philosophy. You should also have noticed that the topic sentence or main idea of the first paragraph comes toward the end of the paragraph rather than at the beginning.

2. In paragraph 2, did you notice that the main idea is the first sentence and that the rest of the paragraph analyzes this main idea?

3. Paragraph 3 introduces Aristotle's notion of philosophy and gives details about what philosophy meant to him.

4. Paragraphs 4 and 5 both begin with a main-idea sentence and proceed to support it with details.

This excerpt has a fairly straightforward organization: General information usually comes before the details. Even when the organization is difficult to follow — when the main idea is implied — you still follow the same procedure as you summarize. You look for the general statement of a paragraph or paragraphs; then you locate the specific information supporting it.

As you continue working through this book, you will be completing several summaries. Your skills will improve with each one.

How to Paraphrase

Instead of dealing with several sentences, a paraphrase may focus on a single sentence. When you paraphrase, you try to make sense of a difficult sentence. Often you cannot understand this sentence because either it is long or the vocabulary is difficult. A *paraphrase* is an accurate,

---

*Vincent Barry, *Philosophy: A Text with Readings*, 2nd ed. (Belmont, Calif.: Wadsworth, 1983), pp. 8–10.

simpler restatement of a phrase, a sentence, or sentences. Unlike a summary, a paraphrase may be longer than the original statement.

Here are some steps to follow when you paraphrase. Most of these suggestions apply to what you read:

1. Read every difficult sentence carefully. Reread the sentence that comes before it and the one that comes after it to place it in the proper context.

2. If the sentence has difficult words, look them up in the dictionary or in the glossary of the textbook. Often confusion comes from not understanding the terminology.

3. Divide long sentences into phrases and clauses. Phrases and clauses are often set off by commas, semicolons, colons, and dashes. In a lecture, listen for the pauses.

4. Determine the subject and verb of the sentence. The subject and verb should give you the core meaning of the sentence.

5. If the statement is written, reread these phrases and clauses; even read these parts aloud if you have to.

6. Write your paraphrase in the margins.

Look at the highlighted sentence in the passage that follows, and use these six steps to paraphrase it correctly. It's the second sentence in paragraph 5 from the excerpt that you just summarized: "No philosopher has a monopoly on wisdom or its meaning. *For us Socrates' critical perspective will do, for it suggests an attitude, a temperament, that underlies other views.* But the other perspectives have merit."

Paraphrase: _____

_____

After writing your paraphrase, see whether you used some of the following strategies:

1. You noticed that the topic of this paragraph is wisdom and that it deals with perspectives on wisdom. Your sentence examined Socrates' perspective.

2. You looked up the words "perspective" and "temperament." You discovered that a perspective is a particular point of view and that temperament is one's emotional nature.

3. You noted that the first comma divides the sentence into two recognizable, balanced parts. The first part, "For us Socrates'," suggests that this statement agrees with this ancient Greek philosopher's point

of view. The part that follows — "for it suggests an attitude" — further explains what Socrates and the author meant.

4. You noted that the subject in the first part of the sentence is "perspective" and the verb is "will do"; the subject in the second part of the sentence is "it [Socrates' perspective on wisdom]," and the verb is "suggests."

5. When you looked at this sentence, you saw that its structure is general-specific. The first part of the sentence introduces Socrates; the second examines what he says.

Having gone through these steps, you were ready to write your paraphrase. It should have said something like "Socrates' understanding of wisdom is helpful; it is a point of view, a feeling that one brings to other views."

Paraphrasing may seem tedious, but as you continue to practice it, your critical reading skills will improve. Most students who cannot paraphrase simply ignore difficult passages and thus have poorer comprehension of the material. With practice in paraphrasing, you will eventually be able to determine whether your difficulty in comprehension is due to difficult words or to long and involved sentences. In other words, you will begin to analyze the author's style. You may find that your paraphrase is a simple statement after all, and that the original author used big words and many words to cover up a simple idea. As you learn more in a particular subject, the easier it will be for you to paraphrase difficult sentences in that field.

Summary

Summarizing and paraphrasing are necessary skills in reading textbooks, listening to lectures, and reviewing your notes. Both are sophisticated skills. In summarizing, you locate main ideas and important details. It is an active process of sorting out the important from the less important and the unimportant. When you paraphrase, you attempt to understand a difficult sentence or sentences. Paraphrasing involves seeing a sentence in its context, looking up new words, and dividing up the sentence into smaller parts. Finally, when you summarize and paraphrase, you put information into your own words, in which form you have a better chance of remembering it.

Did this summary separate the significant from the less significant? Was it worded differently from the original? Do you think it's a successful summary?

You are now ready to practice your summarizing and paraphrasing skills in the following exercises, which also deal with philosophy, and in Part Three on note-taking skills.

Summary Box   *Summarizing and Paraphrasing*

What are they?	*How do you use them?*	*Why do you use them?*
Summarizing: accurately restating material in fewer words	Locate main ideas and significant details and put this information in your own words	To more easily remember large chunks of information
Paraphrasing: accurately and more simply restating difficult material	Read sentence in its context; look up new words; divide up sentences into smaller chunks	To understand difficult sentences that you would otherwise skip over

Topic: Philosophy

All the exercises in Chapter 6 focus on philosophy, a subject you will likely study during your college career. Before you begin these exercises, answer the following questions either individually or in small groups to get some sense for what you already know about philosophy:

1. How would you define the study of philosophy?
2. What is meant by "the good"? wisdom? God?
3. Do you already know about any type of philosophy?
4. How do you think philosophy affects daily life?

Exercise 6.1
Summarizing a
Longer Passage

The following excerpt, from a philosophy textbook, begins to explain what philosophers study. Your job is to underline main ideas and major details. Then, based on your underlinings, answer the five questions that follow. Remember not to underline entire sentences, just the important parts.

Traditional Concerns of Philosophy

(1) Traditionally, philosophy has sought an organized knowledge of the world and our place in it and knowledge about how we ought to live, including the bases for beliefs and interactions with others. Of course, philosophers have approached these general concerns in diverse ways, each emphasizing different aspects. But, in general, philosophy has dealt with such basic questions as: What is knowledge? What is real? What is good? While none of these questions can be considered in isolation, all philosophical questions fall under one or more of these foundational inquiries, which represent the traditional interests of philosophers. Numerous nonphilosophers have also stressed the importance of investigating these subjects.

(2) These traditional concerns suggest the three categories under which all other philosophical problems fall: knowledge, reality, and value. The fields of philosophy that explore these themes are generally termed *epistemology, metaphysics,* and *axiology.*

(3) Epistemology literally means the study of knowledge. A variety of problems are usually discussed as part of epistemology: the structure, reliability, extent, and kinds of knowledge; truth (including definitions of truth and validity); logic and a variety of strictly linguistic concerns; and the foundations of all knowledge (including the conditions under which an assertion is warranted and numerous concerns dealing directly with science and scientific knowledge).

(4) Metaphysics is the study of the most general or ultimate characteristics of reality or existence. Some of the problems that fall under it are the structure and development of the universe; the meaning and nature of being; and the nature of mind, self, and consciousness. Also, the nature of religion can be considered to fall under metaphysics, which includes the existence of God, the destiny of the universe, and the immortality of the soul.

(5) Axiology refers to the study of values. Specifically, axiological problems often involve values in human conduct; the nature and justification of social structures and political systems; the nature of art; and the meaning of art in human experience.

(6) In approaching these areas, philosophy asks critical questions about the obvious and taken-for-granted. This is an important characteristic of the philosophical enterprise, but there are others.*

1. The main idea of paragraph 1 is that

   a. philosophy deals with what knowledge is
   b. philosophy has several traditional subjects of interest
   c. philosophy basically addresses the issues of who we are, what we think, and how we act
   d. each philosopher approaches the field differently

2. Paragraph 2 serves to

   a. introduce entirely new information
   b. name those studies that answer the questions introduced in the previous paragraph
   c. define metaphysics
   d. define axiology and metaphysics

3. The main idea of paragraph 3 concerns

   a. the ways that epistemology studies knowledge
   b. a definition of truth and validity
   c. how language determines what we know
   d. the nature of scientific knowledge

1. _____

2. _____

3. _____

4. _____

5. _____

_____
80%

(score = # correct × 20)
Find answers on
pp. 336–337.

*Barry, *Philosophy,* p. 12.

4. The last sentence in paragraph 4 is a

    a. main-idea sentence
    b. major-detail sentence
    c. minor-detail sentence
    d. none of these

5. Which of the following is *not* a main idea of this excerpt?

    a. Epistemology is the study of knowledge.
    b. Axiology studies the structure of the universe.
    c. Metaphysics studies existence.
    d. Philosophy attempts to organize our knowledge of the world.

Exercise 6.2
Summarizing a
Second Passage

This second excerpt from a philosophy textbook continues the discussion about what philosophy studies. As in the previous exercise, underline the main ideas and significant details in each paragraph. Underline only key sentence parts. From your underlinings, finish the partially completed outline that follows.

The Difficulty of Defining Philosophy

(1) It's not surprising that Liz and Jon had trouble defining philosophy. For almost 3,000 years philosophers have asked, "What is philosophy?" and they have yet to agree. Why?

(2) One thing that makes defining philosophy tough is that it lacks distinct subject matter. Biology, botany, physics, astronomy, psychology, economics, political science — all deal with a specific body of subjects. If you asked botanists, physicists, or psychologists what their studies dealt with, they probably could answer without too much disagreement. Not so with philosophy. Philosophers often disagree on their subject matter. One reason is that philosophy deals more with issues than with specific subjects. Issues make up the content of philosophy. While some issues have remained throughout the development of philosophical thought, many have not. Some have faded with the passage of time or have become part of the subject matter of other disciplines, such as physics or psychology. What's more, even those issues that have remained in the province of philosophy have changed as various thinkers and ages have considered them.

(3) To illustrate, the early Western philosophers were fascinated by a number of questions about the nature of the universe: What does everything consist of? What's the nature of reality? Is reality ultimately material or nonmaterial? Today we may find such questions strange, because we feel that physics is answering them. Of course, 3,000 years ago the science of physics didn't exist as we know it today. Nevertheless, the point remains: What was once a philosophical question might be regarded today primarily as a scientific one and would be so handled. Thus, contemporary physics has been devoted in part to throwing light on the age-old philosophical concern about the nature of the universe.

(4) Take another ancient philosophical concern: human nature. What is it to be a human being? What, if anything, makes human beings

different, perhaps unique? What does it mean to be a human? To a large degree, such inquiries are now taken up by the social sciences in general, and by psychology and anthropology in particular. Again, what was once a question strictly for philosophy is today a concern of many disciplines.

(5) Of course, this doesn't mean that reality and human nature are no longer philosophical concerns. They are, as we'll see in the chapters ahead. But they can no longer be described as exclusively the concerns of philosophy. On the contrary, if you wanted to make philosophical sense out of these areas, you would have to investigate what the appropriate physical, biological, and social sciences were saying about them.

(6) So, because philosophy deals primarily with issues, many of which have been usurped by other fields and altered with the passing of time, it's hard to define philosophy in terms of subject matter. The task of defining philosophy becomes even tougher when you consider competing definitions. For some, philosophy is "the quest for truth," for others it's "the search for God," for still others it's "the study of the logical structure of artificial languages." Such definitions, while valuable, tell us more about the biases of philosophers than about philosophy itself.*

I.

A.

B.

C. Reality and human nature no longer studied just by philosophers

D.

Answers will vary. Ask instructor for sample underlinings and outline.

Ask your instructor for sample underlinings and a sample outline for comparison.

Exercise 6.3
Summarizing a
Third Passage

This third excerpt deals with the issue of the psychologically healthy individual. Yet by explaining a psychological issue, this excerpt again attempts to explain the purpose of philosophy. As with the previous two exercises, underline main ideas and significant details. Then complete an outline—this time without any help—summarizing the main ideas and major details.

Worth and Meaning in Philosophy

(1) Some modern psychologists, Abraham Maslow among them, point out that humans have needs other than maintenance ones, which they term *actualizing needs*. While more difficult to describe than maintenance needs, actualizing needs appear to be associated with self-fulfillment, creativity, self-expression, realization of your potential, and, in a word, being everything you can be. Why mention these?

---

*Barry, *Philosophy*, pp. 6–7.

Because evaluating the worth of courses and disciplines in terms of their job preparation value is to take a narrow view of what human beings need. It completely overlooks higher-level needs. This doesn't mean, of course, that studying philosophy will necessarily lead to self-actualization. But philosophy assists by promoting the ideal of self-actualization, or what psychotherapist Carl Rogers terms the "fully functioning person."

(2) Consider some characteristics of the self-actualized or fully functioning person. One is the ability to form one's own opinions and beliefs. Self-actualized people don't automatically go along with what's "in" or what's expected of them. Not that they are necessarily rebels; they just make up their own minds. They think, evaluate, and decide for themselves. What could better capture the spirit of philosophy than such intellectual and behavioral independence?

(3) A second characteristic is profound self-awareness. Self-actualized people harbor few illusions about themselves and rarely resort to easy rationalizations to justify their beliefs and actions. If anything, philosophy is geared to deepen self-awareness by inviting us to examine the basic intellectual foundations of our lives.

(4) A third characteristic is flexibility. Change and uncertainty don't level self-actualized people. Indeed, they exhibit resilience in the face of disorder, doubt, uncertainty, indefiniteness, even chaos. But they are not indifferent or uncaring. Quite the opposite. They are much involved in their experiences. Because of their resilience, they not only recognize the essential ambiguity of human affairs but also develop a high ambiguity tolerance. They are not upended by a lack of definite answers or of concrete solutions. When seriously undertaken, the study of philosophy often promotes what some have termed a philosophical calm, the capacity to persevere in the face of upheaval. This stems in part from an ability to put things in perspective, to see the "big picture," to make neither too much nor too little of events.

(5) A fourth characteristic of self-actualized or fully functioning people is that they are generally creative. They are not necessarily writers, painters, or musicians, for creativity can function in many ways and at various levels. Rather, such people exhibit creativity in all they do. Whether spending leisure time or conversing, they seem to leave their own distinctive mark. Philosophy can help in this process by getting us to develop a philosophical perspective on issues, problems, and events. This means, in part, that we no longer see or experience life on the surface. We engage it on deeper levels, and we interact with it so that we help to fashion our world. In another way, because philosophy exercises our imaginations, it invites a personal expression that is unique and distinctive.

(6) Finally, self-actualized or fully functioning people have clearly conceptualized, well-thought-out value systems in morality, the arts, politics, and so on. Since a fundamental concern of philosophy is values and since philosophy often deals directly with morals, art, politics, and other value areas, it offers an opportunity to formulate viable assessments of worth and find meaning in our lives. For some psychologists, the search for meaning and values constitutes the human's primary interest.

the search for meaning and values constitutes the human's primary interest.

Write your outline of this passage here:

> Answers will vary.
> Check your
> underlinings and your
> outline with the sample
> underlinings and
> outline on pp. 337–339.

*Exercise 6.4
Paraphrasing
Sentences in
Paragraphs*

Two paragraphs on Buddhist philosophy follow. See if you can apply what you have learned so far about philosophy to determine the kind of philosophical questions Eastern philosophers ask. You will be asked to paraphrase certain sentences from both paragraphs. Apply the rules for paraphrasing to these sentences; then read through the four choices and select the paraphrase that is most like yours. Place all of your answers in the answer box.

Eastern Views

(1) When we speak of Eastern philosophy, we refer to those systems of thought, belief, and action espoused by many peoples in the Near and Far East. (2) Because Eastern thought offers many views of human nature, it is impossible to mention them all. (3) Buddhism's view is particularly noteworthy for several reasons. (4) First, it represents a large number of Eastern thinkers. (5) Second, many Westerners have been converted to Buddhism. (6) Third, it contrasts sharply to most Western views. (7) At the same time, we must acknowledge the rich diversity of Buddhist sects: Theravada, Mahayana, Bodhisattva and Pure Land, and Zen. (8) The treatment of Buddhism and Eastern

thought in this book will likely prove too cursory for most Westerners, but our intention is not to exhaust the subject but to provide a vital transcultural perspective as well as evidence of the global view of philosophy.*

1. Which of the following is an effective paraphrase for sentence 1?

    a. Eastern philosophy refers to what people do in the East.
    b. Many people in the East and the Far East believe in Eastern philosophy.
    c. Eastern philosophy refers to how the people of the Near and Far East think and act.
    d. The beliefs, thoughts, and actions of the people in the Near and Far East are too numerous to explain in a single philosophy.

2. Which of the following is an effective paraphrase for sentence 5?

    a. Many Westerners have studied Buddhism.
    b. Many people in the West have taken on the beliefs of the East.
    c. Many Westerners do not understand the Buddhist beliefs.
    d. The beliefs of the West are becoming like the beliefs of the East.

3. Which of the following is an effective paraphrase for sentence 6?

    a. The belief systems of Buddhism are very different from those in the West.
    b. Western views are always in conflict with Buddhist beliefs.
    c. Buddhist ideas are more sharply focused than Western ideas.
    d. Buddhist and Western ideas agree on only a few issues.

4. Which of the following is an effective paraphrase for sentence 7?

    a. Zen is a different belief system from Theravada.
    b. There are many conflicting types of Buddhist beliefs.
    c. There are many interesting and different types of Buddhist beliefs.
    d. Buddhist religions are rich in material wealth.

5. Which of the following is an effective paraphrase for sentence 8?

    a. This textbook only presents a brief explanation of Buddhism.
    b. This textbook attempts to explain how Buddhism influences Western thought.
    c. Westerners will likely not understand Eastern beliefs, yet they need a world perspective to place Eastern thinking in its proper place as a philosophy.
    d. This textbook will probably not fully explain Eastern philosophy, but it will attempt to show how Western and Eastern beliefs

---

*Barry, *Philosophy*, p. 56.

compare and how Eastern philosophy fits into the general goals of philosophy.

(9) Central to Buddhist thought is the belief that all existence is characterized by constant movement and change. (10) Since "all is change," there is no fixed or static human nature. (11) Nevertheless, like existentialists, Buddhists do make statements about the human condition, which can be summed up in the Buddhist doctrine of the Four Noble Truths.

(12) The first of these truths is the existence of suffering. (13) From birth to death, life is a succession of physical and psychological torments that no one avoids. (14) Yes, for a time we may ward off suffering with youth, health, and riches, but ultimately we experience it. (15) Suffering is a universal problem in a finite and ever-changing world.

(16) The Second Noble Truth states that we suffer because we desire or crave things. (17) The insidious nature of these "thirsts" is that the more we try to satisfy them, the worse they become. (18) The more we get, the more we want and the more we must have.*

6. Which is an appropriate paraphrase for sentence 9?

   a. Buddhism believes that nothing stays the same in life.
   b. Buddhism believes that few things change in life.
   c. As we exist, Buddhists say, we move.
   d. Movement and change are a part of Buddhism.

7. Which is an appropriate paraphrase for sentence 10?

   a. Everything changes the human being.
   b. The human being refuses to be static.
   c. Human nature can never be identified because it is in a constant state of change.
   d. Human nature can never change because it is always fixed.

8. Which is an appropriate paraphrase for sentence 13?

   a. The human being consistently faces pain — to the mind and the body.
   b. Life is a series of struggles that few can avoid.
   c. Few succeed in avoiding the pain of life.
   d. In life, the mind and the body are constantly at war, and this causes endless pain.

9. Which is an appropriate paraphrase for sentence 15?

   a. The world is changing, and that is why we suffer.
   b. The world is not infinite, but the universe is.
   c. We all suffer in a world that has an end.
   d. All human beings suffer in a world that changes and will finally end.

1. _____
2. _____
3. _____
4. _____
5. _____
6. _____
7. _____
8. _____
9. _____
10. _____

70%

Ask instructor for answers.

---

*Barry, *Philosophy*, pp. 56–57.

10. Which is an appropriate paraphrase for sentence 17?

    a. Our desire for things make us angry.
    b. Our desire for things makes us want more things.
    c. The desire for things is finally an evil that humans must endure.
    d. Desire is like a thirst; it may go away for awhile, but it finally comes back.

Exercise 6.5
More Paraphrasing
of Sentences in
Paragraphs

The following paragraphs continue the discussion of Eastern philosophy. Read through the paragraphs carefully; then, using your paraphrasing skills, write appropriate paraphrases for the listed sentences. If you did not complete the previous exercise, read it through to get a sense for how this excerpt begins.

Eastern Philosophy

(1) The Third Noble Truth is that release from this seemingly endless round of pleasure pursuit is possible by realizing that the true nature of self is not found in trying to satisfy our desires, but in fortifying ourselves with values that are contrary to these desires. (2) When we do this, we ease pain, suffering, and unhappiness.

(3) The values that express the true nature of self are found in the Fourth Noble Truth: that we gain release from suffering through the Noble Eightfold Path. (4) This path consists of the following steps:

1. *Right understanding.* (5) Humans must realize that the only way out of pain and suffering is to know their true selves, to abandon ignorance about the self, and to eliminate craving and desire. (6) Without understanding we do not know how to escape our predicament.

2. *Right intention of purpose.* (7) We must want release from our dilemma and commit ourselves to discovering self-knowledge. (8) Without purpose we will not do what we must to find peace.

3. *Right speech.* (9) One sign that we are serious about attaining enlightenment is that our speech is above reproach. (10) We must never lie, gossip, slander, boast, flatter, or threaten.

4. *Right conduct.* (11) Just as speech reflects the quality of our intention, so does conduct. (12) Seekers of enlightenment never kill or harm any living creature. (13) Neither do they pollute their bodies with meats and liquors.

5. *Right way of livelihood.* (14) How we earn a living must be compatible with our goal of enlightenment. (15) Seeking material self-enrichment, such as money and status, excites desires and leads us from the path of true self-knowledge. (16) Working in the service of other people helps to quell these desires and to keep us directed toward our goal.

6. *Right effort.* (17) Speech, conduct, and way of living are not substitutes for discipline. (18) Right effort involves constantly checking desires and cravings and conceding no morsel of gratification to them.

7. *Right mindfulness.* (19) The interior life is as important as the exterior; what we think is as important as what we do. (20) Just as we must not give in to our desires, so must we not even think of them. (21) All action originates in thought. (22) When the thought is right, so is the action.

8. *Right concentration.* (23) The best way to ensure right mindfulness is through meditation and concentration, the spine of the Eightfold Way. (24) Through reflective practices and concentrated voyages into the interior self, we can gain enlightenment.*

Paraphrase the following numbered sentences:

7. _____

9. _____

11. _____

18. _____

24. _____

70%

(score = # correct × 20)
Find answers on p. 339.

Exercise 6.6
Using Paraphrasing
and Summarizing
Skills in a Longer
Passage

The following excerpt contains several paragraphs on the Buddhist way of life, a continuation of the discussion in the previous two exercises. The underlined sentences will require paraphrasing on a separate sheet of paper or in the margins. When you have completed your reading, answer the five questions that follow. In answering the questions, you may refer to the passage. Place all your answers in the answer box.

The Buddhist Way of Life

(1) What are the basic beliefs of Buddhism, and how do they determine how Buddhists should live? The Buddhists believe in two important concepts of living—one, the significance of human action, and two, the ways that morality and wisdom work together.

(2) First, Buddhists strongly believe that our actions determine our destiny. We are what we have done previously, and what we will be is determined by our previous actions. So in a sense, we can never escape our past; therefore, we must try to live as responsibly as we can. Thoughtless action breeds a thoughtless life.

---

*Barry, Philosophy, pp. 57–58.

(3) The second major point is that the living of a good or moral life makes the individual a wise person. A person who considers how to act responsibly, how to be good, how to care for others is automatically engaged in wise thoughts. By being both virtuous and wise, the individual comes to consider those issues that are most important to the human being.

(4) By adhering to Buddhist moral standards, one is allowed to contemplate nirvana. *Nirvana* is defined as enlightened wisdom, the highest spiritual place a practicing Buddhist can be. Buddhists emphasize that nirvana cannot be achieved by blindly following the principles of their religion. The true believer must want to follow the Noble Truths; that is, the motivation must come from within. Buddhists thus focus on personal experience and common sense rather than on rules and commandments.

(5) An important Buddhist teaching is the respect people should have for life. Buddhists do not tell their followers what they can and cannot eat or whether they should ever use violence. They simply ask people to respect life and, by respecting life, to determine whether animals should be killed for food or whether murder of humans is ever justified. By grappling with these never-answered questions, one attains wisdom.

(6) Another important precept that practicing Buddhists live by is not to take what is not given to you. This precept does not simply say "Do not steal!" It is asking believers to be patient, to wait for something to be given to them. Instead of focusing on what they want, Buddhists practice patience and serenity, for they believe that what is due them will be given in time. And what they aggressively take is not due them. Taking what they want will harm their spiritual life.

(7) This is just an introduction to the complex and fascinating belief system of Buddhism. It is clearly a philosophy and a religion that focuses on making one's own reasoned decisions. It is a questioning rather than a dictating philosophy. It asks its followers to listen and to accept life, not to speak over others or to reject what others have to say before listening attentively.*

1. The main idea of paragraph 2 is

   a. all that people have are their actions
   b. the way one acts determines how one lives
   c. our past always follows us
   d. Buddhists do not favor thoughtless actions

2. The best summary of paragraph 4 is

   a. nirvana is enlightened wisdom
   b. nirvana is not achieved simply by acting properly
   c. nirvana—enlightened wisdom—is achieved when the believer chooses to follow the Noble Truths

---

*Adapted from Barry, *Philosophy*, pp. 58–60.

    d. Buddhist standards must be followed in order to achieve nirvana; none of the Buddhist precepts can be ignored

3. A major detail in paragraph 5 is

    a. Buddhists ask each believer to determine whether it is morally right to slaughter an animal for food
    b. Buddhists encourage their followers never to use violence
    c. Buddhists teach a respect for life
    d. Buddhist philosophy presents several questions to its believers

4. The main idea of paragraph 6 is

    a. do not steal
    b. an important belief for the Buddhists is to take whatever you can from life
    c. an important belief for the Buddhists is to take only what you receive from life
    d. Buddhists practice serenity as a way of determining what to accept from life

5. The best summary for paragraph 7 is

    a. Buddhism is a philosophy that asks you to listen carefully to life
    b. Buddhism is a philosophy that asks you to question life
    c. Buddhism asks its believers to question, listen, and accept rather than to have fixed answers and to force them on others
    d. Buddhism is both a philosophy and a religion that asks its followers to understand its principles and to live a decent life

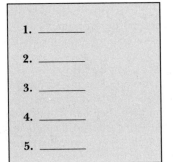

1. _____

2. _____

3. _____

4. _____

5. _____

Now answer the following five questions with a short phrase or sentence:

6. Reread paragraph 1. List the two points that this excerpt intends to cover.

7. Reread paragraph 2. From the evidence in this paragraph, why do you think that Buddhism asks its followers to live responsibly?

8. Paraphrase the underlined sentence in paragraph 2.

9. Paraphrase the underlined sentence in paragraph 4.

10. Paraphrase the underlined sentence in paragraph 6.

80%

(score = # correct × 10)
Ask instructor for
answers.

Exercise 6.7
Writing a Paragraph
Using Summarizing
and Paraphrasing
Skills

Your job is to go back to the excerpt on Buddhism and to find the information to answer the following questions. Much of this information can be found in your paraphrases and your answers to the summary questions. From your responses to the three questions, answer the essay question that follows.

1. How are actions an important part of Buddhist morality?

2. What is nirvana?

70%

Ask instructor for answers.

---

3. How are acceptance and serenity an important part of Buddhist morality?

Essay question: In one paragraph, discuss the most important ways Buddhism advises its followers to live. In your discussion, focus on how Buddhist morality understands the following: action, nirvana, serenity.

Exercise 6.8
Using Summarizing
and Paraphrasing
Skills on a Textbook
Excerpt

The following is a philosophy textbook excerpt on Western law, providing you with a different response to ethics and morality than the one you have been considering in the previous exercises on Eastern philosophy and Buddhism. Read through the excerpt quickly to get a sense for its organization. Then go back and read it slowly, paying particular attention to longer sentences that you may want to paraphrase. You may also want to underline the key main ideas and major details. When you finish, answer the five questions that follow, and place your answers in the answer box. You may refer to the excerpt in deciding on your answers.

Law

(1) Traditionally, the line of demarcation between the individual and society has been the *law*, by which we mean a rule or a body of rules that tells individuals what they may and may not do.

(2) Our Western legal system, which we have inherited from the Judeo-Christian tradition, is a hierarchy of laws. For example, when a town law and a state law conflict, the state law takes precedence. Likewise, federal laws take precedence over state laws. Does anything take precedence over federal law, over the so-called law of the land? Both the Jewish and the Christian traditions maintain allegiance to a law that transcends any state, which they have historically referred to as the "law of God." We find a similar concept in ancient Greek philosophy.

(3) The Stoics, members of a school of thought founded by Zeno around 300 BC, believed that the world does not operate by blind chance but involves divine providence. The universe, they believed, is

rational, in the sense that it operates according to laws that the human mind can discover. This orderliness or world reason the Stoics variously termed "Zeus," "nature," and "*logos*" ("word"). Since people are happy when they act in accordance with nature — with the order of the universe — the purpose of institutions, according to the Stoics, is to enact laws that reflect this single universal law. Thus, what we today call "civic laws" have their basis in natural law. *Natural law* generally refers to (1) a pattern of necessary and universal regularity holding in physical ratio or (2) a moral imperative, a description of what ought to happen in human relationships. It's the second definition that concerns us here.

(4) The Christian philosopher and theologian Saint Augustine presented a well-thought-out scheme of law in his *City of God*. In fact, Augustine's thought influenced Saint Thomas Aquinas, who in the Middle Ages distinguished among several kinds of law. First is divine or eternal law — that is, God's decrees for the governance of the universe. According to Thomas, all things obey eternal law, and how they behave simply reflects this law. Thus, a flame rises and a stone falls. God, then, is the lawmaker of the universe; things behave as they do because He so decrees it; they cannot behave otherwise. But Thomas also applied this concept to the affairs of states. For Thomas, laws applying to the universe — what we today call physical laws — found their counterpart in the lesser communities called states.

(5) Thomas defined natural law as divine law applied to human situations. This description is not of much help until one takes a closer look at Thomas's morality. Morality, as Thomas conceived it, is not an arbitrary set of rules for behavior; rather, the basis of moral obligation is built into the very nature of the human in the form of various inclinations, such as the preservation of life, the propagation of the species, and the search for truth. The moral law, then, is founded upon these natural inclinations and the ability of reason to discern the right course of conduct. The rules of conduct corresponding to these inherent human features are called natural law.

(6) A good part of Thomas's theory of natural law had already been worked through by Aristotle. In *Ethics*, Aristotle distinguished between natural and conventional justice. According to Aristotle, some forms of behavior are wrong because they violate a law that has been made to regulate the behavior. To use a contemporary example, consider the law in many places against jaywalking. Since there's nothing in nature that requires people not to jaywalk, such a law is conventional, not natural. In contrast, Aristotle argued that some laws are derived from nature; the behavior that they prohibit has always been wrong. Murder and theft might be two examples. These are wrong not because any human-made law forbids them but because they run counter to the nature of human beings. Both Aristotle and Thomas believed that humans can discover the natural basis for human conduct through reason. But Thomas went further, contending that the human's existence and nature can only be understood in relation to God.

(7) For Thomas, then, law deals primarily with reason, which is the rule and measure of acts. Law consists of these rules and measures of human acts and is therefore based on reason. What's more, the natural law is dictated by reason. Since God created everything, human nature

and natural law are best comprehended as the product of God's wisdom or reason.

(8) In summary, for Thomas, natural law consists of that portion of the eternal law that pertains directly to humans. The basic precepts of the natural law are preservation of life, propagation and education of offspring, and the pursuit of truth and a peaceful society. These precepts reflect God's intentions for the human in creation and can be discovered and understood by reason.

(9) Although these precepts do not vary, their enforcement does. Since different societies are influenced by different topographies, climates, cultures, and social customs, Thomas believed that different codes of justice are needed. He called these specific codes of justice human law. The function of rulers is to formulate human law by informing themselves of the specific needs of their communities and then passing appropriate decrees. So, whereas natural law is general enough to govern the community of all humans, human law is specific enough to meet the requirements of a particular society.

(10) For Thomas, then, there are two points of difference between human law and natural or divine law. First, human law applies to a specific group, society, or community; second, it is the expressed decrees of a human agent and not the laws operating in the universe at large. Nevertheless, a human law is a law because it articulates divine law. That is, human law is not law because it emanates from a legislator or ruler but because it implements divine law.

(11) From Thomas's theory of law we can draw one conclusion that is particularly relevant to our discussion: Subjects have the right to rebel. This conclusion follows from his idea that human law must be obeyed only when it expresses divine law. Since humans are capable of poor judgment, rulers can pass unjust laws that are not "an ordinance or reason for the common good." In Thomas's view an unjust law is not a law at all and is therefore not binding.*

1. Which is an appropriate summary of paragraph 2?

   a. In interpreting laws, one finally goes back to the law of God.
   b. The law of God is the most difficult one to locate and understand.
   c. State law is more important than town law.
   d. Federal laws are more powerful than state laws.

2. The main idea of paragraph 3 concerns

   a. natural law
   b. the two types of natural law
   c. a description of how people should respond to each other
   d. natural law and its relationship to regularity and morality

3. The main idea of paragraph 5 concerns

   a. *City of God*
   b. how morality is related to natural law

---

*Barry, *Philosophy*, pp. 188–190.

    c. how reason determines action

    d. rules of conduct

4. A major detail in paragraph 6 is

    a. Aristotle's *Ethics*

    b. Aristotle's influence on Saint Thomas Aquinas

    c. the idea that some laws prohibit irregular behavior

    d. the concept that murder does not go against human nature

5. What is the main idea or conclusion of paragraph 7?

    a. Laws are reasonable, but few people understand them.

    b. Laws explain human behavior.

    c. God created laws, so people naturally follow them.

    d. What humans are and how they should act are a part of what God is.

1. _____

2. _____

3. _____

4. _____

5. _____

    Now read the following questions; then go back and reread the excerpt. After you have read the excerpt, answer the following questions without looking back.

6. Paraphrase this sentence from paragraph 8: "The basic precepts of the natural law are preservation of life, propagation and education of offspring, and the pursuit of truth and a peaceful society." (2 points)

7. Paraphrase this sentence from paragraph 9: "Since different societies are influenced by different topographies, climates, cultures, and social customs, Thomas believed that different codes of justice are needed." (2 points)

70%

Ask instructor for answers.

---

8. Why does Aquinas believe that it is sometimes right for human beings to go against the law? (1 point)

Follow-up on the Philosophy Exercises

Now that you have completed these exercises, it may be helpful to see how your reading has changed some of your ideas about philosophy as a field of study. You may want to go back to these exercises and reread them just for their content or for the way they introduce various types of philosophy. Then answer the following questions either individually or in small groups.

1. How would you now define *philosophy*?

2. What are some of the beliefs of Eastern philosophy?

3. What parts of Eastern philosophy do you agree with? Can it help us respond to some of our world problems?

4. What issue in philosophy do you now want to study further?

7 Reading and Listening for Inferences

MAKING INFERENCES

Terms of qualification

Word choice: connotations

Details:
▶ General?
▶ Specific?

Now that you have begun to identify various organizational patterns in writing and speech and you are summarizing and paraphrasing what you read and hear, you are on your way to reading and listening more critically. But sometimes knowing the main idea, the details, and the organizational pattern is not enough. Books and lectures often leave much unsaid, and you must "read between the lines." Making judgments and drawing conclusions about what is suggested is called *making inferences.* The effective student is an efficient inference maker, gleaning important points from what is suggested. It is the correct inference that instructors are looking for on exams and essays. You can make inferences about most material by looking for the terms of qualification in a sentence, the author's or speaker's word choice, and the kinds of details used.

Terms of Qualification

A single word or phrase can change the message of a sentence. It can give strong support for a statement or add doubt. A *term of qualification* is a word or phrase that limits the truth of a statement. In most cases, the speaker or writer will not tell you the degree of certainty intended in a statement; you need to infer this certainty from the term of qualification.

Terms of qualification can be divided into four categories: terms expressing no doubt, terms expressing a little doubt, terms expressing some doubt, and terms expressing much doubt.

Words and Phrases That Express No Doubt

all	surely	assuredly	there is no doubt
none	conclusively	undoubtedly	without reservation
never	clearly	absolutely	without hesitation
always	unequivocally	constantly	it is a proven fact
certainly	precisely	undeniably	it is undeniable
definitely	plainly	without a doubt	without question

Let these words and phrases become signals to you that what you are reading or listening to carries certainty. You can also use them when you write particularly strong statements.

See how the use of the word "absolutely" adds conviction to the following statement: "Mozart is absolutely the most brilliant musician ever to write classical music." The writer here evidently has positive feelings about Mozart and uses "absolutely" to establish these positive feelings. Sometimes, when you find such strong terms of qualification, you may want to underline them and make a marginal comment like "strong statement."

Now consider terms that express a small degree of doubt:

Words and Phrases That Express a Little Doubt

most	seldom	there is little doubt	it is believed
mostly	rarely	almost never	almost always
usually	slightly	with little reservation	
consistently	one can safely say	the consistent pattern	

When you find such words and phrases, ask yourself what the exceptions to the statement might be. These exceptions are often not discussed by the author. By failing to notice the term of qualification, you might wrongly conclude that the statement has no exceptions.

Consider how in the following statement the word "usually" plants a question in your mind: "College students usually find Mozart's opera *The Marriage of Figaro* to be the most exciting work they study in the course." If the author does not discuss the exceptions, it would be wise for you to underline the term of qualification and write in the margin something like "When do students not enjoy this opera?" Also begin using these terms in your own writing when you want to show a little doubt.

Now look at this list of terms expressing some doubt. If these terms are used, you need to consider the exceptions, which are often not elaborated upon by the writer.

Words and Phrases That Express Some Doubt

many	ostensibly	it seems
frequently	apparently	one can infer
often	somewhat	one can say with some
may	likely	reservation
might	this might mean	the hypothesis is
perhaps	this could mean	the theory is
one would assume	the results imply	it is possible that
the assumption is	possibly	it is probable that
one would infer	at times	
it is suggested that	it appears	
seemingly		
generally		

The following sentence uses the term of qualification "it appears." How does this term alter the meaning of the statement? "It appears that rock music will continue to be an important musical experience for teenagers." Because the writer includes "it appears" in this statement, you cannot conclude that rock music will always be teenagers' preferred form of music. In a marginal comment, you might ask "What are the author's reservations?" You can also start using these terms in your own writing when your statements are not definite.

Finally, consider the following words, which suggest much doubt. When you see or hear these words, you should question the truth of these statements.

Words and Phrases That Suggest Much Doubt

supposedly	it is suspected that
it is guessed that	it is rumored that
it is conjectured that	

Look how "it is rumored that" makes the following statement questionable: "It is rumored that the federal government is trying to ban rock concerts that sell over 10,000 tickets for one show." Because this statement is rumor, you cannot include it in any serious discussion of rock concerts. Many irresponsible speakers and publications use rumor as the basis for their arguments. Never cite these speakers or publications as sources in a serious essay or speech.

Word Choice

You can make many inferences about a passage by analyzing the kinds of words that a speaker or author uses. *Connotations*, the hidden meanings of words, tell you whether an author or speaker has a positive, neutral, or negative attitude toward the topic. Authors and speakers often do not directly tell you their attitude toward the topic because they do not want to be accused of being biased. But you can infer these attitudes from the connotations of their words.

Look at the following sentence on Duke Ellington and see if you can locate the word with a strong positive connotation: "Duke Ellington continues to be one of the most revered figures in the history of American jazz." Do you see that "revered" is a positive word, suggesting that Ellington still commands a great deal of respect among jazz historians? To be revered is to be greatly respected, almost worshipped. In a marginal note about this sentence, you could include a comment like "'Revered' suggests great respect, almost worship."

Look at the use of "destructive" to see how it gives negative associations to this sentence about heavy metal music: "Heavy metal music clearly has a destructive effect on the behavior of young people, particularly at concerts." Do you see that "destructive" has antisocial and violent associations? Although the author does not directly state that young people lose their sense of right and wrong, such a meaning is suggested in the connotations of "destructive." A marginal comment noting the connotations of this word would help you remember the author's intent.

Some statements avoid using words or phrases with obvious connotations. Notice how this statement uses neutral language: "The swing era in jazz lasted for about fifteen years, from 1935 to 1950." Do you see that the author uses no words suggesting that the swing era was either a positive or negative musical event? Here the author may be purposely using neutral language so as not to express an opinion about swing.

The total effect of an author's choice of words on a particular passage is called its *tone*, or the feeling that a reader gets from the words used in a passage. A passage's tone can leave the reader with positive, negative, or neutral feelings toward the topic. After you read a work, ask yourself what overall feeling it gives you. Then try to see what type of language in the work makes you feel this way.

Details of Support

In longer written passages or in longer lectures, you can infer something about the author or speaker from the details that are presented. If the details are presented logically, you can infer that the speaker or author is in command of the material. But if the details are disorganized, you can infer that the speaker or author is poorly prepared. You also can infer something by studying the sources used in the work. If known publications or experts are cited, you can more likely value the argument. If the speaker or author does not mention sources, you would be justified in questioning the thesis. Again, the author or speaker will probably not comment on the nature of the details; it is up to you to determine the value of the work from the nature of the details.

Look at the following paragraph on the Beatles. What do the details say about the competence of the writer?

> The Beatles were a very famous rock group several years ago. There were four of them, and they acted and dressed strangely. Their appearance and behavior made people like them even more. They made their first appearance in the United States in the early sixties on a popular television show.

Even if you agree with the thesis of the excerpt, the evidence is vague. The author does not name who these Beatles were, nor does she mention how they acted and dressed. The author also does not name the show they appeared on. Because these details are vague, you can infer that the writer, although logical, is not well prepared. Therefore her argument is not convincing.

Study the details of this second passage on the Beatles, and again try to infer something about the author:

> The Beatles were decidedly the most famous rock group to emerge from England in the sixties. There were four of them: John, Paul, George, and Ringo. Fans in America and Europe loved them for their long hair and their often irreverent sense of humor. They gained great notoriety in the United States in 1964 when they appeared on the "Ed Sullivan Show," the most popular variety show on television at the time.

Doesn't it seem that the author of this excerpt has done more research on the subject? She knows the names of each member, how they acted and looked, and the name of the show that made them famous in the United States. You will likely read this writer carefully, because the material is both logical and detailed.

When you write your own critical essays, be sure to cite your sources and present accurate details. If you do, your reader will read your work more carefully. You will learn more about effective essay writing in Chapter 16.

Summary

An *inference* is an insight you gain from something that is not stated directly. By making correct inferences, you better understand the material. You make inferences by noting terms of qualification, word choice, and the nature of the details. You should make marginal comments on your inferences.

The more you read and listen, the more sophisticated your inferences will become. You will begin comparing past knowledge with what you are currently learning. And your learning will be that much more rewarding.

Summary Box   *Inferences*

What are they?	*How do you make them?*	*Why do you need them?*
Insights or deductions made by a reader or listener but not directly stated	By studying terms of qualification, word choice, and details	To give more meaning to your reading and listening To become more questioning of what you read and hear

Topic: Music History

The exercises in this chapter all deal with the issue of music history, a course that you might one day take in college. Before you begin these exercises, answer the following questions either individually or in small groups to get some sense for what you already know about music history.

1. How would you define *music history*?
2. What do you know about classical music? Who are some of the great classical composers?
3. Are rock music and jazz in any way like classical music?
4. What is your favorite type of music? Why?

Exercise 7.1
Making Inferences
from Details

You can make inferences from the examples an author uses. If the examples are accurate, you can infer that the author is credible; if the examples are inaccurate, you can infer that the writer is unprepared.

Read the following paragraphs carefully, and determine whether the author is being detailed or vague. All of the paragraphs describe musical instruments. Write *D* in the answer box if the paragraph is detailed and *V* if the paragraph is vague.

The Instruments of the Orchestra

(1) The string instruments are very important to an orchestra: They make up about half of all of the instruments. They include the violin, viola, cello, and double bass. What makes these instruments different is their relative size. Their differing sizes produce different pitches or sounds.

(2) How does a string instrument make sound? Part of the instrument is hollow. Another part transmits the sound to the body. Then the body changes the sound. This change in sound makes each instrument different.

(3) Woodwinds are another type of orchestral instrument. As their name suggests, these instruments rely on wind to make their sound, and each one is made of wood. Examples of woodwind instruments are the flute, piccolo, oboe, English horn, clarinet, and bassoon. Each of these instruments has a hollow body and holes along the length that let air in and out.

(4) The flute is a peculiar instrument. In recent times the material it is made of has changed. The flute and piccolo produce a particular sound. This sound is made by air moving and colliding with other air. The flute also has a particular sound range.

(5) The oboe is another interesting orchestral instrument. The wood that oboes are made of is specially treated. The reeds used in oboes are an important part of the instrument's sound. The range of sound that the oboe produces is not very wide.

(6) The saxophone is sometimes included in an orchestra. It is considered part of the woodwind family, even though its body is made of metal. What makes it like other woodwind instruments is the reed that

1.	_____
2.	_____
3.	_____
4.	_____
5.	_____
6.	_____
7.	_____
8.	_____
9.	_____
10.	_____

80%

(score = # correct × 10)
Find answers on p. 339.

it uses to produce its distinctive sound. Although it is only an occasional member of the orchestra, the saxophone is always part of concert and jazz bands.

(7) Brass instruments make up another musical family. They are unlike woodwinds. The unique sound of a brass instrument is its buzzing. Brass instruments come in various sizes, and the size of each instrument can be changed.

(8) What types of brass instruments does the orchestra use? In most orchestras, three trumpets, four French horns, two tenor trombones, one brass trombone, and one tuba are included. Of these instruments, the trumpet has the highest pitch. Its pitch is altered by changing the length of its tubing. There are three piston valves in a trumpet that alter its size and therefore its range.

(9) Another instrument in the brass family is the cornet, which is similar to the trumpet. The cornet's tube is shaped like a cone. It produces a mellow sound. Finally, a cornet is also equipped with a mute, which softens its tone even more.

(10) The trombone has a different sound from the trumpet. It is also shaped differently from the trumpet. Also, the trombone's sound is powerful. Its sound is unique but very difficult to describe.*

Exercise 7.2 Locating and Analyzing Terms of Qualification

The following paragraphs discuss Johann Sebastian Bach (1685–1750), one of the great classical composers. In these paragraphs are five terms of qualification, which are underlined. In the spaces provided, explain how each term of qualification alters the meaning of the sentence. Comment on whether the term makes the statement stronger or casts doubt on it. You may want to refer to the lists of terms of qualification on pp. 126–127.

Example: Almost every student of music knows Bach's work and is impressed by it.

Explanation: This is a strong statement about Bach's abilities, but the use of "almost" suggests that not all students of music find him to be great.

Johann Sebastian Bach

(1) Most students of music would say that Johann Sebastian Bach is one of the greatest composers of all time. Bach's life was uneventful. The most important biographical detail is that he was part of an extremely talented musical family that spanned six generations.

(2) What is Bach's appeal? Why is he an undeniably dominant figure in music history? Scholars of music constantly refer to his skill in writing counterpoint. The way that he ordered musical relationships, it seems, has a pleasing effect on the listener's mind.

---

*Adapted from Charles R. Hoffer, *The Understanding of Music*, 6th ed. (Belmont, Calif.: Wadsworth, 1989), pp. 52–57.

(3) The *fugue* is Bach's greatest musical contribution. In a fugue, lines of music imitate each other in carefully organized ways. Scholars <u>generally</u> agree that the fugue evolved over several generations and with several composers.

(4) Analyzing a Bach fugue shows how fugues are <u>frequently</u> structured. Bach's Fugue in C Minor begins with a melody divided into four parts. This main melody is called the subject, and this subject is expressed by various imitations called voices, which constantly reinterpret the subject.*

1. *Term:* _____

   Explanation: _____

2. *Term:* _____

   Explanation: _____

3. *Term:* _____

   Explanation: _____

4. *Term:* _____

   Explanation: _____

5. *Term:* _____

   Explanation: _____

Now read the following series of paragraphs, continuing the discussion on Bach. In these paragraphs are five additional terms of qualification. This time they are not underlined. Locate them and determine what effect they have on the sentence. Place each term and explanation on the lines provided at the end of the excerpt.

(5) The fugue is certainly not the only form of music that Bach wrote for the organ, although perhaps it can be seen as the most important. Two others known as the *chorale variation* and the *chorale prelude* also use the fugue format, but these two musical forms vary the main musical theme each time it is introduced into the composition.

(6) Another type of music Bach wrote for the organ is called the *passacaglia*. This musical form continues one musical theme throughout but adds variations over it. The passacaglia is usually seen as a fascinating, demanding listening experience. Without question, one of Bach's finest works is the Passacaglia in C Minor.

---

*Adapted from Hoffer, *Understanding of Music*, pp. 185–188.

(7) There is no doubt that anyone interested in seriously studying European music will spend time experiencing this amazing composer — J. S. Bach.*

6. *Term:* _____

  Explanation: _____

7. *Term:* _____

  Explanation: _____

8. *Term:* _____

  Explanation: _____

9. *Term:* _____

  Explanation: _____

80%
Ask instructor for answers.

---

10. *Term:* _____

  Explanation: _____

Exercise 7.3
Commenting on Word Choice in Sentences

The following paragraphs describe the life and music of Wolfgang Amadeus Mozart (1756–1791), a German composer who came after Bach. The writer of these paragraphs has a definite attitude toward Mozart. Read these paragraphs carefully to determine what he is saying about Mozart and what his attitude toward him is; then go back and reread the underlined words to see how they alter the meaning of the sentence they are in. You may want to consult a dictionary or thesaurus as you complete this exercise to determine the meanings of the underlined words. Place your explanations on the lines provided at the end of the excerpt.

Example: Mozart was one of the <u>dazzling</u> composers of the eighteenth century.

Explanation: To dazzle is to overpower by intense light. The author is suggesting that Mozart was clearly an overpowering and brilliant composer of his time.

---

*Adapted from Hoffer, *Understanding of Music*, pp. 185–188.

Mozart's Music and Life

(1) Wolfgang Amadeus Mozart is nothing less than a musical <u>miracle</u>. His compositions are consistently clear, delicate, and simple, yet they defy a simple musical analysis.

(2) Mozart was a child prodigy, composing his first pieces at the <u>astonishing</u> age of five. He was performing at six, and by the age of thirteen, he had written concertos, symphonies, and an opera.

(3) Mozart had a <u>phenomenal</u> musical memory. He was able to do the seemingly <u>impossible</u> task: compose entire musical pieces in his mind. He has been quoted as saying that when he committed a musical piece to paper, he had worked it all out in his mind beforehand.

(4) Although Mozart possessed an <u>unfathomable</u> musical gift, his personal life was <u>disastrous</u>. He was naive when it came to his finances and consistently found himself in debt. At thirty-five he died of uremic poisoning, and he did not have the money for a respectable funeral. This musical <u>giant</u> died a pauper.

(5) His short life notwithstanding, Mozart completed a remarkable number of musical compositions. He <u>explored</u> many musical genres: operas, symphonies, concertos, and string quartets. With each type of music he composed, Mozart left an <u>indelible</u> musical style. His works consistently reveal different aspects of his musical <u>genius</u>, so he continues to be studied by musical scholars, performers, and musical composers today for what he has to say about classical music.*

1. *Explanation:* _____

2. *Explanation:* _____

3. *Explanation:* _____

4. *Explanation:* _____

5. *Explanation:* _____

6. *Explanation:* _____

7. *Explanation:* _____

8. *Explanation:* _____

9. *Explanation:* _____

10. *Explanation:* _____

70%
(score = # correct × 10)
Find answers on p. 340.

---

*Adapted from Hoffer, *Understanding of Music*, pp. 210–212.

Now go back to reread the passage. What do you think is the overall tone of this passage? What words suggest this tone?

_____

_____

Exercise 7.4
Making Inferences
in a Longer Passage

In the following passage on rock music, you will be asked to make inferences based on details, word choice, and terms of qualification. Read the passage carefully, marking the text for main ideas and major details as well as commenting on any word choice that seems particularly interesting to you. Then answer the questions that follow. You may refer to the passage when answering the questions. Place all answers in the answer box.

Rock Music in the Fifties and Sixties

(1) It seems that rock music got its start in 1955 when Bill Haley and the Comets sang "Rock Around the Clock" in the movie *Blackboard Jungle*. This film was about a group of rowdy teenagers in an urban high school. The simple blues-like music of the Haley song, coupled with the feelings of discontent among teenagers, seem to have laid the foundation for rock music, a kind of music that seems to speak to almost all teenagers today.

(2) Elvis Presley soon followed on the heels of Bill Haley. His striking good looks and sexually suggestive movements as he performed added more excitement to his singing. Songs like his "You Ain't Nothing but a Hound Dog" continued the simple yet catchy beat of "Rock Around the Clock." Presley was undeniably the most significant contributor to rock music in the fifties. Although he has been dead for over fourteen years, his legacy lives on in both the now middle-aged fans who remember him and the teenagers who know him today through his music.

(3) Rock music in the sixties became a more complex, more thoughtful type of music. There seemed to be a singing style for everyone in this decade: Motown, the Beatles, the Rolling Stones, as well as the folk music of balladeers like Bob Dylan and Joni Mitchell. By the sixties, some rock music had developed a keen social conscience. Good looks and physical movement would no longer always sell a lyric. Singers and songwriters like Bob Dylan and the Beatles began to introduce social questions into their lyrics. Many antiwar rock songs emerged as a response to the war in Vietnam, which began to escalate in the sixties and create violence and discontent in the entire nation.

(4) What defined rock music in both the fifties and the sixties was a clear beat and an often refreshing experimentation with musical form. Moreover, the musical instruments that rock employed were decidedly different from those used before the fifties. The saxophones and trumpets of the forties gave way to electronic instruments, especially guitars and organs. Rock music also often used music technology in interesting ways, amplifying the sound and playing with it through the engineer's skillful use of mixing and multiple tracks.

(5) What seemed to separate rock music of the fifties from that of the sixties was the electrifying popularity of the group in the sixties over the solo performer. The advantage of the group was that it was able to play several instruments—particularly electric guitar, electric organ, and drums—as it sang. Fans could now select their favorite group member among the several who performed in concert and on television.

(6) Thanks to the contributions of performers in the fifties and sixties, rock music seems to be here to stay. Its variety today seems to have provided for a larger listening audience—from teenagers, its original audience, to young adults and middle-aged adults who grew up and in a sense were nourished on rock.*

1. What terms of qualification are used in paragraph 1?

   a. "seems" and "got"
   b. "seems" and "almost all"
   c. "almost" and "kind"
   d. "simple" and "this"

2. Which word from the following sentence in paragraph 2 has positive connotations? "His striking good looks and sexually suggestive movements as he performed added more excitement to his singing."

   a. looks
   b. movements
   c. performed
   d. striking

3. What term of qualification is used in the following sentence in paragraph 2? "Presley was undeniably the most significant contributor to rock music in the fifties."

   a. significant
   b. contributor
   c. undeniably
   d. fifties

4. Which word or words from this sentence in paragraph 3 have positive connotations? "Rock music in the sixties became a more complex, more thoughtful type of music."

   a. complex
   b. thoughtful
   c. both a and b
   d. neither a nor b

---

*Adapted from Hoffer, *Understanding of Music*, pp. 511–516.

```
1. _____
2. _____
3. _____
4. _____
5. _____
```

5. Which word or words in the last sentence of paragraph 3 has negative connotations?

    a. emerged
    b. discontent
    c. response
    d. nation

Now answer the following five questions with a short phrase or sentence.

6. What do you think the writer means in paragraph 4 by the phrase "an often refreshing experimentation with musical form"?

7. Locate a word in the last sentence of paragraph 4 that positively describes the music engineer.

8. What do you think the writer means in paragraph 5 by the phrase "electrifying popularity of the group"?

9. What term of qualification is used in the first sentence of paragraph 6? How does it alter the meaning of this sentence?

10. What do you think is this author's overall attitude toward rock music in the fifties and sixties? Which words or statements help suggest this attitude?

```
    80%
Ask instructor for
answers.
```

Exercise 7.5
Writing Your Own
Paragraph Using
Main Ideas and
Major Details

Your job in this exercise is to go back to the passage on rock music in Exercise 7.4 and determine the major characteristics of rock music in the fifties and sixties. As you locate this information, jot it down in the outline below. From the information in the completed outline, answer the essay question in one paragraph.

I. Characteristics of Early Rock Music

    A. In the fifties: _____

    _____

```
    70%
Ask instructor for
answers.
```

    B. In the sixties: _____

    _____

Essay question: Rock music developed in interesting ways in its first two decades. What were the characteristics of rock music in the fifties and sixties? In what ways was the music in these two periods similar? How was it different?

*Exercise 7.6
Determining Main
Ideas and Major
Details and Making
Inferences from a
Textbook Excerpt*

The following is an excerpt from a textbook on jazz, an American musical movement that came before rock. Read through the excerpt quickly to get a sense for its organization. Then go back and read it slowly, paying particular attention to the way jazz is described. There are many technical terms that you will not need to know to answer the questions that follow. You may refer to the excerpt in deciding on your answers.

Traditional Jazz

(1) The roots of jazz reach back to black Americans' African heritage. But other elements have also influenced jazz: minstrel show music, work songs, field hollers, funeral marching bands, blues, French-Creole and Spanish-American music, and, more recently, West Indian music. Jazz did not develop until about the beginning of the twentieth century. Basin Street in New Orleans is traditionally considered its birthplace, although clearly jazz did not just pop into being in one spot and at a fixed historical moment. It was brought to public attention by the funeral procession. On the way back from the cemetery the band played tunes in a way quite different from the somber sounds that accompanied the march to the gravesite. The players shifted the emphasis from the strong to the weak beat and launched into a decorated version of the melody. When Storyville, the New Orleans red-light district, was closed down in 1917, many jazz musicians lost their jobs and sought work in other cities. Jazz moved up the Mississippi River through Memphis and St. Louis to Chicago and the rest of the United States.

(2) Two types of Afro-American folk music existed before and during the early years of jazz and later merged with it. One of these was *ragtime*. It featured the piano, occasionally in combination with other instruments. The music sounds like a polished, syncopated march with a decorated right-hand part. Early musicians associated with ragtime are Scott Joplin in Sedalia, Missouri, and Ben Harvey, who published his *Ragtime Instructor* in 1897.

(3) The other type of music involved with early jazz was the folk *blues*. Its musical characteristics will be discussed shortly. Some of the most famous names associated with blues are Leadbelly, whose real name was Huddie Ledbetter; W. C. Handy, who was known for his "Memphis Blues" and "St. Louis Blues"; and Ferdinand "Jelly Roll" Morton, whose first published blues appeared in 1905—the "Jelly Roll Blues."

(4) Like folk music, jazz was created by generally untutored musicians who could not have written down what they played or sang, even if they had wanted to. Jazz is different from most folk music in two respects, however. It has sprung from the cities rather than the fields and forests; it is an urban form of music. And for most people, it is a spectator experience. Usually only a few people perform, although listeners may contribute a little hand clapping and foot stomping.

Musical Elements of Jazz

(5) What is traditional jazz? It has several elements.

(6) *Melody.* The most significant feature of jazz melodies is the *blue note*. These notes are derived from an altered version of the major scale. The blues scale merely lowers the third, fifth, and/or seventh steps. Many times the performer shifts between the regular note and its lower alternative as if searching for a sound, which in a sense is what is happening. The blue-note interval is an approximation of a microtone, roughly half of a half step in this case. African music is the influence behind its use in jazz. Blue notes are a source of subtle color. Their effect in jazz is further enhanced by the fact that the chord in the harmony usually contains the particular note at its expected pitch while the lowered blue note is sounded in the melody. This combination creates an interesting and characteristic dissonance.

(7) *Harmony.* Traditional jazz harmony is as conservative as any church hymn. The typical chords are the same three that form the backbone of traditional tonal harmony: tonic (I), dominant (V), and subdominant (IV). More recently, sophisticated types of jazz have employed the advanced harmonic idioms of Debussy, Bartók, and Stravinsky. The appeal of jazz, however, does not lie in its harmony.

(8) *Rhythm.* Rhythm is one of the most important features of jazz. Although its meter is nearly always two beats per measure, with irregular meters occurring only rarely, the jazz musician employs an endless variety of syncopated patterns and rhythmic figures over this regular pulse. Syncopation — the redistribution of accents so that the rhythmic patterns do not occur as the listener expects — is the lifeblood of jazz.

(9) Jazz rhythms do not fit well into the usual divisions of time into sixteenths, eighths, and quarters. Jazz musicians perform rhythm with small deviations of timing and accent that cannot be rendered in notation. Players even make slight alterations of the patterns of conventional notation when reading them. These deviations in rhythm are one reason why traditionally trained musicians often cannot achieve an authentic jazz sound.

(10) *Timbre.* The basic timbre sought by jazz instrumentalists is perhaps an unconscious imitation of the black singing voice: a bit breathy with a little vibrato (rapid and slight variance of pitch on a single tone). Certain instruments, therefore, have become associated with this idiom. The saxophone was intended to be a concert instrument, but it was taken up by jazz musicians because it can produce the desired quality. Mutes — metal or fiber devices inserted in or over the bell of brass instruments to change the tone quality — are often used, and their names are as distinctive as the sounds they produce: *cup, wah-wah,* and *plunger* (like the end of a rubber sink plunger). Many jazz trumpeters use a particular type of mouthpiece that helps them produce a more shrill sound and makes high notes easier to play. In jazz style the clarinet is played in a manner that produces a tone quality like that of the saxophone. The timbres of other instruments also vary according to whether they are playing orchestral music or jazz.

(11) Some jazz timbres, like the bongo and conga drums and the Cuban cowbell, are from Afro-Cuban sources, while others, such as the Chinese woodblock, cymbals, and vibraphone, have an Oriental flavor.

(12) *Repetition of Material.* Jazz has no form that is true for all its styles. Generally it is a series of stanzas based on the chords to a popular tune. The form of the blues is more definite. A line is sung and immediately repeated; then a third line concludes the stanza. Sometimes the singer does not sing all the way through a section, and an instrumentalist fills in with a short solo called a *break.*

(13) *Text.* The metrical scheme of the text is often one of the standard poetic meters. It is not uncommon to find iambic pentameter in verses of the blues. The texts seldom have literary value, but some are quite moving.

(14) *Improvisation.* Improvisation is a fundamental component of jazz. Traditionally jazz is not written down because it is made up on the spot. This extemporaneous creativity is what gives jazz its ever-fresh quality. Sometimes people confuse a sexy or "hot" popular song with jazz. Jazz does not exist unless someone improvises on a tune.*

Place the answers to the first five questions in the answer box.

1. The first paragraph

   a. discusses jazz's roots
   b. focuses on the influence of the African-American culture on jazz
   c. discusses the types of jazz
   d. both a and b

2. In the first sentence of paragraph 4, what term of qualification is used?

   a. jazz
   b. untutored
   c. generally
   d. not

3. What word in the last sentence in paragraph 6 has a positive connotation?

   a. combination
   b. dissonance
   c. interesting
   d. creates

4. The main idea of paragraph 7 is

   a. jazz has a conservative harmony
   b. jazz's attraction is not based on the type of harmony it uses
   c. jazz has used some of the music styles of Debussy and Stravinsky
   d. both a and c

1. _____

2. _____

3. _____

4. _____

5. _____

---

*Hoffer, *Understanding of Music*, pp. 501–504.

5. The last sentence in paragraph 8 uses a word with a positive connotation. The word is

   a. lifeblood
   b. listener
   c. rhythmic
   d. accents

   Read the following questions, then go back to reread the excerpt. Finally, without looking back, answer the following questions in phrases or short sentences.

70%

Ask instructor for answers.

---

6. Describe three of the seven most important characteristics of jazz. (3 points)

7. How and where did jazz develop? (2 points)

Follow-up on Music History Exercises

Now that you have completed these exercises, it may be helpful to see how your reading of this topic has changed some of your ideas about music history. You may want to go back to these exercises and reread them just for content or for what they have to say about music history. Then answer the following questions either individually or in small groups:

1. How would you now define *music history*?
2. What do you now know about Bach and Mozart?
3. What do you now know about rock and jazz? How are they similar? different?
4. What area in music history would you now want to pursue further?

8 Reading Graphs and Tables

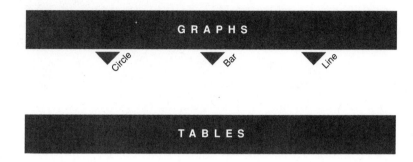

Reading graphs and tables is a necessary college skill. A graph is a visual representation of information; a table presents information compactly. If you learn more easily visually, graphs should help you learn. For each kind of graph, you need to use a specific strategy.

Circle Graphs

Circle graphs show how the whole is broken up into recognizable parts. The entire circle equals 100 percent, and the divided sections represent the parts. When you study circle graphs, you must first determine the subject. Then you should see how the parts relate to this subject and to one another.

Look at the graph in Figure 8-1, which depicts the elements in the earth's crust. If you had to remember the elements making up the earth's crust for an ecology exam, this circle graph would help you. Answer the following questions as you study this graph:

1. What does the whole circle represent?
2. How are the parts organized — smallest percentage to largest? largest percentage to smallest?
3. What are the three most plentiful elements in the earth's crust?

In studying this circle graph, you should have noted that the entire circle represents the composition of the earth's crust, or its ten most plentiful elements. You should have then noticed that, as you move clockwise, the percentages become smaller, from the most plentiful (oxygen) to the least plentiful (titanium).

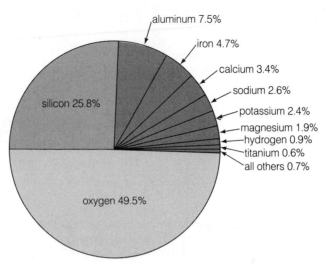

Figure 8-1   *Earth's crust. (Source: G. Tyler Miller, Jr.,* Living in the Environment, *4th ed. [Belmont, Calif.: Wadsworth, 1985], p. 235. Used by permission.)*

Bar Graphs

Bar graphs are usually a series of rectangles comparing the parts of a whole, much like circle graphs. Each rectangle represents 100 percent and is often divided up into parts of this 100 percent. You should ask the same questions that you would when studying a circle graph:

1. What is the subject?
2. How do the parts relate to this subject?
3. How do the parts relate to one another?

Look at the bar graph in Figure 8-2, showing the crops of the world. Determine the subject, what each bar represents, and how these bars relate to one another.

In studying this material, you should have determined that this bar graph represents the relative world use of various crops, each bar representing the crop's supply in millions of metric tons. Did you determine that four crops—wheat, rice, corn, and potato—account for most of the world's food?

Bar graphs are effective study aids when you need to remember a great deal of information.

Line Graphs

Line graphs may give you more trouble than circle or bar graphs do. Line graphs are made up of three important parts: the vertical axis, or the line going up and down; the horizontal axis, or the line going from side to side; and the diagonal line, or the line going either up, down, or parallel to the horizontal axis. Line graphs always illustrate relationships, usually cause-effect relationships. In business or economics ma-

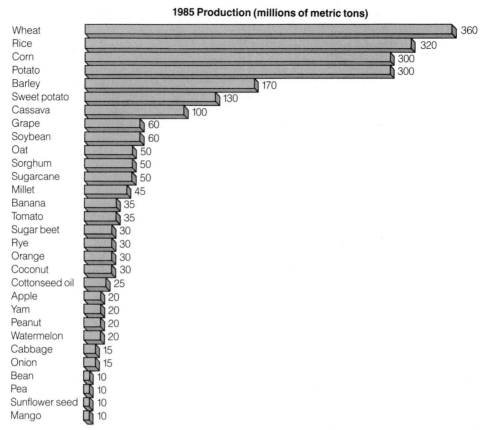

Figure 8-2   *World food crops (1985 production in millions of metric tons). (Source: G. Tyler Miller, Jr.,* Living in the Environment, *5th ed. [Belmont, Calif.: Wadsworth, 1988], p. 235.)*

terial, the line graph often shows how the supply of a particular product affects its demand — how, for example, lowering the supply increases the demand. In biology material, the line graph often shows how a biological activity is affected by a particular variable or change — how, for instance, temperature (a variable) affects cell movement (a biological activity).

As with circle and bar graphs, when studying a line graph you need first to determine the subject of the graph and what the numbers on the vertical and horizontal axes mean. Unlike circle and bar graphs, you then need to study the vertical and horizontal axes as well as the diagonal line to determine the nature of the relationship. Determining this relationship is crucial. Without it, you will not understand the details of the line graph or the meaning of the diagonal's movement.

Look at the line graph in Figure 8-3, which shows how consumer prices fluctuated in the United States from 1947 to 1986. First determine what the numbers on the vertical and horizontal axes represent. Then decide what the diagonal's upward movement suggests.

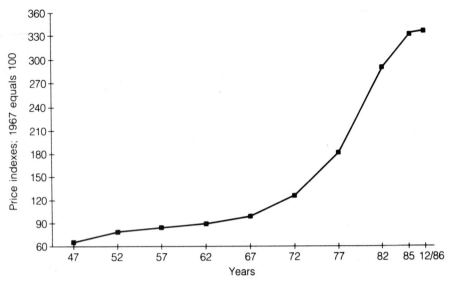

Figure 8-3   *Consumer price indexes, 1947–1986. (Source: Adapted from Philip C. Starr,* Economics: Principles in Action, *5th ed. [Belmont, Calif.: Wadsworth, 1988], p. 215.)*

In studying this graph, did you determine that the consumer price index increased over this time span shown in the graph, that it almost doubled between 1947 and 1972, and that it more than tripled between 1967 and 1985?

With line graphs, you may have a problem in correctly estimating where the diagonal meets each axis. Using a small ruler to locate a particular point on the diagonal will help your calculation. Use a ruler to find the consumer price index for 1977 in Figure 8-3. Did you come up with 180?

Sometimes line graphs get more complicated, with two or more diagonals or variables for you to consider. And sometimes these diagonals intersect. No matter how complicated the line graph, however, your strategy should be the same as in reading a line graph with one diagonal: (1) Determine the subject of the graph, (2) determine what the numbers on each axis represent, and (3) determine how the diagonals relate to one another.

Look at the line graph in Figure 8-4, on crude oil prices in the United States. Determine the subject, what the numbers on each axis mean, and how the two diagonals relate.

In studying this more complex line graph, you should have determined that it is comparing the price of crude oil between 1973 and 1986 in terms of 1973 dollars and 1986 dollars. The vertical axis measures the price per barrel, and the horizontal axis lists the years from 1973 to 1986. The diagonal lines suggest that oil prices went up sharply in the years 1979 through 1981 and then declined rather sharply. Furthermore,

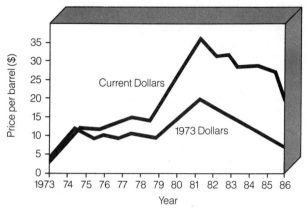

Figure 8-4 *Average world crude oil prices between 1973 and 1986. (Source: G. Tyler Miller, Jr.,* Living in the Environment, *5th ed. [Belmont, Calif.: Wadsworth, 1988], p. 340. Data from Department of Energy and Department of Commerce.)*

because of inflation, the purchase of a barrel of oil with 1986 dollars was much more expensive than the purchase of a barrel of oil with 1973 dollars. In 1981, for example, purchasing a barrel of oil with 1986 dollars cost almost twice as much as purchasing a barrel of oil in 1973.

By carefully reading a line graph with two or more diagonals or variables, you can extract a great deal of information.

Tables

Unlike graphs, tables are not visual. They simply present information concisely. Tables are especially helpful study aids because they present much information in a small space. When you read tables, as you did with graphs, first determine the subject; then establish what each category and subcategory represent. If you do not know what a particular part of a table means, you may not be able to use the table efficiently. Unlike a line graph, whose diagonal shows a trend (up, down, or staying the same), a table does not spell out these trends for you; you need to make these inferences from the data in the table. If you note a trend in a table, make a marginal note stating what that trend seems to be.

Look at Table 8-1 on the damage caused by plants and animals imported in the United States. Note the categories of the table, and note the order of each entry. What inferences can you draw from the data?

The table presents five causes of damage, plus where each cause came from, how it was brought over to the United States, and the type of damage that it caused. The agents causing damage seem to have come from Asia, Europe, and Latin America. Insects and plants seem to have caused the greatest damage—for example, the camphor scale insect damaged 200 species of plants, chestnut blight destroyed nearly all American chestnut trees, and Dutch elm disease destroyed millions of elms. Finally, it seems that damage is caused both by plants and animals.

Table 8-1   *Damage Caused by Plants and Animals Imported into the United States*

Name	Origin	Mode of Transport	Type of Damage
Mammals			
European wild boar	Russia	Intentionally imported (1912), escaped captivity	Destruction of habitat by rooting; crop damage
Nutria (cat-sized rodent)	Argentina	Intentionally imported, escaped captivity (1940)	Alteration of marsh ecology; damage to levees and earth dams; crop destruction
Birds			
European starling	Europe	Intentionally released (1890)	Competition with native songbirds; crop damage, transmission of swine diseases; airport interference
House sparrow	England	Intentionally released by Brooklyn Institute (1853)	Crop damage; displacement of native songbirds
Fish			
Carp	Germany	Intentionally released (1877)	Displacement of native fish; uprooting of water plants with loss of waterfowl populations
Sea lamprey	North Atlantic Ocean	Entered via Welland Canal (1829)	Destruction of lake trout, lake whitefish, and sturgeon in Great Lakes
Walking catfish	Thailand	Imported into Florida	Destruction of bass, bluegill, and other fish

Source: G. Tyler Miller, Jr., *Living in the Environment*, 5th ed. (Belmont, Calif.: Wadsworth, 1988), p. 302. From *Biological Conservation* by David W. Ehrenfeld. Copyright © 1970 by Holt, Rinehart and Winston, Inc. Modified and reprinted by permission.

Do you see how densely packed with information this table is? Most tables that you will come across are equally informative. As you continue to read tables, you will be able to make more subtle inferences and determine more patterns that are suggested in the data. You will also find yourself relying on tables more for study purposes.

Summary

Graphs are visual, concise means of presenting information. There are three kinds of graphs: circle, bar, and line. Circle and bar graphs show the composition of something. Line graphs show relationships among two or more variables and are sometimes difficult to understand. Unlike graphs, tables are not visual; rather, they present information in categories. In reading a table, you need to make inferences regarding the patterns that emerge from the data.

Name	Origin	Mode of Transport	Type of Damage
Insects			
Argentine fire ant	Argentina	Probably entered via coffee shipments from Brazil (1918)	Crop damage; destruction of native ant species
Camphor scale insect	Japan	Accidentally imported on nursery stock (1920s)	Damage to nearly 200 species of plants in Louisiana, Texas, and Alabama
Japanese beetle	Japan	Accidentally imported on irises or azaleas (1911)	Defoliation of more than 250 species of trees and other plants, including many of commercial importance
Plants			
Water hyacinth	Central America	Intentionally introduced (1884)	Clogging waterways; shading out other aquatic vegetation
Chestnut blight (a fungus)	Asia	Accidentally imported on nursery plants (1900)	Destruction of nearly all eastern American chestnut trees; disturbance of forest ecology
Dutch elm disease, *Cerastomella ulmi* (a fungus, the disease agent)	Europe	Accidentally imported on infected elm timber used for veneers (1930)	Destruction of millions of elms; disturbance of forest ecology

Graphs and tables are often effective study aids, because much information is presented in a small amount of space. You may choose to create your own graphs and tables for study purposes when you want to condense the material you are studying.

Summary Box   *Graphs and Tables*

What are they?	*Why use them?*

Graph: visual way to present information in circles, bars, or lines
Table: concise way to relate information by setting up categories and subcategories
	Graph: to present information visually and to help you learn material more easily
	Table:
	  to present information concisely
	  to show relationships among facts and figures
	  to gain insights about material you are studying
	  to help you remember information for exams

Skills Practice

Exercise 8.1
Reading Graphs and Tables

Use the strategies you have just learned to answer the following questions concerning graphs and tables. The topics are those you encountered in the exercises in previous chapters. Place all answers in the answer box.

1. Table 8-2 concerns

   a. poverty
   b. person above the poverty level, by race
   c. the poorest and richest people of the United States
   d. the percentage of various races under the poverty level in the United States

Table 8-2   *Persons Below the Poverty Level as a Percentage of Total Population by Race*

	Race			
Year	*White*	*Black*	*Other**	*Everyone*
1965	13.3	NA	NA	17.3
1970	9.9	33.5	NA	12.6
1975	9.7	31.3	26.9	12.3
1980	10.2	32.5	25.7	13.0
1984	11.5	33.8	28.4	14.4

Source: Philip C. Starr, *Economics: Principles in Action*, 5th ed. (Belmont, Calif.: Wadsworth, 1988), p. 172. Data from *Statistical Abstract of the United States, 1982–83* and *1986*.
*Includes people of Spanish origin and people of all other races.

2. The race in the United States that seems to have the largest percentage below the poverty level is

a. other
b. white
c. black
d. none of these

3. Poverty among whites between 1965 and 1984 seems to have

a. gone down considerably
b. gone down somewhat
c. increased
d. none of these

4. The subject of the bar graph in Figure 8-5 is

a. how much gas automobiles use in European countries
b. how much gas automobiles use in various countries
c. how much gas automobiles use in the United States
d. how gas consumption in the United States compares with that in Japan

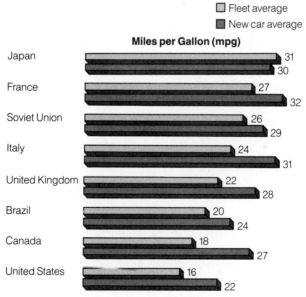

Figure 8-5 *Automobile fuel economy for selected countries (1982). (Source: G. Tyler Miller, Jr.,* Living in the Environment, *5th ed. [Belmont, Calif.: Wadsworth, 1988], p. 388.)*

5. The country that uses gas most economically is

   a. the United States
   b. Italy
   c. Canada
   d. Japan

6. In which country is the mileage for fleet cars almost twice as efficient as it is in the United States?

   a. Soviet Union
   b. Japan
   c. Canada
   d. Italy

7. Which is the only country in which the fleet average mileage is *more* than the new car average?

   a. United States
   b. France
   c. Japan
   d. Brazil

8. In Table 8-3 what form of energy did the federal government seem to support the most in 1979?

   a. fossil fuel
   b. nuclear
   c. wind
   d. breeder fission

9. About how many billions of dollars did the federal government spend on energy research in 1979?

   a. 3
   b. 4
   c. 4½
   d. 5

10. About how much does one nuclear-powered aircraft carrier cost?

   a. $3 billion
   b. over $2 billion
   c. over $1 billion
   d. $388 million

1. _____

2. _____

3. _____

4. _____

5. _____

6. _____

7. _____

8. _____

9. _____

10. _____

_____

80%

(score = # correct × 10)

Find answers on p. 340.

Table 8-3   *Expenditures for Energy Research in 1979*

Program	Millions of Dollars	Total Energy Budget	Approximate Military Expenditure Equivalents
Nuclear energy	1,132	29	One missile-carrying submarine
Breeder fission	608	15	Two conventional submarines
Conventional fission	297	8	One conventional submarine
Fusion	227	6	Three long-range bombers
Conservation	792	20	One conventional aircraft carrier
Fossil fuel energy	577	15	Four destroyers
Basic energy research and technology development	338	9	Four long-range bombers
Solar energy	321	8.6	Three long-range bombers and one F-15 fighter plane
General science and research	307	8	Three B-1 bombers
Environmental research and development	186	5	Two long-range bombers
Geothermal energy	133	3	One destroyer
Wind energy	54	1.4	Four F-15 fighter planes
Biomass energy	24	0.5	Two F-15 fighter planes
Hydroelectric energy	23	0.5	Two F-15 fighter planes
Total	3,887	100.0	Three nuclear-powered aircraft carriers

Source: G. Tyler Miller, Jr., *Energy and Environment: The Four Energy Crises,* 2nd ed. (Belmont, Calif.: Wadsworth, 1980), p. 157. Used by permission. Data from staff report 1978h.

Exercise 8.2
Reading More
Graphs and Tables

Here are two more graphs and another table on topics that you are familiar with, each followed by questions. Place your answers in the answer box.

1. From Figure 8-6, determine the improvement in miles per gallon of gas for new cars in the United States between 1973 and 1985.

   a. 11.5
   b. 12.5
   c. 13
   d. 20

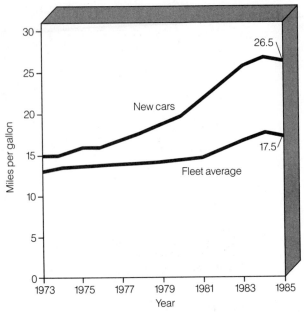

Figure 8-6 *Increases in the average fuel efficiency of new cars and the entire fleet of cars in the United States between 1973 and 1985. (Source: G. Tyler Miller, Jr.,* Living in the Environment, *5th ed. [Belmont, Calif.: Wadsworth, 1988], p. 390. Data from U.S. Department of Energy and the Environmental Protection Agency.)*

2. Determine the improvement in miles per gallon for fleet cars between 1973 and 1985.

   a. 2.5
   b. 7.5
   c. about 3
   d. about 4

3. What does this graph suggest about the relationship between miles per gallon and fleet and new car gas use?

   a. Fleet cars are less efficient.
   b. New cars seem to be improving more than fleet cars.
   c. Both a and b are true.
   d. The graph does not say.

4. What is the main point of the line graph in Figure 8-7?

   a. As time goes on, there are more older Americans.
   b. In 1900 fewer than 3 million Americans were over sixty-five years of age.
   c. The number of older Americans seems to double every twenty-five years.
   d. The number of older Americans will decrease after the year 2000.

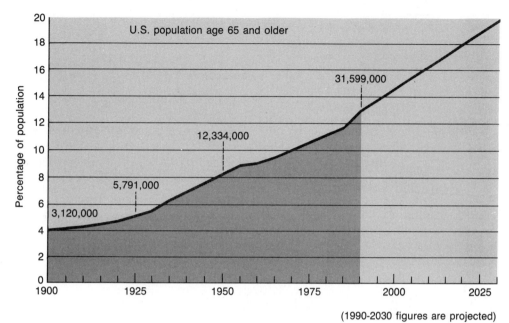

(1990-2030 figures are projected)

Figure 8-7   *The graying of America (1990–2030 figures projected). (Source: Thomas Dye,* Power and Society, *5th ed. [Pacific Grove, Calif.: Brooks/Cole, 1990], p. 265. Data from U.S. Bureau of the Census,* Statistical Abstract of the United States 1988 *[Washington, D.C.: U.S. Government Printing Office, 1988], p. 15.)*

5. What does the shaded area in Figure 8-7 represent?

    a. ninety-year representation of the numbers and percentages of older Americans
    b. fifty-year representation of the numbers and percentages of older Americans
    c. increase in percentage of older Americans over a seventy-five-year period
    d. decrease in percentage of older Americans over a ninety-year span

6. The percentage of older Americans between 1900 and 1990 seems to have

    a. doubled
    b. tripled
    c. quadrupled
    d. increased fivefold

7. The projections for the years 2000–2025 suggest that

    a. the number of older Americans will decrease
    b. the number of older Americans will increase, but their percentages will decrease

1. _____

2. _____

3. _____

4. _____

5. _____

6. _____

7. _____

8. _____

9. _____

10. _____

_____
80%
Ask instructor for
answers.

c. older Americans will increase to about 32 million

d. the percentage and number of older Americans will continue to increase

8. Table 8-4 analyzes

a. the population by numbers of the largest and smallest cities in the United States

b. the population by numbers of the twenty-five largest cities in the United States

c. the percentage of increase in population between 1980 and 1986 in the twenty-five largest American cities

d. both b and c

9. In percentages, which city has had the greatest decrease in population?

a. Milwaukee

b. Cincinnati

c. Pittsburgh — Beaver Valley

d. Cleveland

10. As of 1986, what was the population of Kansas City?

a. 1,518,000

b. 151,800

c. 15,180

d. none of these

Exercise 8.3
Writing a Paragraph
with a Main Idea
and Supporting
Details from
Information in
a Graph

In this writing exercise, you are to use only the information presented in the circle graphs and bar graphs in Figure 8-8 to answer the following essay question. This material concerning the Hispanic population in the United States comes from a sociology textbook.

Use the following outline to jot down notes that you will use in your paragraph.

I. Basic Information on Hispanics in the United States

A. Where Hispanics generally come from: _____

B. Where they live: _____

C. Income: _____

D. Education: _____

_____
80%
Ask instructor for
answers.

Essay question: In an organized paragraph, discuss where most Hispanics have come from, the most heavily populated Hispanic areas in the United States, the Hispanics with the highest and lowest incomes, and their educational levels compared to the U.S. average. Where appropri-

Table 8-4   *Largest Metropolitan Areas in the United States*

Metropolitan Area	Population	
	1986 Total (Thousands)	*Percentage Change, 1980–1986*
1. New York–Northern New Jersey–Long Island, NY–NJ–CT	17,968	2.4
2. Los Angeles–Anaheim–Riverside, CA	13,075	13.7
3. Chicago–Gary–Lake County (IL), IL–IN–WI	8,116	2.3
4. San Francisco–Oakland–San Jose, CA	5,878	9.5
5. Philadelphia–Wilmington–Trenton, PA–NJ–DE–MD	5,833	2.7
6. Detroit–Ann Arbor, MI	4,601	3.2
7. Boston–Lawrence–Salem–Lowell–Brockton, MA	3,705	1.1
8. Dallas–Fort Worth, TX	3,655	24.7
9. Houston–Galveston–Brazoria, TX	3,634	17.2
10. Washington, D.C.–MD–VA	3,563	9.6
11. Miami–Fort Lauderdale, FL	2,912	10.1
12. Cleveland–Akron–Lorain, OH	2,766	−2.4
13. Atlanta, GA	2,561	19.8
14. St. Louis, MO–IL	2,438	2.6
15. Pittsburgh–Beaver Valley, PA	2,316	−4.4
16. Minneapolis–St. Paul, MN–WI	2,295	7.4
17. Seattle–Tacoma, WA	2,285	9.1
18. Baltimore, MD	2,280	3.7
19. San Diego, CA	2,201	18.2
20. Tampa–Saint Petersburg–Clearwater, FL	1,914	18.6
21. Phoenix, AZ	1,900	25.9
22. Denver–Boulder, CO	1,847	14.1
23. Cincinnati–Hamilton, OH–KY–IN	1,690	1.8
24. Milwaukee–Racine, WI	1,552	−1.2
25. Kansas City, MO–KS	1,518	5.9

Source: Adapted from Thomas Dye, *Power and Society*, 5th ed. (Pacific Grove, Calif.: Brooks/Cole, 1990), p. 295. Data from U.S. Census Bureau, *Statistical Abstract of the United States 1988* (Washington, D.C.: U.S. Government Printing Office, 1988), p. 28.

ate, provide specific figures. Start with a topic sentence discussing where Hispanics generally live and how their lifestyle compares to that of average Americans.

Exercise 8.4 Determining Main Ideas and Major Details and Interpreting a Table in a Textbook Excerpt

The following is an excerpt from an economics textbook; it concerns economic programs instituted in Ronald Reagan's years as U.S. President. Read through the excerpt quickly to get a sense of its organization. Then go back and read it slowly, paying particular attention to the two tables and their relationship to the excerpt. When you finish, answer the five questions that follow. You may refer to the excerpt in deciding on your answers.

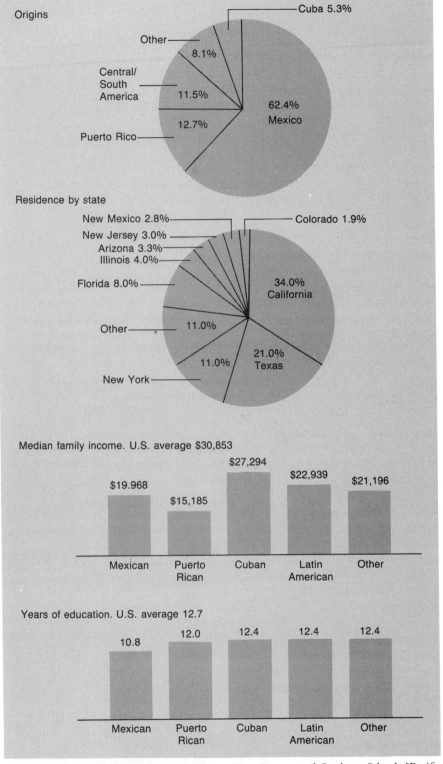

Figure 8-8 *Hispanic Americans. (Source: Thomas Dye,* Power and Society, *5th ed. [Pacific Grove, Calif.: Brooks/Cole, 1990], p. 241. Data from U.S. Bureau of the Census,* Statistical Abstract of the United States 1988 *[Washington, D.C.: U.S. Government Printing Office, 1988].)*

Connections Between Tax Cuts, Inflation, and Federal Deficits

(1) The central point of this section is that the effectiveness of discretionary fiscal policy depends on whether the price level is going up and down. In the course of explaining the connection between the price level and fiscal policy, we will show how federal deficits (and consequent increases in the national debt) have escalated in recent years.

(2) The early years of the Reagan administration illustrate the central point of this section. Beginning with President Ronald Reagan's election in 1980, his administration was determined to reduce the size and scope of the federal government's activities. Central to Reagan's policies were (1) an income tax cut (called the *Kemp-Roth* bill) amounting to 25 percent over three years, (2) an equal cut in *nondefense* government spending, and (3) a halt to double-digit inflation.

(3) The tax cut bill became law. Double-digit inflation was stopped cold, but Congress was unable to cut nondefense spending by enough to prevent very large deficits. Few of Reagan's staff members realized at the time the connection between getting rid of inflation and budget deficits.

(4) To bring down inflation, the Federal Reserve Board of Governors (the details of their operations are in the next chapter) instituted an extremely tight money policy whereby consumer and business loans became very expensive to obtain because of high interest rates. Suffice it to say here that the effect on the economy was drastic—business slowed down so much that we had the highest unemployment rate since World War II. But prices *did* come down.

(5) The connection with federal deficits is this: When prices come down, union members with cost-of-living-adjustment (COLA) agreements automatically see a slower increase in their paychecks, and everyone else has less reason to demand higher wages. As increases in incomes slow down, the federal government's tax revenues also increase at a slower rate. The automatic stabilizers are at work. Table 8-5 shows the deficits and the year-to-year changes in the consumer price index (CPI) during an 8-year period, 1978–85. (We're starting two years before President Reagan's election in 1980.)

Table 8-5 *Deficits (in Billions of Dollars) and the Inflation Rate*

Year	Federal Tax Receipts	Federal Expenditures	Deficits (col. 2 − col. 3)	Year-to-Year Changes in the CPI
1978	$399.6	$458.7	− $59.1	7.7%
1979	463.3	503.5	− 40.2	11.3
1980	517.1	590.9	− 73.8	13.5
1981	599.3	678.2	− 78.9	10.4
1982	617.8	745.7	− 127.9	6.1
1983	600.6	808.3	− 207.7	3.2
1984	666.5	851.8	− 185.3	4.3
1985	734.1	946.3	− 212.2	3.6

Source: Economic Report of the President, 1987.

(6) One can see at a glance that the deficits jumped in size beginning with 1982 and that in that same year, the inflation rate came way down from a high of 13.5 percent in 1980 to 6.1 percent in 1982. We need to dig somewhat further into the table to see what was happening. If we divide the 8-year period into two 4-year periods, we can see more clearly the changes that occurred in the government's tax receipts and expenditures. Table 8-6 shows these changes in percentage terms.

(7) The table shows that 1982 was indeed a watershed year. Up to 1982, receipts, expenditures, and prices increased rapidly. The increase in receipts was undoubtedly aided by the high rates of inflation and the effects of the automatic stabilizers that increased the federal government's share of everyone's increases in income.

(8) After 1982, when the drastic drop in price increases occurred, the increases in tax receipts slowed way down, thereby creating the scenario for larger deficits. Experts in the Reagan administration, in particular David Stockman, then Director of Reagan's Office of Management and the Budget, realized what was going on — specifically the need to offset falling tax receipts with drastic cuts in domestic programs. But as we observe often in this book, cuts in government spending are politically extremely difficult to achieve. Table 8-6 shows that *increases* in government spending did come way down in the second 4-year period. (Actual *cuts* in total spending were never achieved.) But in both 4-year periods, the increases in spending exceeded the increases in tax receipts; deficits had to result.*

1. The main idea of paragraph 1 suggests that

    a. Reagan's policies were carefully thought out
    b. Reagan's economic policies did not succeed completely
    c. Reagan's economic policies favored the poor
    d. the cuts in federal spending were reasonable

Table 8-6   *Percentage Increases in Federal Tax Receipts and Expenditures During Two 4-Year Periods, 1978–81 and 1982–85*

	Percentage Increases in Tax Receipts	*Percentage Increases in Expenditures*	*Percentage Increases in Consumer Prices*
1978–81	50	73	39.4
1982–85	19	27	11.4

Source: Economic Report of the President, 1987.

---

*Philip C. Starr, *Economics: Principles in Action*, 5th ed. (Belmont, Calif.: Wadsworth, 1988), pp. 309–311.

2. The main idea of paragraph 2 is that the Reagan administration believed the federal government

    a. was too large
    b. did too much
    c. was controlled by Congress
    d. both a and b

3. In paragraph 3, the author suggests that the Reagan administration

    a. understood the causes of inflation
    b. could accurately predict the budget deficit
    c. did not understand how inflation and the budget deficit were related
    d. really did not want to bring down inflation

4. In Table 8-5, what year shows the largest federal deficit?

    a. 1979
    b. 1983
    c. 1984
    d. 1985

5. What does Table 8-6 suggest?

    a. The federal government brought in more money than it paid out.
    b. The government spent more money than it brought in.
    c. Consumer prices went up from 1978 to 1985.
    d. The federal budget was probably balanced in 1985.

Now read the three questions that follow; then go back to reread the excerpt. Finally, answer the following three questions in a phrase or sentence without looking back at the excerpt.

6. How did the Reagan administration try to bring down inflation, or a general rise in prices? (2 points)

7. What economic reason did the Reagan administration give for cutting federal programs? (1 point)

8. What happens when an increase in federal spending is greater than the government's tax receipts, or the money the federal government takes in? (2 points)

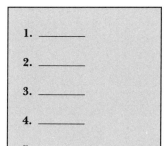

1. _____

2. _____

3. _____

4. _____

5. _____

_____
70%
Ask instructor for answers.

Lecture and Study Notes

In this part, you will learn several note-taking skills that you can successfully use in listening to lectures and in study reading. You will find that when you take effective notes, you are using several of the reading and listening skills that you acquired in Part Two. When you master these note-taking techniques, your studying for exams will become both organized and worthwhile.

9 Characteristics of Lectures

CHARACTERISTICS OF LECTURES

Who is the speaker?   What is the subject?   What are the students' obligations?

Lectures are a special kind of communication. A lecture is a dialogue between you and the speaker. Your response to the lecturer is often in the form of notes rather than oral comments. Accurate notes are important, for they are your only record of what your lecturer said. In this part of the book, you will learn how to write useful notes. Consider the following aspects of a lecture: the lecturer's speaking style, the subject of the lecture, and your obligations as a listener.

The Speaker

Lecturers' speaking styles are as varied as writers' styles. Some lecturers speak loudly, others softly. Some lecturers speak quickly, others slowly. It is up to you to adjust your listening strategies to the speaker's style. The average lecturer speaks at 125 words per minute, whereas the average reading rate is 250 words per minute. With a lecturer who speaks quickly, you may have a difficult time getting down all of the information. With a lecturer who speaks slowly, your mind may wander and you may become bored. But whatever the lecturer's style, you need to focus on the main ideas and the major details of the material.

If a lecturer presents too much information, consult with classmates, who may have written down some of the information that you did not get. If a lecturer speaks slowly and presents too little information, you need to concentrate on the important points of the lecture.

Also, you should realize that most instructors are not professional speakers. Their delivery will usually not be polished and humorous. Lecturers are not entertainers; they are trained to impart information, not to be comedians. Some students have even commented that the entertaining lecturers are generally not the most informative.

Most instructors present organized lectures, so your focus must be on the instructor's organization, which often centers on general and specific bits of information. Instructors often use the same signal words in their lectures that you find in written material. In fact, good lecturers use these signal words to direct you to important information. Good lecturers realize that students can reread what is in writing, but that "relistening" without a tape recorder is impossible. Successful lecturers also understand that lectures are not as formal as written discourse. So they repeat themselves and make obvious comments such as "This is important" or "Write this down."

Along with repeating themselves and using signal words, lecturers use visual and vocal signals to punctuate their speaking. A lecturer's most effective visual aid is the chalkboard. When an instructor writes a term on the board or draws a chart or map, be sure to write this material down. A lecturer may also list important steps on the board or say "There are three steps to remember." Jot these steps down. In addition, a lecturer's tone of voice or rate of speech may change when an important point is made. Lecturers who speak rapidly often slow down when they say something important. Lecturers who normally speak softly may present a key point in a louder tone. Get acquainted with each lecturer's speaking style, and look for the verbal signals.

Finally, lecturers may sometimes read directly from the textbook. You should write down the page number of these passages, because they are probably important points.

A few lecturers are disorganized in their presentation, making your note taking a difficult chore. They may not consistently present main ideas and major details in proper proportion, and they may digress often so that main ideas lose their focus. Unfortunately, you will need to compensate for this lack of organization by noting what information is missing. You will then need to rely more on your textbooks and on library material. You may also need to consult with classmates who may have understood more of the lecture.

The Subject of the Lecture

All of the skills you have learned so far in this book should be used when you take notes. Lecturers will organize their material around main ideas, major details, and minor details as well as the seven patterns of organization. Thus you should listen for the words that signal a particular organizational pattern. You will also use your paraphrasing skills when a lecturer speaks in difficult sentences, and you will need to make appropriate inferences when a lecturer is being indirect.

Although you will be using all of these skills when you listen to lectures, you also need to know how lectures are different from writing. Lecturers are often repetitive, whereas writing is not. Consider repetition in lecture as a kind of rereading; what a lecturer repeats is often important and difficult to understand the first time.

A lecturer may also digress, or get off the main point. A lecturer may occasionally relate a humorous anecdote that is related to the lecture. These digressions would not make sense if you were to read them.

Because writing is often concise, digressions in writing are seen as flaws. When you hear digressions in lecture, you should see how they apply to the topic as well as enjoy them. See digressions as unique to speaking, a feature that makes speech more intimate than writing.

The subject matter of the lecture also dictates the kinds of notes you will take. You will often take notes using main ideas and major details in the arts and humanities, the social sciences, and some biological sciences. In a history lecture, for example, you will often group your information around main ideas and details of support. On the other hand, in physical science and math courses, you will need to copy down solutions to problems and ignore the traditional note-taking format. The successful note taker in a math or science course accurately writes down the steps in a problem. Finally, in a foreign language course you will be responding orally, so your notes will be brief—a grammatical rule or a new vocabulary word. With each course, you need to be flexible and devise a note-taking style that best fits the subject matter.

Student Obligations

The key to successfully listening to lectures finally rests on you. You must see listening to lectures as a concentrated activity. You must anticipate the instructor's comments and determine the structure of the lecture.

Here is a list of hints that should help you become a more effective note taker. Some of these points have already been discussed in this chapter, but it will help if you see them put together.

1. Listen attentively for the topic, the main idea, and details of support. Train yourself to hear both general and detailed statements. Keep asking yourself: Is this the topic? the main point? What details relate to this main idea?

2. Listen for signal words that introduce a particular organizational pattern. When you identify the proper organizational pattern, you will better understand the logic of the lecture.

3. Look for visual cues and listen for auditory cues—what the lecturer puts on the board and when and why the lecturer's tone of voice changes. These cues often suggest important points.

4. Familiarize yourself with the topic before you begin listening to the lecture. If an instructor assigns a chapter before she lectures on it, read the material even if you do not understand all of it. The more exposure students have to a topic, the less difficult they tend to find the material. Going to lecture without having done the assigned reading is unwise.

5. Listen attentively during class discussions. Do not assume that because a student is speaking you do not need to listen. What students ask or say often are the same questions and answers that you have.

Sometimes, even student comments are worthy of being placed in your notes. Also, listen to the instructor's response to student comments. You will learn a lot about your instructor by listening to his responses to students' ideas. You may find that a particular instructor likes original thinking, while another is looking for the conventional answer. These inferences can help you in studying for exams in these courses.

6. Try to see the lecture material from the instructor's point of view. You have every right to disagree with the instructor, but only after you have listened to what he or she has said. Students often tune instructors out when they do not agree with their point of view. By not listening to the several points of view on each topic, they are being unfair both to the material and to the instructor.

Mastering these hints may take some time. But once these suggestions become habit for you, you will be able to anticipate the direction of the lecture—knowing beforehand when the lecturer will introduce a new topic or main idea or what organizational pattern the instructor intends to use. When you are able to anticipate information and structure, you will find that listening to lectures becomes both interesting and challenging.

Your other obligation is to assess the value that is assigned to lecture material in each of your courses. By the second or third week of the semester, you should have determined the value of notes in each of your courses. You should have determined whether the lectures are like or unlike the material in textbooks. And by the first examination, you should have determined how much of the exam came from your notes. You will find that some instructors rely on the textbook when making up an exam; others rely on their lecture notes. Most instructors divide up their exam questions evenly between textbook and lecture material. It is you who must resolve all of these issues, and you should do so early in the semester.

Some students think that attending lectures is a waste of their time—that they can learn everything from the textbook and from the notes of others. Except for the very bright student, not attending lectures is a bad idea. Even if most of the instructor's lectures follow the textbook, by attending lecture you will develop an appreciation for the subject that you cannot get from your textbook. You will also get to know your instructors from their lectures—both their personality and their attitude toward the material. If your instructor loves the subject, some of this enthusiasm will rub off on you. From the very best lectures, you will learn details and hear anecdotes that you cannot find in textbooks. And it may be in a particularly exciting lecture that you will decide to major in that subject—a decision that can affect the rest of your life.

Summary

Lectures are dialogues between the instructor and you. When you attend lectures, you must remember that speech is different from writing. Instructors repeat themselves in lectures, and they may digress. You should use all of the reading skills that you have learned to listen to lectures effectively. Each course you take requires a different listening and note-taking style, which you must determine early on in the semester.

Attending lectures gives you an appreciation for a particular course that reading will not give you. If you listen critically to lectures, you will have another important educational tool at your disposal.

Summary Box   *Lecture Material*

What is it?	Why do you need it?
An oral means of transferring information from the speaker to you	To gather information in a particular area
A dialogue between the speaker and you	To record the speaker's attitude toward a subject
Information that is usually organized around main ideas and major details	To appreciate a subject — something you cannot acquire just by reading your textbook
Information that is not as concise as writing and that requires active listening	

Skills Practice

***Exercise 9.1
Inventorying a
Lecture***

Choose an instructor whose lectures are difficult for you. Then complete the following inventory on one of his or her lectures. This inventory may help you understand why you are having difficulty taking notes on the lecture material.

1. Name of instructor: _____

2. Name of course: _____

3. Place a check next to those qualities that describe your instructor's lecture style:

_____ a. speaks rapidly

_____ b. speaks slowly

_____ c. speaks loudly

_____ d. speaks softly

_____ e. does not use the chalkboard

_____ f. is disorganized

_____ g. makes statements you do not agree with

_____ h. other: _____

The following are some suggestions for dealing with the characteristics that you checked in item 3, lettered to correspond to the list of problems.

a. If the instructor speaks too fast, you must try to keep up with the pace. Don't get upset if you cannot write down all of the important points. Just keep listening for main ideas and supporting details. Check classmates' notes to see what you may have missed.

b. If the instructor speaks too slowly, you may get bored, and your mind may wander. Keep listening for the lecture's focus: main ideas and details of support.

c. Notice when the instructor's voice gets softer or louder. A change in loudness may signal that an important point is going to be made.

d. If the instructor speaks softly, you need to listen more actively; try to find a desk nearer to the instructor. Notice when his or her voice changes volume and see whether this change signals important information.

e. If your instructor doesn't use the chalkboard to highlight important points, see whether he or she uses any other cues. Does your instructor repeat key words and phrases or use hand gestures that signal important material?

f. If your instructor is disorganized, you will need to listen more carefully, jotting down those questions that your instructor leaves unanswered. In this case, you will need to rely more on your textbook, library material, and your classmates.

g. If your instructor makes remarks you disagree with, try to follow his or her train of thought. You are free to disagree with your instructor, but you need to follow his or her line of argument first.

h. Bring any other problems that you may have to your study skills instructor. You may even choose to present your complaint to the instructor who is giving you difficulty. State what your criticism is and what you would like to see changed. Some instructors will take your criticisms seriously and try to change their lecture style.

Exercise 9.2
Inventorying Your
Notes

Choose one course whose notes you are not entirely satisfied with. Then complete the following inventory.

1. Name of course: _____

2. Place a check next to those qualities that describe your note-taking style:

_____ a. too brief

_____ b. too wordy

_____ c. disorganized

_____ d. inaccurate

_____ e. messy

_____ f. any other problem: _____

The following are some suggestions for dealing with the problems that you checked in item 2, lettered to correspond to the list.

a. If your notes are too brief, you need to listen for supporting details. You are probably concentrating too much on main ideas. Remember, you also need to recall supporting details. Keep in mind that supporting details may be examples, characteristics, steps, causes, or effects. So listen carefully for names, places, and numbers. However, remember that brief notes are acceptable in a foreign language course.

b. If your notes are wordy, you are probably trying to write down everything. Remember that minor details usually do not need to be part of your notes. Wordy notes obscure main ideas and supporting details. Before writing, ask yourself: Is this statement significant? Will it give support to the main idea? Is this statement a restatement of something I've already written? Does this statement further elaborate on a previous detail? Approximately two to three written pages of notes in an hour's lecture is adequate.

c. If your lecture notes are disorganized, you probably cannot differentiate well between main ideas and supporting details. You will learn more about this issue in the next chapter. For now, remember that separating general from specific information is a key to learning and remembering. You may want to review Chapters 3 and 4, which treat main ideas and supporting details.

d. If your notes are inaccurate, you must start listening more carefully. Inaccurate notes are often caused by a daydreaming note taker. In-accuracy is especially problematic in a math or science course, where the right number or correct sequence is essential to a correct solution. Leave your personal life outside of class, so you can listen to the lecture material with full concentration. Anyone can listen more attentively; it just takes discipline.

e. If your notes are messy, go over them soon after class is over and rewrite any words that are hard to read. If your handwriting is poor, you may need to write more slowly, even if you write less. Notes with less information are better than those that you cannot read.

f. If you have any other problems with your notes, speak with your study skills instructor.

10 *Traditional Note-taking Techniques*

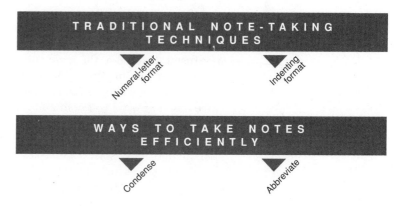

Now that you have made an inventory of your strengths and weaknesses as a note taker, you are ready to study the note-taking techniques that have helped many students. The two most common techniques are the numeral-letter format and the indenting format. However, you will find that taking notes in math and science courses requires different note-taking strategies. In all three cases you can use abbreviations to save time. You can use these suggestions for both your lecture notes and the notes you take as you read.

Numeral-Letter Format

You have already studied the numeral-letter format in the beginning chapters' discussions of main ideas and major details. In this format, you identify main ideas with Roman numerals (I, II, III) placed at the far left margin. You identify major details with capital letters (A, B, C) and indent them under the Roman numerals. Look at the following example:

I. Two Characteristics of Private Enterprise

    A. The right to private property
    B. Freedom of choice

In some cases you may want to include a minor detail in your notes. Your can represent minor details with Arabic numerals indented under your major details. Study the following example:

I. Adam Smith's *Wealth of Nations*

    A. A discussion of a market economy

        1. Market economy relying on the theory of supply and demand

Many rules go along with the numeral-letter format, but you don't need to know all of them. If you try to follow all the rules, you may get confused. Just follow the main rule: Place main ideas at the left edge of your paper, and indent major details.

By now you should realize that main ideas and major details organize much of what you read and listen to. Main ideas must be attached to major details; both types of information are meaningless alone. You need a general and a specific context. Knowing that the business department offers a series of courses is much less meaningful than knowing that business includes many disciplines, like marketing, finance, and accounting. On the other hand, knowing that finance is a course of study is much less meaningful than knowing that it is part of the larger study of business administration. This detail does not make much sense unless you connect it to the more general statement.

When you use the numeral-letter format, you need to adhere to two minor procedures. First, be sure to place a period after the numeral or letter (I. or A.). The period separates the number or letter from the words you write and thus shows that the numbers and letters are divisions and not part of your comments. Second, skip a line between Roman numerals (the main ideas). By separating main ideas, you give more emphasis to them and make them easier to locate when you study your notes. Look at the following example:

I. Current Trends in the Study of Business

    A. Scarcity of resources
    B. International business
    C. The challenge of technology

II. Reasons for Studying Business

    A. As a career choice
    B. As a way to own a business

By leaving a space between I and II, you clearly separate two distinct chunks of information.

Don't expect to write down all of the major details you hear. As when summarizing, write down only the significant details, or those that most directly support the main idea. If for some reason you miss a few major details in lecture, ask to see a classmate's notes.

Indenting Format

The indenting system, another popular format, does away with letters and numbers entirely. You simply place main ideas to the left, major details indented underneath, and minor details indented under major details. You separate general from specific statements by their positioning on your paper. Here is an example:

Forming a partnership
    Contractual agreement required
        Establishes legal relationship between partners

As you can see, the information gets more specific as you move to the right.

Many students prefer this format to the numeral-letter format because they do not have to remember the correct sequence of numerals and letters. They do not need to go back in their notes to see if their previous main idea was, for example, a II or a III. Some students also complain that the numerals and letters clutter their notes.

Remember, however, that both formats rely on the same idea. The farther to the right you put information, the more specific this information is. Try both techniques to see which one fits your own listening and writing style.

Notes in Mathematics and Math-Related Courses

In math and science courses, you will often find that the numeral-letter and indenting formats are inappropriate. The math or science instructor often presents solutions to problems on the board, writing each step in sequence. You cannot separate main ideas from major details. In a sense, every step to the solution is a main idea.

Consider the following hints for taking notes in math and science courses:

1. Listen carefully when your instructor presents laws, axioms, theorems, or properties. When possible, write these statements down word for word as you would a definition. In the margin, identify the particular statement as a law, axiom, theorem, or property. Look at the following example:

associative property $a + b = b + u$ | $5 + 3 = 3 + 5$

                   $a \times b = b \times a$ | $5 \times 3 = 3 \times 5$

Numbers may be added or multiplied in any sequence.

2. When an instructor solves a problem on the board, copy it down step by step. The problems an instructor writes on the board are probably

important ones. These solutions will often be like the solutions to homework problems and problems on exams. Number each step, and make comments after any step that is unclear to you. Put question marks next to those steps that you cannot follow. Try to answer these questions before you come to the next class. Look at this example:

Problem 3: $2(5x + 5) + 4x = 80 - 20x$. Solve for x.

Do operations in parentheses first.

(1)	$10x + 10 + 4x = 80 - 2x$
(2)	$14x + 10 \quad\quad = 80 - 2x$
(3)	$16x = 80$
(4)	$x = 5$

$+2x$ balances both sides of the equation.

3. Leave spaces next to those problems that you did not complete. When you review your notes, try to complete the solution.

4. Leave extra spaces between problems or draw a line across your page of notes to show where one problem ends and another begins.

5. Reread your notes after every lecture. Math and science are disciplines that build on information you have previously learned. If you are unclear about Monday's solutions, Wednesday's will be even more confusing.

6. Use the numeral-letter and indenting formats whenever the instructor presents material not requiring problem solving.

How to Condense Information

Learning to condense information will help you write down more information in a shorter period of time. When you summarize, you locate main ideas and major details from long passages. When you *condense*, you write the key elements in a sentence and delete unnecessary words and phrases. What you usually write down are the subject, verb, and object of a sentence. Often you reduce a complete sentence to a phrase. Look at how the following sentence has been condensed: "In a sense, a corporation is a group of people acting like one person created by the law" is condensed to "Corporation like legal person." In condensing, you are often left only with the "who" or "what" and with the "what was done" of the sentence. In the sample sentence, the who is the corporation and the what is a legal person. In lecture, listen for names and for what these names did.

Sometimes it is preferable to copy information exactly as it is stated. You have already seen the importance of copying down a mathematical or scientific law or theorem or of the steps in a solution. When you hear a definition, try to write it down exactly as you hear it. Definitions are the tools for understanding a subject, so it's best to write down their exact meanings.

I. Market

    A. Def: group of potential customers with the authority and ability to purchase a particular product*

Except for definitions and mathematical solutions and laws, you will often not be copying information exactly as you hear it. So condensing is a key skill to learn, as important as summarizing. You cannot write down everything that the instructor says unless you know shorthand. By condensing each sentence into the "who" or "what" and the "what was done," you clarify the significant elements of the lecture. You will have several opportunities to condense lecture and textbook material in the exercises in this chapter and in chapters that follow.

Note-taking Tips

Now that you have studied the numeral-letter, indenting, and math-science outlining formats and learned about condensing, you are ready for the following note-taking tips:

1. The notes that you take for each course should be written in a separate bound notebook or in a three-ring notebook with dividers for each class. Three-ring notebooks are especially useful because you can add supplementary material to your notes, you can take out material when you want, and you can insert notes for a lecture that you may have missed. Also, you can keep all of your lecture notes in chronological order. Further divide each class section into two sections: one for your lecture notes and another for your reading notes. (More is said about preparing reading notes in Chapter 13, which covers the SQ3R study system.) You may think that all of this organization is a waste of time, but you will find that it pays off when you have to study for an exam. You do not want to be one of those students who has trouble studying for the exam because lecture notes are missing or disorganized.

2. Put the title of each day's lecture at the center of the top line of a clean sheet of paper. Put the date at the top right-hand corner of the same page. Look at the following title:

                          Marketing Terminology   *11/24/92*

3. Use a ballpoint, fountain, or felt-tip pen when you take notes—except in math and science courses. When figuring and refiguring are required, use pencil.

4. Write on only one side of the page. Draw a line (preferably red) 2½ inches from the left side of the page. Use this margin for extra

---

*Adapted from Joseph T. Straub and Raymond F. Attner, *Introduction to Business*, 4th ed. (Boston: PWS-Kent, 1991), p. G-9.

comments that you make as you go over your notes. You can also use the reverse side of the page for any additional comments that you might make during the semester.

5. You can also use the left-hand margin during lecture to remind yourself of important due dates: when a project is due, an examination date, and so on. In this margin, you can also ask a question about the lecture. Often you cannot interrupt a lecturer with your question. Look at how comments are incorporated into the following lecture excerpt on management:

Management Roles

I. How a Manager Performs Different Functions

What do
figurehead
and liaison mean?

First test 3/18

    A. Figurehead
    B. Leader
    C. Liaison
    D. Monitor of information

6. Identify the kinds of details that you write in the margins, either during or after lecture. The abbreviations that you will most commonly use are: "def" for definition, "ex" for example, "eff" for effect, and "char" for characteristic. "Cause" and "step" have no abbreviations. As you identify the details, you will better understand the lecture's organization. See how the abbreviation "ex" is used in the following lecture note:

Manager's Interpersonal Skills

Ex | Intervening in a personal problem between two co-workers

7. Do not recopy your notes. Recopying does not require much thinking, and it is time that you can better spend doing other assignments. You must edit your notes, however. After class or within twenty-four hours, reread your notes. Reviewing information right after it has been introduced helps you remember it. During your review, rewrite any words that are unclear, and answer those questions you posed in the left-hand margin (preferably in a different color of ink). You may also use this margin to summarize the important points of the lecture or to record any new insights. Look at this example:

Management Levels

I. Top-Management Skills

   A. Conceptual — seeing the organization as a whole
   B. Human — interacting successfully with other people
   C. Technical — knowing the specialty responsibility area

What is specialty responsibility? Knowing practices of particular part of the business

8. Write legibly, even if you thereby write less; students lose time trying to decipher their handwriting.

How to Use Abbreviations

Now that you have learned several note-taking systems, you are ready to use abbreviations to save even more time when you take notes. You can use these abbreviations for both lecture and study notes. Like condensing, abbreviating reduces sentences to their essential meaning.

Abbreviation Symbols. Here is a list of commonly used symbols that students use when taking notes; commit them to memory.

=	equals
= ly	equally
≠	does not equal
" "	when you repeat the same information
⟶	causes
⟵	is caused by
⟶ ⟵	is both cause and effect
>	greater than
<	less than
+ or &	and or more
−	less or minus
∴	therefore
⊃	implies or suggests
#	number
%	percentage
¶	paragraph
//	parallel

See how the following sentence can be rephrased with abbreviations:

The percentage of those in middle management is greater than those in top management.

% middle management > % top management.

Words Commonly Abbreviated.   Below are abbreviations for words and phrases that you will commonly see in textbooks and hear in lectures. Study these abbreviations; then commit them to memory.

yr(s) = year(s)	pos = positive
c = century	neg = negative
re = regarding	incr = increase
ft = foot	decr = decrease
m = meter	maj = major(ity)
yd = yard	min = minimum
in. = inch	sig = significant
c = centimeter	imp't = important
mi = mile	lg = large
lb = pound	mt = mountain
g = gram	N = north
1st, 2nd, 3rd, 4th = first, second, third, fourth	E = east
nec = necessary	S = south
wd = word	W = west
mn = main	orig = original(ly)
ea = each	co = company
pt = point	cf = compare
prin = principal	w = with
usu = usually	w/o = without
genl = general(ly)	vs = versus, or against
ie = that is, that is to say	intro = introduction
pl = plural	concl = conclusion
ant. = antonym	cont'd = continued
syn = synonym	thru = through
def = definition	chpt = chapter
Am. = American	p = page
log. = logic(al)	pp = pages
inc = incomplete	subj = subject
sp = spelling	eg = for example
dept = department	
amt = amount	
specif = specific(ally)	
fem = feminine	
masc = masculine	

If you study this list carefully, you will find that four words end with a period (in., Am., ant., log.). You need to use a period after an abbreviation if the abbreviation spells out an actual word. The period corrects the confusion. For example, "ant" without a period could be mistaken for an insect rather than an antonym.

Once you have learned these abbreviations, you will be able to take down more information during lectures. See if you can write down the following statement concisely:

> A large increase in defense spending results in higher taxes or major cuts in other areas.

> lg incr defense spending → higher taxes or maj cuts

Once you have memorized these abbreviations, they become easy to read and do not slow down your reading rate.

Rules to Follow When You Create Your Own Abbreviations. As you develop skill in using abbreviations, you will find other ways to condense your notes. Whatever system you use is fine, as long as you can figure it out later.

1. If the word is one syllable, write it out. It takes about as much time to write "tax" as to write "tx."

2. When you decide to leave out letters, leave out vowels rather than consonants. You can recognize a word more easily if you see the consonants. For instance, you will probably recognize the abbreviation "bkgd" as "background."

3. Use only the first syllable of a long word if that first syllable gives you enough information to identify the word. In your history class you might use "fam" for "famine" without getting confused. But "ty" does not easily equate with "tyranny," so write out two syllables, "tyran."

4. You can sometimes use an apostrophe to delete a syllable or syllables of a word. For example, "requirement" can be written as "requir't"; "unnecessary" can be abbreviated to "unnec'y."

5. To make an abbreviation plural, add an "s" to it as you would normally add to the entire word. For example, "wds" would be the plural for "words."

6. Generally, use a numeral instead of writing out a number. You can write "65" more quickly than "sixty-five." But "45 million" (or "45 mil") is easier to write than "45,000,000." In writing numbers, choose the method that will save you the most time.

7. Often you will be writing down a key word or a phrase several times during a lecture. Early in the lecture, make up an abbreviation for that word or term. The first time you use the term, write this abbreviation and the complete word in the left-hand margin. For example, if you are studying consumer behavior in a marketing lecture, you could abbreviate consumer behavior to "CB" and in your margins write: "consumer behavior = CB."

8. Quickly learn the symbols and abbreviations that your math and science instructors use. You will be regularly using these abbreviations and symbols when you read the textbook, take lecture notes, and solve problems.

9. Edit your notes soon after the lecture. When you edit your notes, be sure that you completely write out any abbreviated words that are not immediately clear to you. If you wait too long, you may not be able to decipher your abbreviations.

10. Use abbreviations even more when your lecturer speaks quickly or presents a great deal of information. When you are pressed for time, using abbreviations will help you get down more information.

11. Do not overuse abbreviations. You want to make sure you know what the abbreviations stand for when you begin reading over your notes.

Summary

The two most common note-taking techniques—the numeral-letter format and the indenting format—are similarly organized. Both have main ideas at the left-hand margin and details indented to the right. Main ideas and major details are the key elements of your notes. Train your listening so you automatically look for details when you hear a main idea. With practice, you should be able to balance main ideas and major details properly. Do not expect to write down all of the details, only the significant ones. Try to condense whatever you hear to the "who" and the "what" of each statement.

Lecture notes in math and science courses are structured differently. In these courses you do more copying, mainly of solutions to problems. Still, in your notes you should comment on the steps to a solution that you do not fully understand.

Remember to review your notes daily, making comments and corrections. Because you will be using these notes all semester, they need to be legible.

You will find that abbreviations help you write down more information during lecture. Abbreviations are either symbols or shortened words. Memorize the most common abbreviation symbols and abbreviated words. In your review of your notes, be sure that you write out the complete word or phrase for those abbreviations that you cannot immediately read.

Summary Box   *Note-taking Techniques*

What are they?	*Why do you use them?*
Numeral-letter format: places main ideas (I) at the left and indents major details (A, B, C) to the right	To give order to your lecture notes and separate main ideas from major details
Indenting format: places main ideas to the left and major details to the right; use no numerals or letters	To write down significant information from lectures
Math-science format: accurately lists and describes the steps necessary for solutions to problems; allows marginal comments when a step is not understood	To help you remember important material for exams
Abbreviations: shorten words or substitute symbols for words or phrases	To write down more information To save time when taking notes

Topic: Consumer Behavior

The exercises in this chapter all deal with consumer behavior. Before you begin these exercises, answer the following questions, either individually or in small groups, to get some sense of what you already know about the field of consumer behavior:

1. What is consumer behavior?
2. What kinds of questions do you think researchers in consumer behavior ask?
3. How do you think a knowledge of consumer behavior benefits the customer?
4. Do you think consumer behavior research can really predict what a customer will buy?

Exercise 10.1 Condensing Sentences from a Lecture

The following ten sentences are taken from an introductory lecture on consumer behavior. Your job is to read each sentence and then condense it into a phrase in which only the essential information remains. You will find that sentences from a lecture tend to be wordy, a style much different from what you normally read. Use the abbreviations "def" and "ex" where appropriate.

1. We must first define the term "consumer behavior." Let's say it is what people do when they are involved somehow with market items—in buying, selling, or producing.

    _____

2. I want to emphasize that consumer behavior as a study is part of many other studies—that is, it is interdisciplinary, and I think it relies heavily on such fields as sociology, anthropology, and psychology.

    _____

3. How is sociology involved in the study of consumer behavior? I think in its focus on group behavior patterns, sociology helps us understand how consumers act.

    _____

4. Psychology also plays a role in our study. In its focus on the individual, psychology shows us how people typically act when they buy something. "Motivation" is an example of a psychological term that we can apply to an individual consumer's activities.

    _____

5. How do you think anthropology is related to our study of consumer behavior? Anthropology, I think, gives us a picture of the culture that determines a person's buying behavior. Ethnic preference is an example of how we use anthropological knowledge in our study of consumers.

    _____

6. Another term that we must define early in this semester is "consumer." Let's say for now that a consumer is anyone who purchases or uses a product.

    _____

7. How should we define "purchasing"? It is a more complicated term. I want to focus on one part of its meaning today. Purchasing on one level simply refers to obtaining an item from someone who sells.

    _____

8. In this course we will later pursue other areas of consumer behavior—specifically where people buy particular products and how they use them. I want to explore these topics only after we have a better understanding of certain key terms.

_____

9. Other issues that I think you will find of interest in consumer behavior involve psychology and economics: how frequently people tend to purchase certain products and the decisions they use in deciding on a particular purchase.

_____

_____
70%
(score = # correct × 10)
Find answers on
pp. 340–341.

10. Finally, I want you to place yourselves in these particular explorations of consumer behavior. Analyzing how you purchase certain items will assist you in understanding your sociological, psychological, and anthropological motives.*

_____

Exercise 10.2
More Condensing
Sentences from a
Lecture

Here are ten more sentences, again from an introductory consumer behavior lecture. Condense these sentences into phrases that pick up the significant information. Where necessary, use the abbreviations "def" and "cause."

1. Often consumer behavior scholars first look at the cultural influences of a particular group's purchasing choices. This is often defined as the macro perspective.

_____

2. In contrast, the micro perspective is often seen as what the individual in a group decides to purchase and the reasons why.

_____

3. I also want to add that an additional discipline I did not consider in the last lecture is economics. It influences consumer behavior in several ways, but particularly it shows us how an economic system like ours distributes its wealth.

_____

_____

*Adapted from Harold W. Berkman and Christopher C. Gilson, *Consumer Behavior: Concepts and Strategies* (Belmont, Calif.: Dickenson, 1978), pp. 5–6.

4. Now I want to begin a new section to my introductory remarks on consumer behavior—its history. Did you know that consumer behavior as a serious study is very young, emerging in the late 1940s?

_____

5. Since the late forties, scholarship in consumer studies has increased tremendously.

_____

6. I think the most important cause of increased studies in our field is the many uses we have found for the computer, so that we can now project with the help of the computer what a consumer will likely do in particular situations.

_____

7. We now have several journals that study consumer behavior, and they have added a greater seriousness to our field.

_____

8. What has also been a major factor in making consumer behavior a serious study is how we have recently begun to use theory to explain how consumers behave.

_____

9. Often consumer behavior scholars study theoretical models. I would define a model in our field as the application of a certain behavioral theory to a particular problem in consumer behavior.

_____

10. I would say that the most popular study that we use to develop theoretical models is the discipline of psychology. I will be talking later on in the semester about various behavioral models that are based on psychological theory.*

_____

> **80%**
>
> Ask instructor for answers.

Exercise 10.3
Using Note-taking
Techniques on Short
Lecture Passages

Read the following lecture excerpts on the cultural and social influences on consumer behavior. After you have read and condensed the information into main ideas and major details, complete the outlines that follow. Because you are reading an instructor's lecture, you will find some of it repetitious.

_____

*Adapted from Berkman and Gilson, *Consumer Behavior*, pp. 6–7.

1. I want to start today's lecture by focusing on how our American culture influences what we in the United States tend to buy. From a consumer standpoint, the one aspect of our culture that seems to go beyond particular ethnic groups is our interest in purchasing material goods. This goal of wanting material wealth is also tied in to other values that seem to be American. I'm thinking about our belief in the self and our basic optimism for the future. We also seem to value order over disorder.

   I.

      A.

      B.

      C.

      D.

2. But can we really say that these values define American culture? Is there really such a thing as an American culture? In some ways Americans seem to be moving away from a focus on material wealth. And though we are not a poor country, the recent economic problems we have seem to make some of us question whether the American culture is still as optimistic as it was, say, twenty years ago. Also, some consumer scholars have argued that the American focus on self-reliance has made some Americans terrified of being alone and on facing life's problems alone. Also, many people interested in the environment have begun to question just how valuable it is to be ordered. Worded differently, we can ask: Has the order of technology created disorder for the environment?

   I.

      A.

      B.

      C.

      D.

3. There are also a great number of ethnic groups in the United States today who seem to call into question just what we mean by an American culture. African-Americans and Hispanics, I think, provide a huge marketing challenge. In determining what these

groups purchase, we find that many African-Americans and Hispanics fit into what sociologists traditionally think is typically American. Yet in many ways we can see that their buying interests show a different set of values.

I.

   A.

   B.

   C.

4. Along with cultural questions, the student of consumer behavior must also see if class influences people's purchasing decisions. Do the values of the lower, middle, and upper classes shape what the people in each of these groups purchase? Or is this question just as difficult to answer as the question of culture and buying in the United States? Does income influence what a person buys? Or does a person's income determine what sorts of beliefs she or he holds? These are just a few of the puzzling questions that we will try to find answers to as the semester goes on.

I.

   A.

   B.

   C.

   D.

5. Another issue closely related to what people buy is where the family fits into these decisions. The family seems to have much to say about what people buy. The family gives to its members certain values. Yet purchasing decisions are also influenced by which members the product will serve. And purchasing is further complicated by who tends to be more powerful — the father, the mother, or the children. And we must also consider how these decisions change as the family gets older — I mean, as parents and children mature.

I.

   A.

   B.

        C.

        D.

   Now use the indenting format to complete the following lecture material on consumer behavior and the individual. This time you will be given no outline format.

   6. Now that we have talked briefly about some of the questions that consumer behavior researchers have about culture and society, we can turn to how the individual influences consumer behavior. Consumer behavior researchers begin by assuming that people learn to buy in certain ways. That is, they are not born to be a certain kind of consumer. The most important way for us to determine how an individual will react is to look at his or her past experience. Because of habit and experience, marketers try very hard to develop what they call brand loyalties, or a consumer's consistent buying of certain products.

   7. Another individual factor that I want to talk a little bit about today is how perception affects what somebody buys. Marketers now realize that each person perceives a product differently. For some, price is the major concern. For others, it is the look or image that the product presents.

   8. As in our discussion of class, society, and culture, an individual's choice in purchasing leads to no definite conclusions. What we do know is that the question of personality does affect what someone buys. Certain personalities tend to choose a sports car over a station wagon. A woman's personality type also helps determine the shade of lipstick she will buy.

9. Another individual factor that I want to talk about is attitude and buying. That is, how does a person's attitude affect what he or she buys? Here, marketers often try to use sports figures or actors to help sell a particular product. Marketers realize that these stars conjure up many positive and negative attitudes in the viewer. And these attitudes help sell a product.

10. Marketers have found that attitudes, unlike other parts of an individual's makeup, are difficult to change. Yet, this fact in itself becomes a marketing challenge. Can a marketing campaign change a person's attitude? And can this changed attitude make an individual buy a product she would normally not buy? Researchers still do not know how effective a marketing campaign can be in changing a person's attitudes. Your reading assignment will pick up this topic in much greater detail.*

70%

(score = # correct × 2, + 6 bonus points)
Find answers on
pp. 341–342.

---

*Exercise 10.4
Using Note-taking
Techniques on More
Short Lecture
Passages*

For the following three lecture excerpts on consumer behavior terminology, your job is to read each excerpt and then use the numeral-letter format to record notes. An outline is provided for these excerpts. As in Exercise 10.3, condense the information.

1. I want to introduce a few more terms today that should round out the most important terms that we will be using for this course. I want to talk a bit about micromarketing. A definition for this term is the business of marketing. Some of the areas that we will consider in micromarketing include managing a marketing campaign, researching marketing behavior, and creating profitable marketing campaigns.

   In the study of micromarketing, the most important concern is looking for new markets. The challenge today is that new markets are not that easy to come by because today's consumer tends to be more educated and less susceptible to earlier marketing strategies. With each product, marketers need to ask similar questions: Is the market young, or is the market becoming younger? Is the market ethnic or becoming culturally diverse? Marketers need to be secure in the data they receive in answer to these questions. As I have said many times before, these are not easy questions to answer.

---

*Adapted from Berkman and Gilson, *Consumer Behavior*, pp. 8–12, and Straub and Attner, *Introduction to Business*, pp. 628–629.

I. Def.:

    A.

    B.

II.

    A.

    B.

    C.

    D.

2. In an attempt to make their job more manageable, some marketers have looked closely at the audience that would most likely buy a particular product. The segment of the market that a marketer looks at may be very small or very large. It may be a market directed at a restricted group, like retirees interested in golfing, or a large group, like teenagers between the ages of thirteen and eighteen.

    Magazine executives can tell marketers what segment of the population tends to buy their magazines. This is the population that marketers may want to target for the sale of a particular product. Magazines often provide what is called a demographic profile. What does a demographic profile consist of? It often includes the age span of the magazine audience and its average income, as well as readers' educational level. So in a strange way, marketers are finding that sometimes, if they restrict their buying population for a particular product, they are actually allowing for greater profit. Why is this so? By targeting a market well, marketers then have a better chance of attracting a greater percentage of that segment to buy their product.

I.

    A.

    B.

II.

    A.

    B.

    C.

3. I'd also like to talk about the concept of macromarketing. Macromarketing, unlike micromarketing, is concerned with consumer behavior on a larger social level. You might find macromarketers asking questions like these: How is advertising deceptive to the public? How does a particular product adversely affect the environment? How can society be trained to recycle?

In some ways, macromarketing begins with different premises than micromarketing does. I think micromarketers see the consumer as someone they need to persuade so they can sell a particular product. The macromarketer begins by assuming that the consumer is often deceived by advertisements, and they see their role as helping the consumer not be deceived. A healthy market comes about, I think, when macromarketers keep the micromarketers in check. What do you think?

    I. Def.:

        A.

        B.

        C.

  II.

        A.

        B.

        C.

Now use the indenting technique to take notes on the following two passages on the value of studying consumer behavior. This time, you are not provided with skeletal outlines.

4. Thus far I have been presenting you with an overview of our course in marketing. We have discussed important terms and important marketing concepts that we will pursue this semester. I want to talk a little bit today about the value of the study of consumer behavior. I'll try to be as brief as I can.

Because we are a capitalist society, we as a country focus a lot of our energy on consumer behavior. We have studied many reasons why consumers act the way they do and how culture and society affect their purchasing. In a way, consumer behavior studies also help sociologists and psychologists understand their fields a little better.

Let me be more specific about what I mean about the relationship between our discipline and others. When we study consumer perception, we help psychologists understand their research on perception better. And when we explore how class affects purchasing, then we help sociologists understand just what they mean by class. In this way I want you to see consumer behavior as an excellent interdisciplinary study. I'm going to be showing how our field relates to other disciplines throughout the course.

5. I also want to repeat that we have two types of consumer behavior studies: micromarketing and macromarketing. But I will be focusing on the micromarketing studies, except for a few lectures at the end of the course.

Before you can appreciate these micromarketing studies, we must go over other preliminary material. This time we'll be talking about how these studies are organized. So we'll first be looking at theories and models as they relate to consumer behavior. Then we'll be looking at the measurement techniques that our field uses to interpret these models. In this part of the course, we'll be learning some elementary rules about flowcharting, and we'll examine and practice some very common formulas in statistics.*

80%

Ask instructor for answers.

Exercise 10.5 Writing Abbreviations from Memory

Go back to the section called "How to Use Abbreviations" (p. 179) to review all of the abbreviations that are listed. Then, without referring to those pages, complete the following questions. Place all answers in the answer box.

---

*Adapted from Berkman and Gilson, *Consumer Behavior*, pp. 14–16, and Straub and Attner, *Introduction to Business*, p. 526.

Write the abbreviations for the following:

1. equals
2. greater than
3. and
4. imply
5. regarding

6. necessary
7. positive
8. increase
9. large
10. maximum

Now write the correct word or words for these abbreviations:

11. w/o
12. cf
13. vs
14. inc
15. imp't

16. prin
17. cont'd
18. #
19. ∴
20. → ←

1. _____

2. _____

3. _____

4. _____

5. _____

6. _____

7. _____

8. _____

9. _____

10. _____

11. _____

12. _____

13. _____

14. _____

15. _____

16. _____

17. _____

18. _____

19. _____

20. _____

_____
80%

(score = # correct × 5)
Find answers on p. 342.

Exercise 10.6
Making Your Own
Abbreviations

For the following twenty words and phrases relating to consumer behavior, write your own abbreviations, using the rules given in the introduction. Your answers may vary from those devised by other students. Discuss your answers with your instructor and classmates. Place all answers in the answer box.

1. behavior
2. advertising
3. *Wealth of Nations* (used several times)
4. social class acceptance
5. persuasiveness
6. affluence
7. competitive
8. urbanize
9. cognitive dissonance (used several times)
10. consumer behavior (used several times)
11. consumption
12. cultures
13. customers
14. industrial
15. labeling
16. law of diminishing returns (used several times)
17. perception
18. reinforcement
19. marketing
20. macromarketing (used several times)

1. _____

2. _____

3. _____

4. _____

5. _____

6. _____

7. _____

8. _____

9. _____

10. _____

11. _____

12. _____

13. _____

14. _____

15. _____

16. _____

17. _____

18. _____

19. _____

20. _____

80%

Ask instructor for answers.

Exercise 10.7
Reading and Writing
Abbreviations in
Sentences

Assume that the following abbreviated sentences on international marketing techniques are from your consumer behavior lecture notes. Your job is to rewrite each as a complete sentence, changing the abbreviations to words.

1. Mrktng bcmng an international actvty.

   _____

2. Easy to make lrg mistakes in this interntl mrkt.

   _____

3. Mny mrktrs do not undrstnd cultrl setting.

   _____

4. Anthroplgy helps cnsmr beh to undrstnd cultrs.

   _____

5. Anthrplgsts use stdy called cross-cultural resrch (CCR).

   _____

6. CCR studies how cultrs are same and diff.

   _____

7. CCR studies atts re love in cltrs.

   _____

8. CCR also works w politcl power in ea cultr.

   _____

9. CCR studies cultrl mng of color.

   _____

10. In some cultrs blk & gray = good.

   _____

Now write your own abbreviated sentences from the sentences on international marketing techniques that follow. Be sure to condense and to make up your own abbreviations when necessary.

11. Cross-cultural research has shown that the colors yellow, white, and gray are weak everywhere.

   _____

12. Red and black seem to be strong colors in every country.

   _____

13. Some marketers see each culture as unique.

   _____

14. This belief suggests that we focus on local marketing campaigns.

   _____

15. Other marketers believe in standardized marketing plans.

   _____

16. These marketers believe in looking at cultural uniformity in the world.

   _____

17. Therefore, they see several countries as one possible market.

   _____

18. Tourism and the mass media have caused some similar marketing needs.

   _____

19. These marketers see Europe as one country rather than several.

   _____

20. The answers to these questions may have a positive or negative impact on each advertising campaign.*

   _____

80%
(score = # correct × 10
[1–10]; answers will
vary for 11–20)
Find answers on
pp. 342–343.

Exercise 10.8
Outlining Lecture
Excerpts and Using
Abbreviations

The following lecture excerpts discuss particular markets and the strategies marketers use to sell their products to them. Use all your note-taking skills (condensing, abbreviating, and using the numeral-letter format) to outline the first three excerpts.

_____

*Adapted from Berkman and Gilson, *Consumer Behavior*, pp. 93–94.

1. We talked last time about the marketing needs of the single person. Today I want to focus on the marketing strategies used for the elderly and the poor. With the elderly, I think we need to know something about how they live and where they live. In past generations, the elderly usually lived with their children; now they often live away from them. Some live in communities for the elderly. Florida, as an example, has become a popular site for the elderly, where they live away from their children.

2. Here are some more vital statistics about the elderly. Today the elderly tend to be better educated than they were in the past. They often have greater incomes than they had in years past. They tend to be better and smarter shoppers. Also, many do some sort of part-time work. They also tend to want to enjoy their retirement years more. Therefore, you see more elderly traveling than you did in the past.

3. What are some of the markets that speak directly to the elderly? There are several, and I want you to list them in order. First, the elderly have unique housing needs. Second, their health needs are different in many ways from those of the rest of the population. Furthermore, they have a different set of insurance needs — both health and life insurance. To a degree, we can target particular foods that the elderly would tend to buy. Finally, the elderly have a unique set of travel needs. I want to emphasize that these six needs provide marketing challenges for the nineties.

Now use the indenting format to outline the following excerpts on marketing strategies for the poor. Be sure to condense information and use abbreviations where appropriate.

4. I want to turn now to another market. That is the market that concerns the poor. What are the unique needs of the poor? What is their particular profile? We know that the poor tend to spend a larger share of their income on life's necessities. These necessities include such things as food, housing, and medical care. What do you think the poor spend less on? Transportation and clothing are not areas where they spend much of their money. Researchers have also found that the poor spend a large amount of their income on sturdy items like stoves and refrigerators. In terms of automobiles, the poor tend to buy used rather than new cars, as you would expect. In terms of furniture, the poor often buy sets of furnishings rather than individual pieces.

5. What sorts of foods do the poor often purchase, and how do they pay their bills? Of course, they tend to buy low-cost food. They often look for low-cost fresh items rather than prepackaged foods, especially in rural areas. They rarely buy more expensive convenience foods. What about credit? More and more people are using credit cards, but the poor tend to use credit and installment buying more often than the middle and upper classes do. Some researchers have even shown that poor families often have a credit debt that is twice that of higher-income families.

6. What can we finally say about the shopping behavior of the poor? Some of these statistics are surprising, I think. Poor urban people tend to pay more — not less — for products than those who live in wealthier areas. Also, there are fewer supermarkets in the poor urban areas for shoppers to choose from. The poor also tend not to be shrewd shoppers. They often listen to what their family members, friends, or the media say rather than looking into programs that provide reduced rates or reading newspaper ads carefully. Also, the poor often shop in areas close to their homes because transportation is often harder to come by for them. Therefore, their consumer options tend to be restricted.*

> Answers will vary. Ask instructor for sample answers.

Exercise 10.9
Taking Notes on a
Longer Lecture
Passage and Using
Abbreviations

The following is a longer lecture excerpt on consumer behavior and social responsibility. Your job is to take notes on this passage. Use the indenting format, condense information where necessary, and abbreviate where appropriate. After you have taken your notes, give the lecture an effective title.

Title: _____

(1) In this part of the course, I want to talk about issues that have not concerned us up to now. How does consumer behavior relate to ethics? That is, how should consumer behaviorists be concerned with treating the consumer correctly? I want to talk specifically about the key consumer issues relating to ethics: truth in marketing, product quality, and product safety. I will talk about each separately, then come to some conclusions about this issue of ethics and consumer behavior both for the consumer and for the marketer and producer.

(2) Marketers have an obligation to be honest in their presentation of a product. The Federal Trade Commission monitors advertisements to ensure that they are not fraudulent. The Commission has uncovered and put a stop to many mail-order frauds. Recently, the question of packaging and labeling has become an important concern. For example, what does it mean for a product to be low in fat or low in cholesterol? What does it mean for a product to be fat-free? The Federal Trade Commission has now written specific requirements that spell out what these packaging statements mean, and marketers and producers are going to have to follow these regulations.

(3) The next issue that consumers need to consider is how reliable a product is. What can a consumer do if a product fails to operate as promised, or if a product becomes a hazard? Consumers need to read what the warranty promises. Often the warranty insists that consumers either exchange a product or get a refund. Particularly when consumers

---

*Adapted from Berkman and Gilson, *Consumer Behavior*, pp. 133–135, 136–138.

buy an expensive item, they need to see just what the warranty promises and does not promise, so they will not be surprised if the product somehow fails.

(4) What happens when the consumer is not satisfied with the warranty, or if the seller does not live up to the warranty? Does the consumer have any options? The customer can go to court and sue. But this process is lengthy and can prove to be expensive.

(5) Some companies have responded to consumer complaints in a positive way. I want to emphasize here that by serving the customer politely and honestly, many companies have increased, not decreased, their profits. So it can pay to be honest. What some companies have done is to ask customers to be very frank about their complaints.

(6) How can complaints serve both the customer and the company? An honest complaint provides useful information for the decisions a company chooses to make in the future. Furthermore, complaints can make the company rewrite its warranties, so future customers will be even more satisfied with the product and the company. When a customer tells her family and friends that a company actually listened to her complaints and even changed policies because of her, they will often become customers of that company as well.

(7) I want to emphasize here that ethics works both ways. If there are unethical companies, so are there unethical customers. For the marketplace to work well, the company and the consumer need to respect each other. What companies and customers need to realize is that honesty on the part of both parties goes a long way to solidify long-term business dealings. I want to repeat that it does pay to be honest. Profits on the part of the producer and satisfaction on the part of the consumer can result if producer and consumer trust each other.*

Answers will vary. Find sample answers on pp. 343–344.

---

*Adapted from Straub and Attner, *Introduction to Business*, pp. 604–606, 617–618.

Exercise 10.10
Using Lecture Notes
to Answer an Essay
Question

Now use only your lecture notes from Exercise 10.9 to answer the following essay question. Begin with a main-idea sentence, and support it with relevant details from the lecture.

> *Essay question:* In what ways are customers protected from fraudulent companies? In what ways can companies serve their customers even more efficiently? Be specific by using evidence from the lecture.

80%
Ask instructor for answers.

Follow-up on the
Consumer Behavior
Exercises

Now that you have completed these exercises, it may be helpful to see how your reading on this topic has changed some of your ideas about consumer behavior. You may want to go back to reread these exercises before you answer the following questions. Answer them either in small groups or individually.

1. How would you now define *consumer behavior*?
2. In what ways do you now think that a knowledge of consumer behavior can benefit marketers and consumers?
3. What are the most interesting areas of consumer behavior for you? What areas would you now like to study further?

11 *Mapping and the Cornell Note-taking System*

ALTERNATE NOTE-TAKING TECHNIQUES

Mapping

Cornell note-taking system

Now that you have studied three traditional note-taking techniques (numeral-letter, indenting, and math-science), you may find the alternate techniques of mapping and the Cornell system helpful. Mapping, a visual note-taking system, is especially helpful for those who are artistic or who have strong visual abilities. The Cornell system is an effective recall system that uses traditional note-taking techniques as well as a systematic remembering strategy. Both techniques are best used when you are editing your notes.

What Is Mapping?

Mapping is a note-taking technique that uses geometric shapes to show the relationship between main ideas and details. The most commonly used shapes are circles, squares, rectangles, and radiating lines. But mapping is individual; you choose your own design to show the relationship between general and specific. Because maps are individual, they help you to retain the material more easily. Maps, often called study maps or advanced organizers, reduce large amounts of information to the essentials, so they are ideal when you study for exams.

Maps may be large or small. If they are large, they need to be put on a separate sheet of paper. If you place additional information on this page, you take away from the study map and distort the visual picture of main ideas tied to details.

Let's say you are studying your notes in British literature and you come across the following statement: "Alexander Pope and Samuel Johnson are the most famous writers in eighteenth-century English literature." You could map this statement in the way shown in Figure 11-1. In this map, eighteenth-century English literature is the general category, and Pope and Johnson are examples.

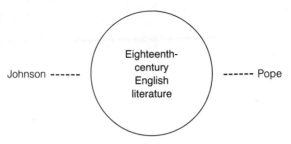

Figure 11-1 *Map of examples.*

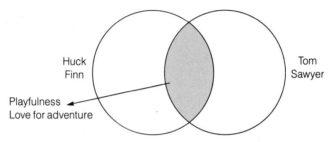

Figure 11-2 *Map of shared traits.*

Let's say you want to show how the two characters Huckleberry Finn and Tom Sawyer in Mark Twain's *Huckleberry Finn* share the traits of playfulness and love of adventure. You can map these similarities by using intersecting circles (see Figure 11-2). Intersecting circles are effective for mapping similarities.

Mapping is also effective in showing sequences. Arrows can join one step to the other. If you came across this statement in your notes, how could you map it? "When a patient contracts this year's Type W influenza, the following symptoms occur, in this order: (1) soreness in joints, (2) upset stomach, (3) vomiting, (4) fever of at least 102 degrees." Do you see how the map in Figure 11-3 shows both the symptoms and their sequence?

A map using arrows is similar to a flowchart, a visualization often used by programmers to set up the logic of their computer program. Flowcharts are now widely used by people outside programming to list the steps in a procedure. Look at Figure 11-4, which shows the career ladder in a computer company. Follow the arrows from bottom to top, each pointing to a higher-level position. Also note that some arrows are joined with broken lines and point in two directions, suggesting the double career option that a person at that level has.

All of the visual techniques mentioned so far can be combined into larger maps that tie together larger chunks of information—several lectures or an entire textbook chapter. Pretend that you are reviewing your notes in anthropology on the evolution of the human species and

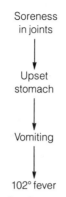

Influenza W Symptoms

Figure 11-3 *Map showing sequence.*

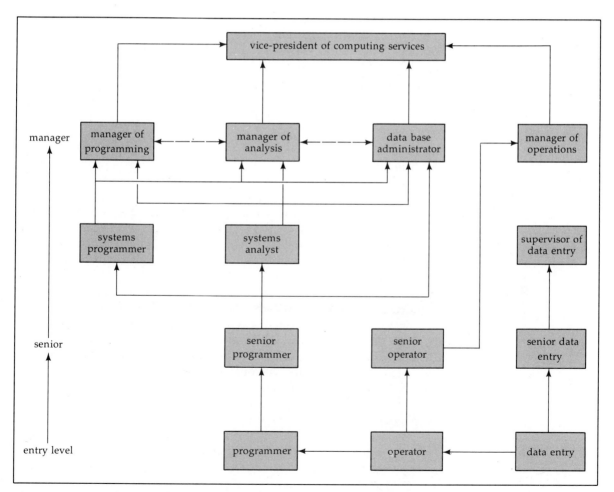

Figure 11-4 *Career ladder. (Source: Perry Edwards and Bruce Broadwell,* Data Processing, *2nd ed. [Belmont, Calif.: Wadsworth, 1982], p 560. Used by permission.)*

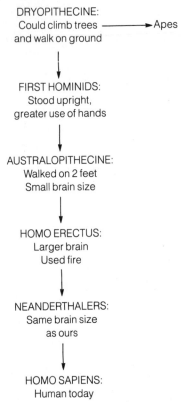

Figure 11-5 *Map of human evolution.*

you want to map this information. Your map could look something like the one shown in Figure 11-5. This map reduces several paragraphs to half a page, listing each human ancestor and noting its important characteristics. It also shows that Dryopithecine evolved into a species different from the apes.

More complex maps can show the relationships among topics, main ideas, and supporting details. The topic is usually in the center, the main ideas branching out from the center, with details of support branching from the main-idea lines (see Figure 11-6). Study maps like these can be used to summarize an entire lecture or a complete textbook chapter.

A second complex type of study map is a tree diagram. The main idea is at the top of the tree, the major details branch out from the main idea, and the minor details in turn branch out from the major details. Figure 11-7 shows the tree study map.

Many students have found that these larger maps are effective study aids for midterm and final examinations. These maps force students to condense and help them see relationships between general and specific types of material. In addition, the visual nature of study maps allows students to "see" the whole and its parts when they take an exam.

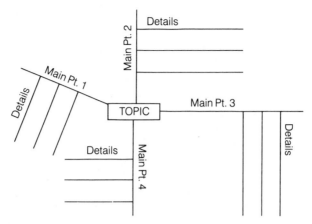

Figure 11-6 *Diagram of a study map.*

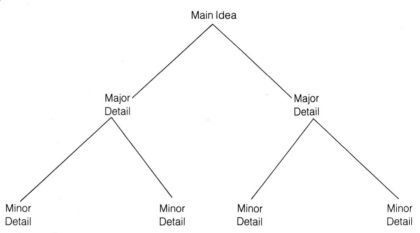

Figure 11-7 *Tree study map.*

Keep in mind that mapping has few rules and is for the most part individual. If you have visual aptitude, make some study maps as you edit your notes. Even if you don't have strong visual abilities, try using study maps to help you study for exams.

What Is the Cornell Note-taking System?

A system developed at Cornell University incorporates several of the note taking strategies that you already know and includes a successful recall strategy as well. To use this system correctly, follow these ten steps:

1. When taking notes, use spiral-bound notebook paper, and place all of your lecture notes in chronological order in a loose-leaf notebook. By using these two items, you can include material without destroying the sequence of the lectures. Also, title each lecture and date it on the top line.

2. Draw a vertical line 2½ inches from the left edge of the page. You will have the remaining 6 inches of paper to write down your lecture notes.
3. During lecture, take notes in any format you prefer: numeral-letter, indenting, or even short paragraphs.
4. Concentrate on writing only main ideas and significant details during lecture.
5. Skip lines between main ideas, and use only one side of the paper.
6. Read through your notes after class, filling in any incomplete information and rewriting any illegible words.
7. As you review your notes, underline all main ideas or outline them with a box.
8. After you have reviewed your notes once, jot down in the 2½-inch margin some key phrases that summarize what you have learned.
9. Cover up the 6-inch side of your notes to see whether you can recall the important parts of the lecture with only these key phrases as clues.
10. Continue this procedure until you can easily recall the important parts of the lecture.*

Look at the following lecture notes dealing with the family. This student has correctly employed the Cornell system:

← *2½ inches*	*6 inches* →
	Nature and Function of the Family *4/12/92*

def of family	Definition and strength of the family
	    Def: "Basic unit of kinship or relatedness
	        through blood"

2 chars of fams in all societies	Most fundamental of social structures All societies have families

3 functs of fams	Functions of families
	    Essential in caring for and raising children
	    Sexual outlet for spouses
	    Emotional and physical comfort

As you can see, the Cornell note-taking system is rather sophisticated. Use this technique only after you have mastered the numeral-letter and indenting systems. The Cornell system is basically a refinement of these two systems. Once you are comfortable with the Cornell system, you will find that you can organize and retain large amounts of study material efficiently and intelligently. You will be asked to use this Cornell system in several of this chapter's exercises.

---

*Adapted from Walter Pauk, *How to Study in College*, 2nd ed. (Boston: Houghton Mifflin, 1974), pp. 126–132.

Summary

Mapping is a relatively new note-taking format. You can most effectively use it when you are editing your notes. The technique is visual and individualistic, allowing you to create your own shapes to illustrate relationships. Mapping reduces information to its essentials and serves as an excellent review for exams. This system works best if you have visual aptitude, but all students benefit if they use it as a study aid. Like the traditional note-taking systems, mapping helps you see the relationships between main ideas and supporting details.

The Cornell note-taking system helps you remember what you learned in lecture. It breaks up a page into 6 inches of lecture notes next to 2½ inches of summary phrases. The Cornell note-taking system is efficient because it makes you review your notes. In Chapter 13 you will study the SQ3R system, which uses a similar recall strategy. By the end of the textbook, you will be successfully applying both the Cornell system and the SQ3R to what you read and study.

Summary Box   *Mapping and the Cornell Note-taking System*

What is it?	*Why use it?*
Mapping: shapes used to relate general and specific information; information reduced to its essentials	To show visually how main ideas relate to major details; to remember more information and prepare better for exams
Cornell system: lecture page divided into 6 inches of notes and 2½ inches of summary; system insists on recall of important points	To help ensure recall of material; to remember more information and prepare better for exams

Skills Practice

In the following exercises you will practice taking notes. Some of the exercises contain material you are already familiar with from your work in Part Two.

Exercise 11.1
Mapping Statements
from Lectures

The following ten statements are taken from lecture notes. Your job is to create, on a separate sheet of paper, a map for each statement that will show the relationship between main ideas and major details. Remember that mapping is individual, so do not expect your maps to be exactly like the ones in the answer key.

1. Impressionism was a school of painting that emphasized the capturing on canvas of a fleeting moment. The most famous Impressionists were Manet, Monet, and Degas.

2. There are only a few pure substances in nature. Gold, diamonds, and sulfur are found in pure form.

3. British literature to 1800 is usually broken up into the following categories: Medieval, Renaissance, and Restoration–Eighteenth Century.

4. There are many kinds of coal. Lignites are the least pure and most immature. Bituminous coal is a medium-quality coal, and anthracite is the most compact and the purest form of coal.

5. F. Scott Fitzgerald is especially known for two novels: *The Great Gatsby* and *Tender Is the Night*. In *The Great Gatsby*, Fitzgerald develops the character of fated idealist Jay Gatsby, and in *Tender Is the Night*, Fitzgerald traces the mental collapse of psychiatrist Dick Diver.

6. Three of the most important causes of the Great Depression of 1929 were (1) a decline in industrial production, (2) an increase in consumer debt, and (3) overpricing of common stocks.

7. Here are three important rules of algebra: (1) the commutative law of addition ($a + b = b + a$), (2) the associative law of addition [$a + (b + c) = (a + b) + c$], and (3) the commutative law of multiplication ($ab = ba$).

8. One of the similarities between whales and chimpanzees is that they both breast-feed their young.

9. Language development usually occurs in four stages. First one understands a language, then one speaks, then one reads, and finally one writes in this language.

10. There are several causes of inflation. The three most commonly mentioned are (1) a large federal deficit, (2) high interest rates, and (3) an annual increase in salaries.

70%

(score = # correct × 10)
Find answers on
pp. 344–347.

Exercise 11.2
Using the Cornell
Note-taking System
on Short Passages

In the following five lecture excerpts,* you will be asked to use the Cornell note-taking system to outline each passage. First use the indenting format, then apply the Cornell strategies to highlight the main ideas and major details.

1. I want to discuss the implications of my statement in the last lecture that the world is divided into two groups—the rich and the poor. Here are some startling facts. One-fourth of the world's population

---

*Adapted from G. Tyler Miller, Jr., *Living in the Environment*, 2nd ed. (Belmont, Calif.: Wadsworth, 1979), p. 118.

lives in the so-called developed, or industrialized, countries. Three-fourths of the world's population lives in the poorer, developing nations. Examples of developed countries are the United States, Japan, and Germany. Examples of developing countries are Guatemala and Nigeria.

Yet one-fourth of the population — the developed nations — effectively controls the world. Isn't that amazing! For example, did you know that the developed countries use 80 percent of the resources of the world and that they account for 85 percent of the total expenditures of the world? What, you ask, are the implications of these facts?

2. I want to make a few comments on the unique properties of water, a substance that you and I cannot live without but generally take for granted. For one, of all the liquids we know, water takes the most amount of heat to make it a vapor. This characteristic makes evaporated water a storehouse of energy. Also, water in liquid form can store amazing amounts of heat. Water, therefore, heats and cools more slowly than other liquids. For this reason, you'll be pleased to know that water protects the Earth from sudden temperature changes.

I also want to discuss how water is used in the human body. It dissolves very easily almost all the substances that our body carries. Water can carry vitamins and minerals throughout our body with ease. Water can also be used to clean the body of its wastes. But you must also remember that, because so many things are soluble in it, water in our body can also be easily polluted by poisons and bacteria.

3. It's strange to realize that our sun, though we think it special to us on Earth, is really quite an ordinary star in the universe. It is as hot and as large as many other stars in the universe. To us, the sun is very impressive, because it is only 93 million miles away. The star that is next closest to the sun is 300,000 times farther away than the sun.

Let's talk a bit about the sun's composition. It is a ball of extremely hot gases. Do you know that it equals 1 million Earths in size? At its surface, its temperature is extremely hot—10,000 degrees Fahrenheit. Scientists think that at the sun's core its temperature is unbelievably hot—25 million degrees Fahrenheit or greater.

4. Last lecture I talked about forests. Today, I want to concentrate on grasslands. Where are they? Grasslands used to cover 40 percent of the land on the earth. Much of this land has since been cleared for agricultural use. The great grasslands today are to be found in South Africa, South America, North America, and the former Union of Soviet Socialist Republics.

What are some of the characteristics of grasslands? First, the land is flat or rolling. Second, remember that grasslands have dry soil. The rainfall on grasslands is approximately ten to thirty inches a year. This rainfall allows grasslands to have a soil composition that is midway between that of deserts and forests. Finally, animals that graze and burrow are often found on grasslands.

5. We are going to spend the next two lectures discussing density. You will need to understand this concept in many of the laboratory problems you will be assigned. Let's first define density as the mass of a substance in relation to its volume. The formula I want you to remember is this one: Density = Mass of a body ÷ Volume of a body. As you can see from studying this formula for a while, a dense body has much mass in a small amount of area.

How is density measured? There are several ways of measuring density. The density of solids and liquids is often measured in grams per cubic centimeter. The gram refers to the mass of an object, and the cubic centimeter measures the volume. The chemical abbreviation I want you to remember is this: gm/cm^3. Sometimes you will see density measured in the English system. This system uses pounds per cubic feet. The chemical abbreviation is lb/ft^3. The density of gases is measured differently.

70%

Ask instructor for answers.

Exercise 11.3
Mapping a Longer
Lecture Passage

Your job is to read the following lecture excerpt on nuclear energy. As you read, take notes — condensing information, using the indenting format, and applying the Cornell strategies. Then, on a separate sheet of paper, create a study map that includes the important points made in your notes. Remember that mapping is individual, so your map may not look like the sample one in the answer key. Complete your study notes in the space provided.

Today my subject is nuclear energy — both its uses and its dangers. First, here are some facts that I want you to know. Current statistics suggest that nuclear energy produces about 8 percent of all electricity in the United States. Scientists predict that by the year 2000 nuclear power will be only slightly more expensive than power from coal.

Are nuclear power plants safe? The facts suggest that the amount of radiation escaping from a nuclear power plant is in fact less than that from a coal-burning plant of equal size. A second point to be made is that nuclear power plants do not let out carbon dioxide as do coal-burning plants.

The important question, I think, is what happens if a nuclear accident does occur. There is a chance for a meltdown or a nuclear accident. The process of meltdown is complex. Meltdowns occur when the nuclear fuel overheats. This overheating can cause the water used to cool the material to turn to steam. This steam can cause pressure that could make the entire plant explode if the steam is not checked. When the plant explodes, then the major problems occur: Radioactive material is sent throughout the environment.

The last consideration I want to talk about today is that of nuclear waste. What happens to the radioactive material that is used, even if it does not explode into the environment? Where can we store it? Radioactive waste, remember, is dangerous and must be removed to central locations. Radioactive materials decay so slowly that they need to be hidden for thousands of years. No nuclear waste has yet been permanently sealed. Yet, plans are to put these wastes in steel cylinders in areas that are not prone to earthquakes and to water exposure. There are no guarantees that these cylinders will still not contaminate the environment.*

Place your lecture notes here, but put your study map on a separate sheet of paper.

*Title:*_____

80%

(score: # correct responses, including title, × 5, + 10 bonus points)
Find answers on pp. 347–348.

**Exercise 11.4
Writing a Paragraph
from a Study Map**

Your job is to write a paragraph from the information that you gathered in the previous lecture on nuclear energy. Use only the information from your study map to answer the following question.

Essay question: In a well-organized paragraph, present the two sides of the nuclear energy argument: Show that nuclear reactors are relatively safe, and present evidence suggesting that nuclear reactors are unsafe, especially if one considers the possibility of meltdown and the problem of storing nuclear waste. Be sure your evidence is accurate.

70%

Ask instructor for answer.

---

*Adapted from Cecie Starr and Ralph Taggart, *Biology: The Unity and Diversity of Life*, 4th ed. (Belmont, Calif.: Wadsworth, 1987), pp. 746–747.

The Library, Study Skills Systems, and Test-Taking Strategies

Having mastered reading and note-taking skills, you are now ready to learn some additional techniques for improving your study skills. In this part you will learn how to use the library and will be introduced to the SQ3R study system, an efficient way to read and remember textbook material. You will also learn how to take objective, essay, and math or science tests. Examinations are important indicators that tell you and your instructor how well you are doing.

12 Library Basics

So far, you have mainly been learning how to organize the information that you read and listen to — around main ideas and significant details. You are now ready to appreciate how libraries are organized and how you can use them to get more information for the courses you are taking. Undoubtedly your college has one or more libraries, and they are all organized in a similar fashion.

Study the information in this chapter to see how it explains your college library or libraries.

The Main Sections of a Library

Libraries are depositories of information and ideas that will help further your education and enhance your life. Librarians run libraries; their major duties are to select and organize new library materials and to assist you in finding material you need in your particular research.

Libraries are typically divided into three sections. The *reference section* holds dictionaries, encyclopedias, and other volumes of brief, specific information that allow you to pursue your research. The *stacks* are where you find books that you can check out. This is invariably the largest section of the library, and it is where you will spend much of your time finding particular books on a topic you are studying. The third section of a library is the *periodical area*, where magazines, newspapers, and journals are found. Here you can locate specific articles on the topic you are interested in studying.

Types of Library Materials

Basically, you will find four types of reading material in libraries: books to borrow, periodicals, reference books, and pamphlets. Each type of reading material will advance your knowledge of your topic in particular ways.

Books to borrow are by far the most abundant type of material you will find in a library. These books are arranged on the shelves by subject matter. College libraries generally have more scholarly texts—that is, books that examine a topic with more detail and analysis. If you are researching the political leader Cesar Chavez, for example, in the stacks you will likely come across books on Chavez's political beliefs, his contributions to the status of the migrant farmer, his biography, and so on. A good college library will have both earlier material on Cesar Chavez and more recent studies.

Periodicals include newspapers as well as magazines and journals published on a weekly, monthly, or quarterly basis. You will probably find titles of articles on your topic in the *Readers' Guide to Periodical Literature*, an index that is published each month. It tells what has been published in that time frame on your topic. If you find a listing in the *Readers' Guide*, you then need to see if your library has the periodical that contains the article. For newspaper articles you can use the *New York Times Index* or *Los Angeles Times Index* to locate information on your subject. If you are researching a book, you can find out what reviewers of that book had to say through the *Book Review Digest*. If your topic is in the arts and humanities, you may want to look through the *Art Index* or the *Humanities Index*. Similarly, if your topic concerns the social sciences, there is also a *Social Science Index*. All of these indexes work like the *Readers' Guide*, telling you what journal or magazine has material on the topic you are studying.

At times you will find the article you want in the magazine or journal itself. At other times the article will be on microfilm or microfiche, which stores a reduced image of the article. With a microfilm or microfiche reader you can enlarge the material so it can be read.

In the reference section, you will likely find a host of encyclopedias and dictionaries. General encyclopedias like the *Encyclopedia Britannica* or the *Encyclopedia Americana* provide you with an introduction to the topic you are studying. The articles in these encyclopedia sets are arranged alphabetically by subject, but the index in the last volume is usually the best place to begin searching. The *Encyclopedia Britannica* is an often-used source for general information. You may want to turn to the *Encyclopedia Americana* for information on issues concerning North America and scientific and technological subjects. Finally, the *New Columbia Encyclopedia* is helpful if you want a short summary of the area you are studying. Your college library is likely to have many other encyclopedias, particularly specialized encyclopedias on art, science, philosophy, and so on. Ask your college reference librarian what types of encyclopedias your college provides.

You will also find several dictionaries in your college library. *Webster's Third International Dictionary of the English Language* is a comprehensive American dictionary on the English language, providing definitions and pronunciations of the words you are interested in. The *Oxford English Dictionary* is another dictionary that you will likely come across. This multivolume dictionary is unique in that it gives the history, or etymology, of each word in the English language, providing a chronology of its use in literary and historical contexts. A number of briefer, collegiate dictionaries are also stored on the shelves in the reference section, as are specialized dictionaries on various fields like music, medicine, and law. Again, your reference librarian will provide you with information about the kinds of dictionaries available to you.

Most libraries also carry pamphlets in a special pamphlet file. These are often government or business publications that may provide useful information on a topic you are interested in. The librarian can help you find any pamphlet on your topic.

How Library Books Are Classified

Library books are commonly organized under two classification systems: The *Dewey decimal* system and the *Library of Congress* system. It is important to have a general understanding of how these two systems work.

The Dewey decimal system is the older of the two. It classifies books by subject. Each subject has a number, and you will find the number on the outside of the book. The number is usually a whole number and a decimal. Here are the general numbers and their subject classifications:

000–099 General works, including bibliography
100–199 Philosophy and psychology
200–299 Religion
300–399 Social sciences
400–499 Language
500–599 Pure science
600–699 Technology, medicine, business
700–799 The arts
800 899 Literature
900–999 History and geography

Underneath the book's Dewey decimal number, you will find additional numbers and letters, which are based on the book's author and title. All of this, called the book's call number, identifies where the book will be located. Figure 12-1 is an example of a Dewey decimal classification and an explanation of its abbreviations.

973.74 — Dewey decimal number for U.S. Civil War history

M138c

First letter of first word of title

Number based on author's last name

First letter of author's last name

Figure 12-1   *Example of a Dewey decimal classification.*

A second system of classifying books in the stacks is the Library of Congress system. It provides more categories than the Dewey decimal system does. These are the nineteen categories:

A   General works
B   Philosophy, psychology, religion
C–D   History and topography (except America)
E–F   History: North and South America
G   Geography and anthropology
H   Social sciences
J   Political science
K   Law
L   Education
M   Music
N   Fine arts
P   Language and literature
Q   Science
R   Medicine
S   Agriculture
T   Technology and engineering
U   Military science
V   Naval science
Z   Bibliography and library science

Often an additional letter next to the first further divides the topic. PL, for example, refers to the language and literature of East Asia and Africa. Figure 12-2 is an example of a Library of Congress classification; it explains what each abbreviation means.

If you are looking for a magazine or journal article, you will likely be searching in one of the periodical indexes in the reference or periodical section of your library. These guides are generally organized alphabetically around subjects. The information given in each entry is sometimes difficult to understand, because much information is squeezed into a small amount of space. Figure 12-3 is an excerpt from the *Readers' Guide to Periodical Literature*, the most widely used index. Notice how abbreviations are used to condense the information.

BF—— Library of Congress letters and numbers for psychology of knowledge

311.

G59—— Letter and number based on author's last name

1990—— Year of publication

Figure 12-2   *Example of a Library of Congress classification.*

Homeless as Authors

Voice for the homeless. B. Marshall.—Author

il | por The Progressive. 55:15 Ag '91

└Name of magazine Volume number Page number Date of magazine

└Abbreviations for "illustrated" and "portrait"

└Title of article

Figure 12-3   *Example of an entry in the* Readers' Guide to Periodical Literature.

Computers in Libraries

Today many large college libraries, perhaps even your own, have computerized their bibliographical information. The traditional card catalogs are drawers full of 3 × 5 cards listing the books and journals of the library, arranged alphabetically by subject, author, and book title. Computers can store the same information in much less space. A computerized index of the library's holdings is often referred to as an on-line catalog. You gain access to this information by using the keyboard and screens in the library. You find information on this terminal by searching for a subject, a title, or an author. Sometimes there is also a printer for your use, which allows you to quickly copy the bibliographical information you need.

What you will find in an on-line catalog is often the same information that you could find in a card catalog. In addition, the computer screen may tell you if the book has been checked out. The advantage to using the computer is that you get an up-to-date listing of all library purchases. Usually a new publication is added to the on-line catalog as soon as it is purchased. More and more libraries are now putting their catalogs on computer, so it is wise for you to learn how to operate one.

When to Use a Library

The library is a very important part of your college, and it will become even more important as you continue your education. Libraries are particularly helpful when you are writing a paper or a report. These assignments call for you to do research in books, magazines, and journals. You will be using all of the information you have learned in this chapter to complete a research paper. In fact, you may want to review this chapter when you begin a research project.

You also need to see your college library as a place to read and browse for pleasure. During those moments when school and work are not too hectic, it is often very relaxing to look through the rows of books or the periodical section. As you continue your education, you will likely find that libraries are special places for lifelong learning.

Summary

A college library is the campus's central location for the information you need to gather as a student. You will find materials in various sections of the library: reference, stacks, and periodicals. The materials are organized either by the Dewey decimal system or the Library of Congress system. This information is often indexed in a card catalog or on-line computer catalog. Libraries are indispensable for your college education as well as for your life-long development as a learner.

Summary Box   *The College Library*

What is it?	Why do you use it?
A central location for scholarly information: materials located in specific sections; books organized according to either the Dewey decimal system or the Library of Congress system and are indexed in a card catalog or an on-line computer catalog	To further your education To find resources for your college research To become a more independent learner To build a background for lifelong interests and pleasures

Skills Practice

Exercise 12.1
Using the Library to
Research a Topic

Choose a topic that interests you, go to the library, and complete the following activities. Your answers will be quite different from those of other students.

1. State your topic: _____

2. Go to the catalog system (either the card catalog or the on-line catalog) and locate five titles that would help you research this topic. Include the author and the title. Also be sure to include the Dewey decimal call number or the Library of Congress call number for each book.

a. _____

b. _____

c. _____

d. _____

e. _____

3. Go to the periodical indexes and locate five magazine, journal, or newspaper entries that you could use to research your topic. Include the author (if listed), the title, the name and date of the periodical, and any other bibliographical information that you find in your search.

a. _____

b. _____

c. _____

d. _____

e. _____

4. Now go to your reference librarian with these titles. Ask if there are any other library materials (such as pamphlets or audiovisual material) that you can use to research your topic even more. Summarize below what you learned from your discussion with the reference librarian:

Answers will vary.

13 The SQ3R Study System

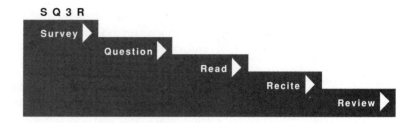

Now that you have practiced locating main ideas and major details and have used several note-taking techniques, you are ready to combine these skills when you study textbooks. SQ3R is a successful study system that gives you strategies for both reading and note-taking from your textbook.

The letters in "SQ3R" stand for survey, question, read, recite, review. Let's look at each of these steps.

Survey

In the survey step, you preview what you intend to read. Research has repeatedly shown that if you survey material before you read it, your comprehension significantly improves.

Surveying is not word-for-word reading; rather, it is selective. You read the titles and headings, note the graphics and other aids, and read the introduction or preface. Before you read, you also determine the length of the reading selection, estimate the time it will take you to read it, determine what material you are already familiar with, and predict whether the other material will be difficult or easy for you to understand. By following these steps, you establish a reading focus.

Surveying an Entire Textbook.   When you first get a textbook, you should briefly survey all the chapters. Consider the following suggestions:

1. Read the preface, which is introductory material written to the reader. The author gives reasons for writing the book, outlines the topics covered, and makes suggestions for using the book.

2. Look carefully at the table of contents, which comes after the preface. Some textbooks have two tables of contents: one short and the other

detailed. Study both of them carefully. See how the book is organized. Is the organization simple or complicated? Are there a few
divisions or several? If there are exercises, do the explanations come
before the exercises, or are all the exercises at the end of the book?
You will be using this textbook all semester, so you need to know the
answers to these questions.

3. See if there is an index, an alphabetical listing of topics found at the
   end of the textbook. Indexes are helpful when you want to find
   information fast. If your textbook has an index, familiarize yourself
   with it so you can use it as a study aid.

4. See if there is a glossary before the index. A glossary defines important terms that are used in the textbook. Instead of referring to a
   dictionary, you can use the glossary. Often students do not even
   realize that their textbook has a glossary.

5. In some math and science textbooks, students will find an appendix
   before the index. In the appendix are charts, graphs, and tables that
   you need for solving problems found in the textbook.

6. You may also discover an answer key in your textbook, often at the
   end. Occasionally you will find answer keys at the end of the exercises
   or at the ends of chapters. Some keys provide all the answers, others
   just some of them. This textbook, for example, gives answers only to
   odd-numbered exercises. In some math textbooks the author provides answers to the even- or odd-numbered problems.

7. Now you are ready to get a sense of the entire textbook. Read
   through parts of the beginning, middle, and end. Notice whether
   the author's style is formal or conversational. It's helpful to have some
   sense for the author's style before you begin reading a specific
   chapter.

Surveying a Chapter.   Consider the following suggestions in surveying a
specific chapter:

1. Study the title of the chapter. Having read the title, do you think you
   know anything about the subject? Has your instructor covered this
   topic in lecture? Or is this an entirely new topic for you? Answering
   these questions will give focus to your reading.

2. At the beginning of many textbook chapters you will find an outline
   or a list of objectives that the author intends to address. Because this
   is the significant information in the chapter, read it over carefully.
   Also, read the introductory paragraphs, which either summarize the
   chapter or introduce an interesting issue that the chapter will cover.

3. Most textbook writers divide chapters into divisions and subdivisions. The headings are usually in boldface print or italics. Thumb

through the chapter. If there are no divisions, read through the chapter's first paragraph, the first sentence of the following paragraphs, and the last paragraph of the chapter. This exercise will help you determine the outline of the chapter.

4. Study all illustrations, graphs, and charts in the chapter. See how this material relates to the chapter's divisions and subdivisions.

5. See if discussion or study questions come at the end of the chapter. By reading these questions beforehand, you will know what topics the author considers most important. Also, see if a bibliography is included at the end. A bibliography lists additional books that you may wish to consult after you have read the chapter.

This chapter survey should take you no more than three or four minutes, but it is time well spent. Having surveyed, you now have a better idea of what to look for in the chapter.

Question

Questions help you identify important information while you read. Sometimes you will make up a question before you read, then look for the answer. Other times you may have a study guide of questions provided by the teacher or printed at the end of the chapter so you can think about the questions before you read or read a chapter part to find the answer. Because you have learned to read for main ideas and supporting details, you may wish to make up your own questions by turning chapter headings into main-idea questions, then reading to determine the main idea and supporting details.

If you choose to make up your own questions, ask yourself about the following issues: What is the chapter topic, and how does the author respond to this topic? What are the major characteristics, steps, events, causes, or results that explain this topic? Are any terms defined?

Making up your own questions may be difficult at first. Start looking at words in boldface print and italics and at the first sentences of paragraphs. From this information make up your own questions. For example, if an economics chapter prints **deficit spending** in boldface, you could write "What is deficit spending?" Or if a consumer behavior chapter begins its first paragraph with "Husbands and wives influence each other's buying preferences," you could turn this statement into a question: "How do husbands and wives influence each other's buying preferences?" By the time you finish reading a textbook chapter, you may have written ten to fifteen questions and answered them.

Read

Only after surveying and questioning are you ready to read. Study reading is an active skill that uses all of the critical reading skills you have learned. Before you begin, arm yourself with your questions and a pen or felt-tip marker (hi-liter). Whenever you come across a main idea or a detail that supports this main idea, mark it by underlining or highlighting the words. But remember: *Do not underline too much*. In most cases, all you need to mark is the part of the sentence that contains the important or core information, material that answers the questions you have made up. If you overmark a page, you will become confused when you review for an exam. You won't know what to review, and you may end up reading over the entire page.

Here are ten tips for marking your textbooks:

1. Mark main ideas with a double line, curved line, hi-liter, or red end of a red and blue pencil. Mark only one main idea per paragraph, and just mark the key parts of this main idea. If the main ideas in a group of paragraphs are related, number them 1, 2, 3, and so on.

2. Mark major details with a single line, hi-liter, or the blue end of a red and blue pencil. Look for definitions, characteristics, examples, steps, causes, or effects. Try not to underline more than two details per paragraph, and mark only the key parts of these detail sentences. If you find that the details follow a pattern, number these details 1, 2, 3, and so on.

3. For very important statements, place an asterisk (*) in the margin next to where they appear. This asterisk will become your signal to study this important piece of information.

4. In some cases you may want to both mark the detail and note its type. If you do so, use the following abbreviations in the margins: "ex," "cause," "eff," "step," "char."

5. Circle the key parts of a definition if the author has not already highlighted it in boldface or italics. Remember the importance of definitions in learning a subject. Place the abbreviation "def" in the margin to direct you to the definition when you review your markings. You may also want to write the term on one side of a 3 × 5 card and its definition on the opposite side. If appropriate, you may want to include an example to help you remember the definition. At the end of the semester, you will have collected all of the important definitions for your course on these cards.

6. If a sentence is particularly difficult to understand even after re-reading it, place a question mark in the margin. When you review, you will be alerted to what you did not understand.

7. Write anywhere in the margins—top or bottom, left or right. But do not include too many written comments in the margins. Reserve this space for short summaries of important points, paraphrases of difficult sentences, and your inferences. For example, if you note that one main idea or supporting detail is more important than the others, you might want to write in the margin "Most important main idea" or "Most important supporting detail."

8. Do not begin marking your chapter right away, because once you have marked something, you will have a hard time erasing it. Read through several paragraphs first. Then go back to underline main ideas and supporting details. Often in rereading you can more easily pick out the important parts of a paragraph.

9. Be consistent with your markings. Use the system suggested above, or make up your own. Just be sure that you use the same underlining symbols and abbreviations throughout the textbook. Otherwise, when you review you will not be able to quickly separate main ideas from supporting details.

10. Think of textbook marking as active reading. Your markings should be the signals that you understand the form and content of the chapter. If you passively mark, you will not retain the important points made in the chapter.

Figure 13-1 is an example of a successfully marked textbook page. The above ten steps show how complex study reading really is.

Sometimes, even after marking your chapter, you will not completely understand what you have read. Almost everyone has to reread all or part of a textbook chapter sometime during the semester. If a chapter is difficult, you may want to put it aside after you have read it once and then reread it in a day or two. If you reread difficult material after it has "settled" for a while, you will often find the material more accessible.

Recite

After study reading and marking the important parts of a chapter, you are ready to write down what you have learned. In the recite step of the SQ3R method, you summarize what you have read. This step is critical because it shows you how much material you have understood and remembered.

When you begin this phase, read for a short time—approximately ten minutes. During this time, mark the passage and make marginal comments. Then close your textbook, and in the section of your notebook designated for this purpose, take notes on what you read. Use any note-taking format that you are comfortable with. Title and date each entry, as in the following example:

Less-Developed Countries, pp. 350–352   10/12/92

You may want to use the Cornell note-taking system when you recite. If you do, write the section title, pages, and date on the top line. To the right of the vertical line, summarize the main idea and supporting details of the section without looking back at the book. Leave spaces to make corrections and additions to your notes. Then look back at the chapter to see if you omitted anything important, and edit your notes

What is the size of military spending?

The Size and Consequences of Military Spending

Amazing figures

Total world military spending in 1983 amounted to more than $811 billion, about 6.1 percent of total world production (world GNP) for that year. The U.S. Arms Control and Disarmament Agency estimates that military spending in 1985 was close to $1 trillion. A look back at Table 21.1 will show you that these levels of spending are more than the combined GNPs of the poorest sixty-seven countries of the world—an indication of what could be done for them if the resources were not used for military spending.

World military spending in real terms (constant dollars) is more than twelve times as great as it was fifty years ago, and the character of the spending is shifting in favor of sophisticated weaponry and away from personnel. This shift is not helping employment in the countries that produce the hardware (mainly the United States, the Soviet Union, France, the United Kingdom, and West Germany) because the hardware is produced by skilled personnel working in high-technology firms. The main effect of the spending is therefore to draw skilled people who are already employed in nondefense industries into industries that produce military hardware.

Cause/effect of Military Spending on employment

One study in the United States estimated that a billion dollars spent on defense in 1975 would have created 76,000 jobs in defense industries, compared with 184,000 jobs in the fields of health and education. The study concluded that defense spending creates less employment than other forms of spending.

The Military-Industrial Complex   *What is the military-industrial complex?*

Def: Military, Industrial Complex

In his farewell address in 1961, President Dwight D. Eisenhower warned the country of the danger of a "military-industrial complex." By that phrase, the President meant that military spending could become so important in terms of employment, money, and votes that Congress would be obliged to vote for ever-increasing military budgets whether the nation needed them or not.

More amazing figures

Despite Eisenhower's warning, U.S. defense spending accounted for one-third of estimated total tax receipts for 1987. The military-industrial complex employs 30 percent of the nation's mathematicians and one of every four scientists and engineers, a development that helps explain America's failure to compete with other industrial nations in civilian markets.

When 10 percent of all jobs in the country depend on defense spending, politicians are pressured to vote for weapons systems whether or not they are considered effective. One example is the B-1 bomber program that, despite misgivings even in the Pentagon about the need for the plane or its effectiveness, now involves contractors in seventeen states producing B-1s at a minimum price of $1.25 billion each.

Military Spending by the LDCs   *How do LDCs affect military spending?*

In rich and poor countries alike, the opportunity costs of military spending can be measured by the loss of public projects aimed at improving health, education, and welfare. But in many LDCs, these costs can worsen a poverty level that is already intolerable.

Figure 13-1   *Textbook page marked during study reading. (Source: Philip C. Starr,* Economics: Principles in Action, *5th ed. [Belmont, Calif.: Wadsworth, 1988], p. 394.)*

as needed. Now you are ready to write the topic, such as "size of the American military," in the column to the left of the vertical. Under the topic, list key words that identify major supporting details, such as "1987 receipts," "number of mathematicians," and "number of scientists and engineers." These notes will be useful study tools for exams. You can fold your notes along the vertical line, read your statement of topic to the left of the vertical line, and attempt to explain it from memory. Reread and recite until your recall is good. You may also want to make study maps of the material. Look at how the Cornell system effectively summarizes material regarding military spending:

	Military Spending, pp. 394–396 *11/12/92*
great amount of military spending	1983: $811 billion in federal money 1985: $1 trillion
military spending's effect on employment	Military spending produces more skilled workers in military and fewer jobs outside of military
def. of <u>military-industrial complex</u>	Military and industrial leaders work together to receive more money for military projects
important employment figures	Military-industrial complex uses ⅓ of all mathematicians and ¼ of all scientists
expense of B-1	B-1 costs $1.25 <u>billion</u> each

In the beginning, your reciting notes may not be very difficult. You may have to review your textbook to see if your notes are both accurate and thorough. As the semester progresses, extend your study reading sessions from ten to fifteen minutes, then from fifteen to twenty. By the end of the semester, you should be able to study read for fifty minutes and accurately recite what you have read. Even the best students can do no more than one hour of concentrated reading of textbook material at one sitting.

With particularly difficult chapters, you may want to break up your reading into shorter sessions. You may even want to write out some short, specific goals. The following goals were set for reading an economics chapter:

1. Read for ten minutes, or complete two pages of the chapter on military spending.
2. Summarize these pages.
3. Break for five minutes.

4. Read for ten more minutes, recite, and take another five-minute break.
5. Complete at least fifty minutes of study reading in this chapter before doing something else.

Review

Review is the final step in the SQ3R method. You will study this step thoroughly in Chapters 15 and 16, which cover test-taking procedures. For now, just realize that reviewing is your insurance for remembering what you worked hard to learn. When you review, you study your lecture notes, reread your text markings, review your study reading notes, and study or design study maps for what you have read. You should then be able to predict the sorts of questions you will be asked on a test of this material. Write your predicted exam questions in your notebook.

You should not review the night before the exam. You need to review throughout the semester. You will retain more of the reading material if you edit and review your notes after every study reading session; you will also do a better job of taking class lecture notes and participating fruitfully in class discussions. Then review all your markings and your study reading notes one week before a major exam. Predict exam questions and create mnemonic devices (as explained in Chapter 14) for memorizing particularly difficult material. Cramming may help you pass the test, but it will not help you retain the material.

Summary

SQ3R is a study system for you to use when reading textbooks. The S stands for survey—taking a general look at your reading task. Q involves questioning—writing key questions whose answers will help you understand the reading. The first R is for read, where you mark up key points and make accurate inferences. In the second R, recite, you summarize what you have read; this step is critical because it tells you what you have learned. The last R stands for review; here, you go over your markings and notes to retain what you have learned.

SQ3R is a sensible study reading system. By using the SQ3R method, you approach your study reading in an orderly fashion: surveying, questioning, reading, reciting, and reviewing.

Summary Box   *SQ3R*

What is it?	*Why do you use it?*
Systematic approach to reading textbook material: S = survey, Q = question, R = read, R = recite, R = review	To understand textbook material To retain textbook material To take better notes in class To ask intelligent questions in class To participate in class discussion about the chapter To recall the material for exams

Skills Practice

In the following exercises, you will practice the SQ3R study system. Some of the exercises contain material that you are already familiar with from your work in Part Two.

Exercise 13.1
Underlining from
Textbook Excerpts

The following three excerpts are from textbooks in various fields. Your job is to read each excerpt. Then, in each paragraph, underline the main idea twice and one or two major details once. Be sure to mark only the important parts of the main ideas and major details. In completing number 2, you may want to review Exercise 7.6 on pp. 138–141.

1. Catching More Fish and Fish Farming

Fish are the major source of animal protein for more than one-half of the world's people, especially in Asia and Africa. Fish supply about 55 percent of the animal protein in Southeast Asia, 35 percent in Asia as a whole, 19 percent in Africa, about 25 percent worldwide—twice as much as eggs and three times as much as poultry—and 6 percent of all human protein consumption. Two-thirds of the annual fish catch is consumed by humans and one-third is processed into fish meal to be fed to livestock.

Between 1950 and 1970, the marine fish catch more than tripled—an increase greater than that occurring in any other human food source during the same period. To achieve large catches, modern fishing fleets use sonar, helicopters, aerial photography, and temperature measurement to locate schools of fish and lights and electrodes to attract them. Large, floating factory ships follow the fleets to process the catch.

Despite this technological sophistication, the steady rise in the marine fish catch halted abruptly in 1971. Between 1971 and 1976 the annual catch leveled off and rose only slightly between 1976 and 1983. A major factor in this leveling off was the sharp decline of the Peruvian anchovy catch, which once made up 20 percent of the global ocean harvest. A combination of overfishing and a shift in the cool, nutrient-rich currents off the coast of Peru were apparently the major factors causing this decline, which also threw tens of thousands of Peruvians out of work. Meanwhile, world population continued to grow, so between 1970 and 1983 the averge fish catch per person declined and is projected to decline even further back to the 1960 level by the year 2000.*

2. Types of Jazz

The 1920s saw the real emergence of jazz, which was given impetus in 1918 by Joe "King" Oliver's famous Creole Jazz Band in Chicago. Other

---

*G. Tyler Miller, Jr., *Living in the Environment*, 4th ed. (Belmont, Calif.: Wadsworth, 1985), p. 153. Used by permission.

musicians soon became prominent: Bix Beiderbecke, who started "white" jazz with his cornet and a band called the "Wolverines"; Paul Whiteman, whose band presented the first jazz concert in 1924, featuring the premiere of George Gershwin's *Rhapsody in Blue*; Bessie Smith, the famous blues singer; Fletcher Henderson and his band; and the notable Louis Armstrong. Through his trumpet playing and vocal renditions, Armstrong had much influence on the basic sound and style of jazz.

Dixieland

The prevailing style in the 1920s was *dixieland*. It is characterized by a strong upbeat, a meter of two beats to the measure, and certain tonal and stylistic qualities that are impossible to notate. It has a "busy" sound because there is simultaneous improvisation by perhaps four to seven players. The result is a type of "accidental" counterpoint that is held together only by the song's basic harmony and the musical instincts of the players. The presence of simultaneous improvisation in both African music and jazz can hardly be a coincidence. Dixieland style is often described is "hot"; it is rather fast and usually loud.

Boogie-Woogie

During the depression of the 1930s the hiring of bands became prohibitively expensive. So pianists enjoyed increasing popularity, especially as they developed a jazz piano style called *boogie-woogie*. It features a persistently repeated melodic figure — an ostinato — in the bass. Usually the boogie-woogie ostinato consists of eight notes per measure, which explains why this type of music is sometimes called "eight to the bar." Over the continuous bass the pianist plays trills, octave tremolos (the rapid alternation of pitches an octave apart), and other melodic figures.*

3. Matter: Types, States, Properties, and Changes

A lump of coal, an ice cube, a puddle of water, air — all are samples of matter. Matter is anything that occupies space and has mass. *Mass* is the quantity of matter in substance.

A substance or pure substance is one of millions of different types of matter found in the world. Any substance can be classified as either an element or a compound. An element is one of the 108 basic building blocks of all matter. Examples include iron, sodium, carbon, oxygen, and chlorine. Scientists have discovered 90 naturally occurring elements on Earth and have made small quantities of 18 others in the laboratory.

A compound is a form of matter in which two or more elements are held together in a fixed ratio by chemical bonds. Water, for example, is a combination of the elements hydrogen and oxygen, and sodium chlo-

---

*Charles R. Hoffer, *The Understanding of Music*, 6th ed. (Belmont, Calif.: Wadsworth, 1989), pp. 505–507.

Answers will vary. Find sample underlinings on pp. 348–350.

ride (the major ingredient in table salt) is a combination of the elements sodium and chlorine. About 5 million compounds of the 108 known elements have been identified, and about 6,000 new compounds are added to the list each week. With proper guidance, you could make a new compound yourself. At least 63,000 compounds are combined in the food we eat, the air we breathe, the water we drink, and the countless products we use.*

Exercise 13.2
More Underlining
from Textbook
Excerpts

The following are three more excerpts from textbooks in different fields. Again, underline main ideas twice and major details once, and mark only the important parts.

1. Early Primate Evolution

The evolutionary history of the primates is not clear-cut, with one form gradually replacing another. Fossils have not yet been recovered for a few critical time periods. Moreover, there are periods in which closely related forms coexisted for some time, with some destined to leave descendant populations and others to become evolutionary dead-ends. What we will be describing, then, are some of the known branches on a very "bushy" evolutionary tree.

The oldest known primate fossils date from the Paleocene (65 million to 54 million years ago). Again, they were morphologically similar to existing tree shrews, with a relatively small brain and a long snout. Although many of those forms died out, some left descendants that evolved into the true prosimian forms of the Eocene (54 to 38 million years ago).

The Eocene climate was somewhat warmer than the Paleocene, and tropical rain forests flourished — as did the early prosimians. These primates were characterized by an increased brain size, an increased emphasis on vision over smell, and more refined grasping abilities. This was the time of divergences that led, eventually, to the modern-day lemurs, lorises, and tarsiers. It was also the time of divergences that led to the first anthropoids.[†]

2. Humans in Nature: Hunter-Gatherers

Early humans survived without claws, fangs, or great speed. That they did so, and multiplied, is due to three major cultural adaptations — all the product of intelligence: (1) the use of *tools* for hunting, collecting, and preparing food and making protective clothing, (2) learning to live in an often hostile environment through effective *social organization* and *cooperation* with other human beings, and (3) the use of *language* to increase the efficiency of cooperation and to pass on knowledge of previous survival experiences.

---

*G. Tyler Miller, Jr., *Chemistry: A Basic Introduction*, 4th ed. (Belmont, Calif.: Wadsworth, 1987), p. 2. Used by permission.
[†]Cecie Starr and Ralph Taggart, *Biology: The Unity and Diversity of Life*, 4th ed. (Belmont, Calif.: Wadsworth, 1987), pp. 644–645. Used by permission.

Our early hunter-gatherer ancestors cooperated by living in small bands or tribes, clusters of several families typically consisting of no more than 50 persons. The size of each band was limited by the availability of food. If a group got too large it split up. Sometimes these widely scattered bands had no permanent base, traveling around their territory to find the plants and animals they needed to exist. Hunter-gatherers' material possessions consisted mostly of simple tools such as sharpened sticks, scrapers, and crude hunting weapons. Much of their knowledge could be described as ecological—how to find water in a barren desert and how to locate plant and animal species useful as food. Studies of Bushmen, Pygmies, and other hunter-gatherer cultures that exist today have shown the uncertainty of success in hunting wild game; thus often most of the food of primitive people was provided by women, who collected plants, fruits, eggs, mollusks, reptiles, and insects.

Many people tend to believe that hunger-gatherers spent most of their time in a "tooth and claw" struggle to stay alive. But research among hunter-gatherer societies in remote parts of the world cast doubt on this idea. These "primitive" people may hunt for a week and then spend a month on vacation. They have no bosses, suffer from less stress and anxiety than most "modern" people, and have a diet richer and more diverse than that of almost everyone else in the world today, rich and poor alike.*

3. Cultural Continuity and Discontinuity

Ruth Benedict (1938) characterized American culture as containing major discontinuities between what is expected of children and what is expected of adults. Children in our culture are not expected to be responsible; they are supposed to play, not work. Few children in America have the opportunity to contribute in any meaningful way to the basic tasks of society. Children take on responsibility only when they become adults. A second major discontinuity is that children are required to be submissive, but adults are expected to be dominant. This is especially true for males. Sons must obey their fathers, but as fathers they must dominate their sons. A third major discontinuity has to do with sex. As children, Americans are not allowed to engage in sexual behavior, and for many people, just the thought of childhood sexuality is repellent. As adults, however, especially as men and women marry, sex is considered to be a normal, even valued, activity.

In great contrast to the discontinuities experienced by the individual learning to participate in American culture is the continuity of socialization among many native American societies. The Cheyenne, a Plains Indian tribe, exhibit a great degree of continuity in their culture. Cheyenne children are not treated as a different order of people from adults. They are regarded as smaller and not yet fully competent adults, although by American standards the competence of Cheyenne children is quite astounding. The play of small children centers on imitation of, and real participation in, adult tasks. Both boys and girls learn to ride

---

*Miller, *Living in the Environment*, p. E2. Used by permission.

horses almost as soon as they can walk. This skill is related to the importance of the horse in traditional Cheyenne culture, in which buffalo were hunted on horseback. By the time they are six, little boys are riding bareback and using the lasso. By eight, boys are helping to herd the horses in the camp. As soon as they can use them, boys get small but good-quality bows and arrows. Little girls who are just toddlers help their mothers carry wood and water. Boys and girls learn these activities in play, in which the routine of family life is imitated. Girls play "mother" to the smallest children; boys imitate the male roles of hunter and warrior and even the rituals of self-torture that are part of Cheyenne religious ceremonies.

Control of aggression is an important value among the Cheyenne, and aggression rarely occurs within the group of adults. A chief rules not by force and dominance but by intelligence, justice, and consideration for others. The needs of the group are more important than the needs of the individual. The Cheynne learn this lesson at an early age. Infants who cry are not physically punished, but they will be removed from the camp and their baskets hung in the bushes until they stop. This is an early lesson in learning that one cannot force one's will on others by self-display. Aggression and lack of control of one's emotions do not bring rewards for either children or adults; rather, they result in social isolation.*

> Answers will vary. Ask instructor for sample underlinings.

Exercise 13.3
Using the SQ3R
System on a Textbook
Excerpt

In this exercise, you will be reading a longer textbook excerpt, continuing the reading of economics material that you began in Chapter 4. You will be asked to survey, make up questions, read, recite, and review. When you have completed these five steps, you will be asked to answer some questions that show how well you understood the excerpt.

A. Survey. Give yourself one minute to survey the following excerpt, noting (1) the title and subtitles and (2) words in italics and boldface type. If you have extra time, begin reading the first paragraph or two. When your time is up, answer the questions that follow without looking back.

Poverty in the Developing Countries

(1) This section is about poverty among nations. Poverty is, of course, a relative matter. Whenever there is any inequality in the distribution of income, some people will always be poor relative to others. But much of the world is so abjectly poor that some observers speak of *absolute* poverty, a condition of life so destitute that its victims are chronically on the verge of death.

(2) Almost 1 billion people—one-quarter of the world's population—are in this category. A quarter of a million people in Calcutta are homeless. They eat, live, and die in the streets. Three million people in

*Serena Nanda, *Cultural Anthropology*, 3rd ed. (Belmont, Calif.: Wadsworth, 1987), pp. 131, 134. Used by permission.

Bolivia (out of a total population of five million) have a life expectancy of thirty years. The average Bolivian eats less than half an ounce of meat per year; in effect, the peasant population is too poor to eat any meat at all.

What Is a "Less Developed" Country?

(3) Several phrases are used to describe countries that are poorer than others: underdeveloped countries, third world countries, sometimes even fourth or fifth world countries. Economists have no specific criteria or explicit definitions of such terms. A nation's position is usually determined by dividing its GNP by population (per capita GNP) so that there is a ladder of countries from rich to poor—from $21,920 per person per year in the United Arab Emirates to $110 per person per year in Ethiopia in 1984.

(4) Usually, all countries are classified as either "more developed" or "less developed." The World Bank in its *Development Report for 1986* uses six subcategories of less developed countries, which we will overlook for the sake of brevity. Instead, we will use just the two categories "more developed" and "less developed" and set the dividing line at $1,000 per person per year, although such a division is arbitrary and often unrevealing. We know that GNP says little about the quality of life. Moreover, a per capita GNP figure conceals the distribution of income within a nation. For example, per capita GNP in Brazil was about $2,000 a year in 1984, but 30 million of Brazil's 133 million people had average annual incomes of $77. Because this section is about the less developed countries, we will use a common abbreviation, LDCs, to indicate that group of about 90 of the 170-odd countries of the world.

The Trouble with Comparing Per Capita GNPs

(5) When we use per capita GNPs to compare countries, we find ourselves trapped by numbers that offer little help in describing real differences in standards of living. Not only is GNP an imperfect measure of welfare or progress *within* a country, it has even less meaning when used for comparisons among countries. Two examples will clarify this point.

(6) In a poor, less developed country (LDC) like Tanzania, with a per capita GNP of $210 per year, the $210 figure is imperfect because it is based primarily on cash transactions. But much of Tanzania's production and consumption typically involves little or no cash. The people in Tanzania's villages feed themselves out of their own production. Therefore, in most cases, per capita GNP figures in poor countries understate their true incomes. Of course, that doesn't mean such people are rich. We could double the numbers, and these people would still be abjectly poor by any standard.

(7) In another example, let's look at the comparative lifestyles of Americans and New Zealanders. In the fall of 1978, New Zealand's per capita GNP was about half that of the United States. But it would be very foolish to conclude that New Zealanders' standard of living was half that of the average American. Fresh food prices were generally half

of U.S. prices, so that with much lower wages, the New Zealanders ate just as well as or better than Americans. Housing costs (rents and home purchase prices) were also about half of ours. Education, medical care, and retirement pensions were all provided from a highly progressive schedule of income taxes. In one specific case, a highly skilled New Zealander construction worker retired from his job at age 60. At the time of retirement, he earned $3.80 per hour—by our standards an abysmally low wage after a lifetime of work. Nevertheless, he owned a home and automobile free and clear, had $50,000 in the bank, and began receiving a pension of 80 percent of his highest earnings. He and his wife were comfortable and content, traveled overseas occasionally, and had no financial worries. However, New Zealanders also have to contend with the high prices of imported products like automobiles.

(8) So how does one evaluate these differences in lifestyles? Can one say that Americans are better off than New Zealanders or vice versa? The question is impossible to answer. Nevertheless, the GNP per capita method of comparison among different countries is the method most commonly used.

(9) In one attempt to improve on the GNP per capita measure, economists devised an index called the **Physical Quality of Life Index (PQLI)**. The PQLI is a composite of a nation's life expectancy, infant mortality, and literacy. The index is 97 for Sweden, 94 for the United States, 35 for Bangladesh. The index reveals the weaknesses of looking only at GNP per capita: GNP per capita in Saudi Arabia is a healthy $10,530 (1984), but its PQLI is only 28.

(10) In this section we review the plight of the LDCs, including the distribution of the world's income, the reasons why the more developed countries (particularly the United States) should be concerned about world poverty, the two major problems of population increase and lack of capital, and some conclusions.*

1. The chapter excerpt has no charts and graphs.

   a. true
   b. false

2. The excerpt does not use italics for emphasis.

   a. true
   b. false

3. The excerpt makes use of boldface print.

   a. true
   b. false

---

*Philip C. Starr, *Economics: Principles in Action*, 5th ed. (Belmont, Calif.: Wadsworth, 1988), pp. 383–385.

1. _____

2. _____

3. _____

4. _____

5. _____

_____
80%

(score = # correct × 20)
Find answers on p. 350.

4. The subtopic "What Is a 'Less Developed' Country?" will likely

    a. define this term
    b. discuss poverty in the United States
    c. discuss the average wages in Europe
    d. discuss the quality of life in North America

5. The title suggests that this chapter will mainly concern itself with

    a. the wealthy countries of the world
    b. the industrialized countries of the world
    c. the poorer countries of the world
    d. overpopulation

B. Question. Now go back to the excerpt, and from the title, subtitles, and terms in boldface print, write four questions that this excerpt appears to address. You will answer these questions as you read the chapter.

1. _____

2. _____

Answers will vary. Find sample outline on p. 350.

3. _____

4. _____

C. Read and Recite. Begin study reading to the end of paragraph 4, underlining main ideas and major details and making marginal comments. Keep your four questions in mind. Then close the book and recite using the indenting format. Finally, apply the Cornell note-taking system to your notes and study the material.

      Now study the rest of the excerpt, and follow the same procedures as those you used to read and recite in the first half of the excerpt.

Answers will vary. Find sample answers on p. 351.

Now look back at your outlines. From them, make up a study map that ties all of the information together.

D. Review. Now study your underlinings, outline, and study map. When you think you have learned the most important points of the excerpt, answer the following questions without looking back.

Examination: Poverty in the Developing Countries

Directions: Choose the letter that correctly answers the following ten questions. Place all of your answers in the answer box.

1. How many people in the world are in absolute poverty?

   a. 4 billion
   b. 3 billion
   c. 2 billion
   d. 1 billion

2. Absolute poverty means that the people

   a. are often sick due to lack of food
   b. sometimes have no food to eat
   c. are on the verge of death from starvation
   d. die from starvation within a year

3. The poorest country in the world by economic standards is

   a. Ethiopia
   b. Bolivia
   c. India
   d. Iraq

4. Which term is *not* used to divide up countries according to poverty?

   a. more developed
   b. mildly developed
   c. less developed
   d. none of these

5. LDCs make up

   a. one-fourth of the world
   b. one-third of the world

c. one-half of the world
d. over half of the world

6. The excerpt suggests that "GNP" is an accurate and informative term.

a. true
b. false

7. The excerpt suggests that Americans are

a. clearly better off economically than people in other countries
b. not better off economically than people in other countries
c. not easily described by the economic terms "GNP" and "per capita"
d. as well off economically as the Japanese

8. "PQLI" stands for:

a. Poor Quality of Life Index
b. Physical Quality of Life Index
c. Population Quality and Life's Illnesses
d. none of these

9. The PQLI considers *all* of the following factors except

a. life expectancy
b. unemployment
c. infant mortality
d. literacy

10. The excerpt ends by suggesting that the United States should

a. not be concerned about world poverty
b. be concerned about world poverty
c. give economic aid in the form of food to the ten poorest countries
d. devise a new system for describing LDCs

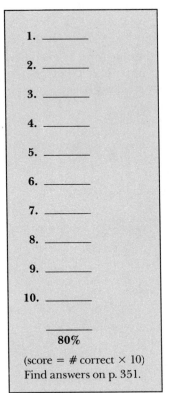

1. _____
2. _____
3. _____
4. _____
5. _____
6. _____
7. _____
8. _____
9. _____
10. _____

_____
80%
(score = # correct × 10)

Find answers on p. 351.

Exercise 13.4
Writing a Paragraph
Using SQ3R

Once again review your textbook markings, study notes, and study map for the textbook excerpt in Exercise 13.3. When you can remember the important points in the excerpt, close your books and notes and answer the following essay question.

Essay question: In an organized paragraph, define "absolute poverty" and "LDCs." Then provide two examples of why it is hard to determine the poverty level of a particular country.

Use the following outline to list the important points that you want to make in your paragraph.

Definitions:

absolute poverty: _____

LDCs:_____

I. Examples of Difficulty in Determining Poverty Levels of a Country

A. _____

B. _____

80%

Ask instructor for answers.

14 Mnemonic Strategies

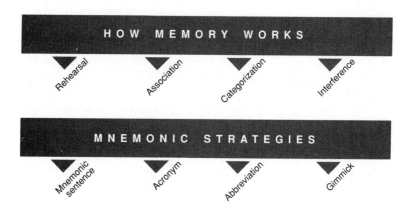

A good memory is a key to learning. Knowing how memory is stored in the brain will give you a better understanding of how to become a more successful student. Also, in understanding how memory works, you can see how memory aids, called *mnemonic strategies*, help you learn.

How Does Memory Work?

The study of the brain and learning, called cognitive psychology, is new. All that students in this field have to work with at this time are theories, at best.

Cognitive psychologists are now suggesting that there are two kinds of memory: short-term and long-term. Everything you learn begins in short-term memory; you read or listen to something, and it enters short-term memory. Almost everything that goes into short-term memory is quickly forgotten, because forgetting is much easier for the brain than remembering. When something stays with you, it has entered long-term memory.

The best way to put information into long-term memory is through *rehearsal*. Rehearsal involves practice; with study material, that would involve rereading, discussing, summarizing, or paraphrasing. When you rehearse information, the brain records it, somewhat as a computer records bits of information on tape or chips. When you learn, the brain records the information with a physical mark on the cerebrum (the learning part of the brain). These marks are called *neural traces*, or memory grooves. Well-rehearsed information creates well-defined neural traces. If you learn something improperly, the neural trace will not be well defined, and it will likely return to short-term memory and be forgotten. Study Figure 14-1 to see how the brain remembers.

How do you keep information in long-term memory? To remember, you should (1) study for short periods, (2) take short rest periods between study periods, (3) review what you have learned, and (4) study different subjects in succession.

Studying for short intervals (twenty-five to fifty minutes) has several advantages. First, realize that the brain forgets more than it remembers; so if you take in less information, you have a better chance of remembering it. Remember, though, that these study periods must be concentrated. You need to reread and recite what you have read. This concentrated reading is what you have learned to do in the SQ3R system.

Another characteristic of the brain is that it tends to rehearse what you have learned even after you have stopped studying. You are unaware of this rehearsal. When you read for a certain length of time, you need to take a relaxing break. Even if the break has nothing to do with what you have studied, your brain will still be rehearsing this new material. Like food being digested, new information needs to sit in the brain awhile before it can enter long-term memory. Remember, though, that you need to carefully schedule your study breaks. Reading for twenty minutes and then taking a three-hour break will not train your brain to remember. If you plan to study in three intervals at night, for example, your breaks should be no more than twenty minutes long.

A third fact to know about the brain is that it tends to forget more during the first twenty-four hours than at any other time. Since you tend to forget more at first, make a point of reviewing what you have learned soon after you have read your textbook or listened to a lecture. What you review today will have a better chance of staying in long-term memory.

A final characteristic of memory is that the brain tends to forget if it is processing similar bits of information. This mental process is known

How the Brain Remembers

Figure 14-1   *How the brain remembers.*

as *interference*. The brain seems to take in more if two chunks of information are different. So it is wiser to study for two dissimilar courses than two similar courses in succession. For example, you will remember more of your psychology chapter if you do some chemistry problems afterward than if you were to follow your psychology reading with reading a chapter of sociology.

Memory Tips

From this very general introduction to learning theory, you can design certain successful learning strategies. Consider the following learning hints:

1. Something learned well the first time is not easily forgotten. Study new information slowly and carefully, asking questions as you go along.

2. Relate new information to several contexts. Putting information into proper context is called *association*. The more contexts that you place information in, the more likely you are to remember this new material. If you are learning the meaning of "ostentatious," for example, it is best for you to learn both its dictionary meaning as well as its synonyms; its history, or etymology; and words related to it, such as "ostensibly," "ostentation," and "ostentatiousness." With each new context that you place the word in, you are creating more memory grooves, all of which are associated with "ostentatious."

   Similarly, the more you read in several fields, the more contexts you make, and the easier it will be for you to attach new information to them. Many composition theorists and language experts are now saying that students learn to speak and write better if they read widely. Creating several contexts seems to be central to successful learning.

3. Organize any information that you read or study into patterns, often into main ideas and major details. Organizing information into recognizable patterns is known as *categorization*. When students categorize information, they have a better chance of keeping it in long-term memory. Even if information seems disorganized, try to find an order; most information is built upon patterns.

4. Reviewing is another important way to remember. Psychological studies have shown that if you have once learned something and have forgotten it, you will have an easier time relearning it. Spaced review helps keep information in long-term memory. Don't leave your reviewing of notes and textbook markings until the night before an exam.

5. On a few occasions, you will be asked to learn a particular sequence or list that has no pattern, such as the colors in the light spectrum or the planets in the solar system. When this happens, use one of the following four mnemonic strategies: a mnemonic sentence, an acronym, an abbreviation, a visualization, or a gimmick.

Mnemonic Sentences. Your biology instructor may want you to remember the order of classifications in the animal kingdom. There is no logic to this nomenclature, so you might want to create a mnemonic sentence that will help you recall each term. Your job is to remember the following divisions in the animal kingdom and their proper sequence: kingdom, phylum, class, order, family, genus, and species. You note that the beginning letters for the classifications are K, P, C, O, F, G, S. Thus, to remember each term, think of a seven-word sentence whose words begin with the seven letters in the biology classifications. You might think of something like: "King Paul called out for Gus and Sam." This sentence will likely stay with you during an exam, when you need to recall this classification sequence.

Acronyms. You use an acronym to abbreviate a phrase. *Acronyms* are made up of the first letter of each word of the phrase; these letters make a word or a new word. NATO, for example, stands for North Atlantic Treaty Organization, and its initial letters can be pronounced as a word. You can make up your own acronyms when you cannot use categorization to remember a particular chunk of information. For example, if you cannot remember the parts of an atom, you can create the acronym PEN to stand for "proton," "electron," and "neutron."

Abbreviations. You can use abbreviations in a similar fashion. *Abbreviations* are made up of the first letter of each word in a phrase. Unlike acronyms, these abbreviations do not spell out a word. MVM could be your abbreviation for remembering the three planets besides Earth that are closest to the Sun: Mercury, Venus, and Mars.

Visualizations. Another successful memory aid is called a *visualization*. In a visualization, you attach what you need to learn to something visual. You have already learned something about visualizing when you studied the spatial-geographic pattern (see Chapter 5). Here, you learned that in biology and geography courses it is helpful to see how one part of an organism or location relates to another.

Visualizing can also prove helpful in learning unrelated pieces of information; you create a picture that incorporates the information into it. For example, if you cannot remember that lapis lazuli is a semiprecious stone, you may want to invent a scene in which a queen has a beautiful stone in her lap. Note the pun on the word "lap." This scene with the jewel on the queen's lap should help you recall the first part of the word and the fact that this stone is precious, worn by queens. You should use such an elaborate visual strategy, though, only when association and categorization have failed to make the proper learning connections for you.

Gimmicks. Gimmicks can also be used to trigger your memory when the conventional learning strategies have failed. *Gimmicks* are simply word games or tricks to help you remember; they are often used in learning to spell difficult words. If you have difficulty spelling "conscience," for example, you might remember its spelling if you learned the slogan "There is a *science* to spelling the word *conscience*." Similarly, if you cannot remember that the noun "principal" refers to a person, you could think of your principal as your *pal*. By remembering "pal," you will no longer confuse *principal*, the person, with *principle*, the rule or belief. Instructors will often teach you these spelling gimmicks, but you may be imaginative enough to make up your own.

Summary

The brain has two storage capacities: short-term and long-term memory. As a student, it is your goal to transfer as much information as possible to long-term memory. You can place more information into long-term memory by studying in short, concentrated periods, by taking spaced study breaks, and by regularly reviewing what you have studied. You will also remember more if you relate what you have learned to several contexts (association). By studying the same material in lecture, in your textbook, and in your study notes, you begin to see it from several perspectives. Categorization is another key learning principle; whenever possible, try to divide information into general and specific categories.

When information has no particular pattern, you may want to use verbal and visual gimmicks to learn it. Generally, though, the most effective way to learn new material is to learn it right the first time — by putting it into logical categories and associating it to what you already know about it.

Summary Box   *Memory Aids*

What are they?	Why do you use them?
Study techniques that help place information into long-term memory Three basic learning principles: rehearsal, association, and categorization Some of the more successful learning gimmicks: mnemonic sentences, acronyms, abbreviations, visualizations, and spelling gimmicks	To help you retain information and easily recall it for examinations

Skills Practice

*Exercise 14.1
Applying Memory
Aids to Study
Material*

Your job is to use a memory aid to learn the following ten pieces of information. Your answers, of course, will vary from those of other students.

1. Think of a gimmick to help you remember the difference in spelling and meaning between *stationery* (writing paper) and *stationary* (not moving).

2. Think of a gimmick that will help you remember the difference in spelling and meaning between *allusion* (reference) and *illusion* (unreal image).

3. Think of a gimmick that will help you remember the difference in meaning between *among* (used in comparing three or more) and *between* (used in comparing no more than two).

4. Think of a gimmick that will help you remember the difference in spelling and meaning between *capital* (meaning chief, or principal) and *capitol* (meaning a building that is the seat of government).

5. Think of a visualization that will help you remember that Nimrod was a mighty hunter referred to in the Bible. Describe the scene in a sentence or two.

6. Think of an acronym that will help you remember the colors of the light spectrum: red, orange, yellow, green, blue, indigo, and violet. Remember that an acronym is a word that is made up of the first letter of each word in the series you want to learn.

7. Think of a mnemonic sentence that will help you remember the first five presidents of the United States: Washington, Adams, Jefferson, Madison, and Monroe.

8. Think of an abbreviation that will help you recall the three most populous cities in the world: Mexico City, Tokyo, and Moscow.

9. Imagine that you need to remember for your anthropology class the three different kinds of societies: egalitarian, rank, and stratified. Think of an abbreviation to help you recall these three types of societies.

10. Assume that you have to learn the meaning of *zealous* (eager or passionate). Use the learning theory of association to help you recall the meaning and uses of *zealous*. Add prefixes and suffixes to this word.

Answers will vary. Find sample answers on pp. 353–354.

Exercise 14.2
Self-Evaluation:
Applying Memory
Tips and Theory to
Your Studies

The following nine questions will test the learning theories that you learned in the introduction. Answer these questions as they pertain to your studies. It would be helpful to share your answers with other students and your instructor; there are no right or wrong answers.

1. To test the theory of interference, study back to back for courses that are similar in content. What problems do you find?

2. To test the theory of interference, study back to back for courses that are different in content. What happens? Do you learn more easily?

3. To test the theory of rehearsal, read for thirty to fifty minutes, but do nothing else. Do not take notes, do not discuss the material, and do not review. Then take a ten-minute break. After the break, recite what you remember. Is your summary complete? What information did you miss?

4. To again test the theory of rehearsal, read for thirty to fifty minutes, but this time take notes, discuss, and review. Then take a ten-minute break. Finally, recite what you remember. Is your summary complete? Is it better than the summary in question 3?

5. To test your rehearsing skills, go over the study notes, lecture notes, text markings, and study maps for one of your classes. See which rehearsal techniques you find most helpful. In a sentence or two, discuss how the following rehearsal techniques helped you remember the material:

   a. underlining: _____

   _____

   b. making marginal notes: _____

   _____

   c. summarizing: _____

   _____

   d. paraphrasing: _____

   _____

   e. making study maps: _____

   _____

   f. reviewing your textbook underlinings and notes: _____

   _____

g. reviewing your study maps: _____

_____

h. other techniques: _____

_____

6. Of the courses you are taking, choose one that requires you to memorize. Make up an acronym to help you remember a chunk of information.

7. Of the courses you are taking, choose one that requires you to memorize certain material. Make up an abbreviation or mnemonic sentence to help you learn this material.

8. Choose a course you are taking that has a difficult word you need to learn. Think of a gimmick that will help you remember either its spelling or its meaning.

9. Find another word for the course that you used for question 8. Create a visualization that will help you remember the meaning of that word.

Answers will vary. Ask instructor for sample answers.

15 Strategies for Objective Tests

So far you have learned to read your textbook critically, take notes from your textbook and from lectures, and use mnemonic strategies when you cannot remember information. You use all of these skills when you prepare for an exam. In most courses, how well you do on exams determines how well you do in the course.

You will be taking two kinds of exams: objective and essay. Each type of exam requires a different strategy. This chapter looks at objective tests.

What Are Objective Tests?

For objective tests, you often need to have learned many details and understood the basic concepts. You will have little or no writing to do, because objective exams are often machine-scored. Thus you are usually required to mark the correct response from two to five choices on the answer sheet. Objective tests are often in three formats: multiple-choice, true-false, and matching. You will study each type later.

How to Prepare for Objective Tests

If your economics instructor announces that you will be taking a 100-question multiple-choice exam the following week, how should you study for it? Cramming the night before, of course, goes against the principle of learning effectively through spaced intervals. Preparing for a 100-question exam should take you three to five days.

In this period, you should first review your textbook markings. You should be looking for highlighted main ideas and supporting details Then read your marginal comments, which often give insights not stated in the textbook. If you come upon any new insights or want to underline additional information, do so at this time.

Third, review your study reading notes. These notes will likely repeat much of what you studied in your textbook, but reading the same information from a new perspective will provide an additional context for you to remember the material. Fourth, review your lecture notes, underlining key points and making marginal comments as you did in your textbook. Study especially carefully those parts of your notes that are not mentioned in your textbook.

As you study your lecture and study notes, you will come across definitions that you need to remember. Put these terms on 3 × 5 cards, with the term on the blank side of the card and the definition on the lined side. The night before the exam, study these cards carefully. Divide your cards into two piles as you study—those terms that you know and those that you don't. By the end of the night, you need to have all of your cards in the "I know" pile. Your cards should look like the one shown in Figure 15-1, which defines "net national product."* Some students prefer to write these definitions on a sheet of paper, with the term on the left side of the page and the definition to the right, as in the following list of economic terms:

Term	*Explanation*
net national product (NNP)	gross national product without depreciation
gross national product (GNP)	sum of government purchases, consumption, investments, and exports
national income (NI)	net national product without indirect business taxes

The only problem with such a study sheet is that you cannot prove you have learned the term, as you can with the cards. On your sheet, you cannot separate the "I knows" from the "don't knows."

Along with note cards and study sheets, you should also design study maps. Look at how the study map in Figure 15-2 relates the same economic terms. The visual nature of study maps may help you remember these terms more easily.

Finally, you should carefully read any instructor handouts. These handouts often present important material, and your instructor may

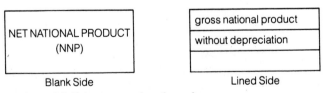

Blank Side   Lined Side

Figure 15-1   *Study card defining* net national product.

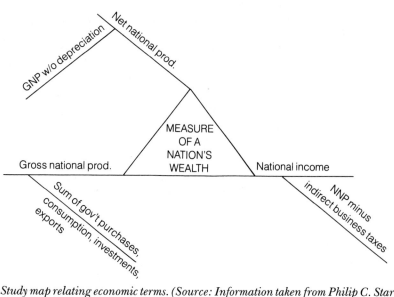

Figure 15-2 *Study map relating economic terms. (Source: Information taken from Philip C. Starr, Economics: Principles in Action, 2nd ed. [Belmont, Calif.: Wadsworth, 1978], pp. 174–175.)*

even design questions from them. Also, if your instructor has provided you with a syllabus, you may want to review the titles of each class meeting to see how the topics relate to one another. If the syllabus does not have titles, review the titles that you have given each lecture.

The night before the exam, concentrate on concepts; do not cram for details the night before the exam.

How to Answer Multiple-Choice Questions

Multiple-choice questions are the most commonly used objective questions. In the multiple-choice format, a question or statement is posed; this section is called the *stem*. Three to five choices follow, which either answer the question or complete the statement. It is up to you to eliminate the incorrect choices and find the correct one. Look at the following multiple-choice example on Sigmund Freud:

stem 1. According to Freud, the three parts of human consciousness are

choices
a. the ego, the id, and the libido
b. the id, the alterego, and the ego
c. the id, the ego, and the superego
d. the child, the adult, and the parent

If you know something about Freudian psychology, you know that the correct answer is c. You either write c on your answer sheet or darken c on your answer grid.

Hints on Taking Multiple-Choice Exams

1. Read the stem and each choice as if it were a separate true-false statement. In the previous example, you would have read "According to Freud, the three parts of the human consciousness are the ego, the id, and the libido." Then determine whether this statement is true or false.

2. If you determine the statement to be false, draw a line through it (if your instructor allows you to mark on the exam), as in the following:

   1. According to Freud, the three parts of the human consciousness are
      a. ~~the ego, the id, and the libido~~

   By crossing out, you eliminate choices. You also save yourself time by preventing your eyes from returning to incorrect choices.

3. Continue to eliminate incorrect choices until you find the correct answer. In some difficult questions, two choices may appear correct to you. If this happens, reread the stem to pick up any shades of meaning in the words; then reconsider the two choices. Look at the following question on short-term memory, from which two choices have already been eliminated:

   2. The best example of the use of short-term memory is
      a. reciting key points in reading material
      b. repeating a phone number just told to you
      c. ~~understanding what categorization means and using this information on an essay exam~~
      d. ~~remembering the name of a friend whom you have not seen for eight years~~

   You can eliminate c and d, because both are examples of information that has been in long-term memory for a long time. Both a and b, however, refer to recently learned information. In rereading the stem, note that the question is asking for the *best* example of short-term memory. Reciting helps put information into long-term memory, so b is the best answer. You need to use your best skills in logic and critical reading when you come upon two choices that both seem correct.

4. Question choices that include absolute terms of qualification, such as "always," "never," and "only." Choices using these terms are frequently incorrect because they need to be true in every case, and few statements are always true. Look at the following question on categorization:

   3. Which statement best describes categorization?

   a. Categorization and association are never both used to learn new information.
   b. Categorization is always used to learn disorganized information.
   c. Categorization is an unsuccessful learning technique.
   d. Categorization is an effective learning technique used by students in several disciplines to learn new material.

You would be correct in omitting both a and b as correct answers, because the qualifiers "never" and "always" insist that these statements be true in every case. If you can think of one exception for each choice, you can eliminate that choice. You are then left with c and d. Knowing that categorization is a basic learning principle, you would choose d as the correct answer.

5. Look for choices that give complete information. Although incomplete answers may not be false, they do not qualify as acceptable choices. Study this question on rehearsal:

   4. Which statement gives the best definition of rehearsal?

      a. Rehearsal is a learning process involving rereading.
      b. Rehearsal is a learning process involving rewriting.
      c. Rehearsal is a learning process that helps put information into long-term memory.
      d. Rehearsal is a learning process that may use all of the senses to place information into long-term memory.

Although choices a, b, and c are all partially correct, choice d is like the main idea for the three preceding choices, so it is the best choice.

6. Read carefully for the terms "not," "except," and "but" in the stem. These words completely change the meaning of the question. If you skip over these terms, you may know the answer yet still choose incorrectly. Consider the following question on rehearsal:

   5. As a learning process, rehearsal includes all of the following activities except

      a. rereading
      b. reciting
      c. discussing
      d. reading

Note how the word "except" reverses the question, asking you to choose the activity that does not involve rehearsal. Choice d is that activity. If you had overlooked "except," you could have chosen a, b, or c — all acceptable rehearsal activities.

7. Be careful to read all of the choices, especially those that say "all of these," "both a and b," or "none of these." Instructors who carefully design multiple-choice questions often make "all of these" or "both a

and b" correct choices. "None of these" frequently serves as a filler choice, when the test maker has run out of interesting choices. Look at the following question on neural traces and see how the option "both a and b" is thoughtfully designed as the correct choice:

6. A neural trace is

   a. a mark on the cerebrum
   b. also called a memory groove
   c. only induced by drugs
   d. both a and b

Had you not read all of the choices, you could have marked a as the correct choice.

8. With multiple-choice questions, make educated guesses. If you can eliminate two of the four choices, you have a 50 percent chance of choosing the correct answer. Be sure that your instructor or the test does not penalize you for guessing. Some standardized tests do. Even if there is a guessing penalty, if you have narrowed your choices down to two, make an educated guess. If you cannot eliminate two or more of the choices, don't spend too much time on that particular question. If there is no guessing penalty, make your choice quickly and move on to the next question. If there is a guessing penalty and you cannot narrow your choices down to two, leave that answer blank.

Many instructors criticize multiple-choice exams, saying that the best indicator of what a student knows is an essay exam. Although this is a valid objection, multiple-choice questions are the most frequently used type of objective question on standardized tests. You will be taking such tests in your college career, so you need to have an efficient strategy for taking them.

How to Answer True-False Questions

True-false questions are also popular on objective exams. Unlike multiple-choice questions, which may have up to five choices, true-false questions have only two. Your chance of being correct is always 50 percent. Instructors emphasize details when they design true-false questions; so when you study for a true-false test, you need to look carefully at the details.

Hints on Taking True-False Exams

1. For a statement to be true, each part must be true. One detail in the statement can make the entire statement false. When you read a true-false statement, look for the following: the "who," the "what," the "why," the "when," the "where," and the "how much." The answer to each of these questions must be correct for you to mark the entire statement true. Look at the following true-false question on Jean

Piaget, and see if it correctly answers the "who," the "what," and the "when":

Jean Piaget made some revolutionary discoveries about child behavior during the nineteenth century.

The "who" (Jean Piaget) and the "what" (child behavior) are correct, but the "when" is not. Piaget did his research during the twentieth century.

Study the key parts of this statement on the Los Angeles School District:

With 48 percent of its 490,000 students Latin speakers, the Los Angeles School District continued to search for competent bilingual teachers in 1987.

With this question, the "who," the "what," and the "when" are correct. The Los Angeles School District was concerned with hiring more bilingual teachers in 1987. But the "how many" is incorrect; the correct enrollment for this school district in 1987 was 590,000. Because this one bit of information is incorrect, you must mark the entire question incorrect.

2. Like multiple-choice questions, true-false questions also may use qualifiers such as "never," "always," and "only." These qualifiers frequently make the statements false. On the other hand, less definite qualifiers like "often," "may," "many," "most," "frequently," and "usually" tend to make the statement true. Read the following true-false statement on association:

The memory technique of association is always used when you learn a new word.

Although association is successfully used in vocabulary learning, it is not always used. The word "always" makes this statement false. If you can think of one case in which the statement is untrue, then the statement is false. But see how a less inclusive qualifier can make the same statement true:

The memory principle of association is often used when a student learns new words.

The word "often" allows for the statement to have some exceptions. Because of the flexibility that "often" gives this statement, you can mark this statement true.

3. In designing true-false questions, instructors frequently match terms with inappropriate definitions. So in preparing for a true-false test,

be sure that you know your definitions and your people. Read this example on categorization:

> Categorization involves placing a word in several contexts in order to remember it. Association, not categorization, is the process of placing a word in several contexts.

The test maker consciously exchanged "association" with "categorization." If you did not know the meaning of both words, you may not have chosen the correct answer.

How to Answer Matching Questions

Of the three kinds of examination questions, matching questions are the hardest to answer correctly by guessing. In answering matching questions, you need to know the information very well. In the matching format, you are given a list of words in one column and a list of explanations of these words in a second column, often to the right of the first list. It is your job to match correctly the word with the explanation.

Hints on Taking Matching Exams

1. Look at both columns before you begin answering. Are there terms in one column and definitions in another? people in one column and descriptions of them in another? people in the left column and quotations in the right column? What pattern do you detect in the following example from learning theory?

1. neural trace	a. a process of placing information into several contexts to ensure retention
2. rehearsal	b. a process of transferring information from short-term memory to long-term memory
3. association	c. a physiological mark on the cerebrum storing a bit of information

   In this set, terms are on the left, definitions on the right.

2. With each correct match, cross out the term and the explanation of it (if your instructor does not plan to reuse the test). In this way, you save time by not rereading material that you have already treated. Look at how crossing out is used for the following matching questions.

___c___	1. ~~neutal trace~~	a. a process of placing information into several contexts to ensure retention
_____	2. rehearsal	b. a process of transferring information from short-term memory to long-term memory
_____	3. association	c. ~~a physiological mark on the cerebrum storing a bit of information~~

3. If the information in the right-hand column is lengthy, begin reading in this column first. Read the explanation; then match it with the approprite term. You save time by not rereading the lengthy explanations.*

How to Take Objective Tests

Here are some strategies to use when you are taking an objective test:

1. Read over all of the directions carefully. Know what you need to do.

2. Plan your time. If your test has three parts—true-false, multiple-choice, and matching—divide your exam hour into equal time allotments. Check your watch so that you do not stay on any one section of the exam for too long.

3. Read through the questions quickly to determine the difficulty level of the exam.

4. Answer the easiest sections first. Since you have a better chance of getting the easier questions right, do not wait until the end of the hour to answer them.

5. Do not spend too much time on any one question. If you are unsure about an answer, make an educated guess. Then place a mark to the left of the question so that if you have time, you can go back to it.

6. Check your numbering so that the number on your answer sheet corresponds to the number on your exam booklet. Students often place a correct answer on the wrong number of their answer grid and get the question wrong.

7. If possible, leave five to ten minutes at the end of the exam to review your answers. Check for carelessness. Change only those answers you are reasonably sure are incorrect. Do not change a guess; more often the guess is correct and the correction is not.

Summary

There are three major types of objective tests: multiple-choice, true-false, and matching. Each type of question requires a different strategy. The multiple-choice question is the most commonly used objective question. With multiple-choice and true-false questions, you can make educated guesses; matching questions, on the other hand, leave little room for guesswork. With matching questions, you need to know names and definitions well.

Multiple-choice questions are frequently used on entrance and professional exams. Thus it is important to develop a successful strategy in answering them.

---

*James Shepherd, *College Study Skills* (Boston: Houghton Mifflin, 1990), p. 247.

Summary Box   *Objective Tests*

What are they?	*How do you take them?*
Examinations, frequently machine-scored, that test the breadth of your knowledge on a subject Three most common types: multiple-choice, true-false, and matching	Multiple-choice: learn to eliminate incorrect answers; cross them out and consider other choices True-false: look for statements that are absolute; they are frequently false Matching: see how the columns are organized; with each match that you make, cross out the statement in one column and the name or term in the other

Skills Practice

Exercise 15.1
Answering Multiple-
Choice Questions

Read the following textbook excerpt about incest taboos from an anthropology textbook. Underline important points and make marginal comments. After reading, recite either by taking notes or by making a study map. When you think you know the material, answer the five multiple-choice questions that follow. Before you answer these questions, you may want to refer to pp. 257–260, which deal with strategies to use when answering multiple-choice questions.

Marriage Rules: Incest Taboos

Every society has rules about mating. In all societies, there are some prohibitions on mating between persons in certain relationships or from certain social groups. The most universal prohibition is that on mating among certain kinds of kin: mother-son, father-daughter, and sister-brother. The taboos on mating between kin always extend beyond this immediate family group, however. In our own society, the taboo extends to the children of our parents' siblings (in our kinship terminology called first cousins); in other societies, individuals are not permitted to mate with others who may be related up to the fifth generation. These prohibitions on mating (that is, sexual relations) between relatives or people classified as relatives are called *incest taboos*.

Because sexual access is one of the most important rights conferred by marriage, incest taboos effectively prohibit marriage as well as mating among certain kin. The outstanding exception to the almost universal taboo on mating and marriage among members of the nuclear family are those cases of brother-sister marriage among royalty in ancient Egypt, in traditional Hawaiian society, and among Inca royalty in Peru. Incest taboos have always been of interest to anthropologists, who have attempted to explain their origin and persistence in human society, particularly as they apply to primary (or nuclear) family relationships. Many theories have been advanced, and we will look here at four major ones.

Inbreeding Avoidance

The inbreeding avoidance theory holds that mating between close kin produces deficient, weak children and is genetically harmful to the species. The incest taboo is therefore adaptive because it limits inbreeding. This theory, proposed in the late nineteenth century, was later rejected for a number of decades on the ground that inbreeding could produce advantages as well as disadvantages for the group, by bringing out recessive genes of both a superior and an inferior character. Recent work in population genetics has given more weight to the older view that inbreeding *is* usually harmful to a human population. The proportion of negative recessive traits to adaptive recessive ones is very high, and in the human animal, inbreeding has definite disadvantages. Furthermore, these disadvantages are far more likely to appear as a result of the mating of primary relatives (mother-son, father-daughter, sister-brother) than of other relatives, even first cousins. It would seem, then, that the biological adaptiveness of the incest taboo as it applies to the nuclear family must be considered in explaining both its origins and its persistence.

The question raised here, of course, is how prescientific peoples could understand the connection between close inbreeding and the biological disadvantages that result. But the adaptive results of the incest taboo need not have been consciously recognized in order to persist; rather, groups that had such a taboo would have had more surviving children than groups without the taboo. This reproductive advantage would eventually account for its universality as groups without the taboo died out.*

Directions: Choose the correct letter to answer the following questions. Place all answers in the answer box.

1. Which of the following is not an example of the incest taboo?

    a. mother mating with son
    b. brother mating with sister
    c. close friends mating with each other
    d. father mating with daughter

2. Exceptions to the incest taboo have sometimes been allowed with

    a. the lower class
    b. royal families

---

*Serena Nanda, *Cultural Anthropology*, 3rd ed. (Belmont, Calif.: Wadsworth, 1987), pp. 205–206. Used by permission.

c. the middle class

d. all of these

3. The inbreeding avoidance theory suggests that incest leads to

a. miscarriages

b. marital problems

c. genetically weak children

d. none of these

4. Recent research in genetics has

a. rejected the inbreeding avoidance theory

b. supported the inbreeding avoidance theory

c. neither supported nor rejected the inbreeding avoidance theory

d. questioned the need for the incest taboo

5. Anthropologists believe that the incest taboo evolved in prescientific cultures because

a. of their strong religious beliefs

b. of their rigid family structure

c. ancient cultures passed on all of their traditions from one generation to the next

d. those who ignored it died out

---

1. _____

2. _____

3. _____

4. _____

5. _____

_____

80%

(score = # correct × 20)
Find answers on p. 354.

**Exercise 15.2
Answering True-
False Questions**

Read the following textbook excerpt on the sun from an environmental studies textbook. Underline the important points and make marginal comments. After reading, recite either by outlining or by making a study map. When you think that you have learned the information, answer the five true-false questions that follow. You may want to refer to pp. 260–262, which present strategies to use in answering true-false questions. Remember that true-false questions often test your knowledge of details.

The Sun: Source of Energy for Life on Earth

Just as an economy runs on money, the ecosphere runs on energy. *The source of the radiant energy that sustains all life on Earth is the sun.* It warms the Earth and provides energy for the photosynthesis in green plants. These plants, in turn, synthesize the carbon compounds that keep them alive and that serve as food for almost all other organisms. Solar energy also powers the water cycle, which purifies and removes salt from ocean water to provide the fresh water upon which land life depends.

The sun is a medium-sized star composed mostly of hydrogen. At its center, the sun is so hot that a pinhead of its material could kill a person over 161 kilometers (100 miles) away. Under the conditions of extremely high temperatures and pressures found in the interior of the sun, light nuclei of hydrogen atoms are fused together to form slightly heavier nuclei of helium atoms. In this process of *nuclear fusion* some of the mass of the hydrogen nuclei is converted into energy.

Thus, the sun is a giant *nuclear-fusion reactor* 150 million kilometers (93 million miles) away from the Earth. Every second, the sun converts about 3.7 billion kilograms (4.1 billion tons) of its total mass into energy. It has probably been in existence for 6 billion years, and estimates are that it has enough hydrogen left to keep going for at least another 8 billion years.*

Directions: Read the following statements. Write A for true and B for false. Place all answers in the answer box.

1. The major element that makes up the sun is nitrogen.
2. In the sun's middle, heat transforms lighter helium to heavier hydrogen.
3. The sun is 140 kilometers (92 million miles) away from the earth.
4. The sun has been called a giant nuclear-fission reactor.
5. The sun was created 8 billion years ago and will not die for another 6 billion years.

1. _____
2. _____
3. _____
4. _____
5. _____

_____
80%

Ask instructor for answers.

Exercise 15.3
Answering Matching
Questions

Read the following excerpt, which defines musical terms from a music history textbook. Underline important points and make marginal comments. After reading, recite either by outlining or by making a study map. When you think that you know the material, answer the five matching questions that follow. You may want to refer to pp. 262–263, which present strategies to use in answering matching questions.

Musical Terminology

Certain musical terms are basic to an understanding of music literature. The first term to learn is *music*, which is defined as a combination of sounds that are organized and meaningful, occurring in a prescribed span of time and usually having pitch. In the definition of music is another term, *pitch*, which is defined as the degree of highness or lowness of a sound. Related to pitch is *interval*. Interval is defined as the distance between two pitches. The most fundamental interval is an *octave*. Finally, *melody* is defined as pitches sounded one after another, presented in a logical series that forms a satisfying musical unit.†

---

*G. Tyler Miller, Jr., *Living in the Environment*, 4th ed. (Belmont, Calif.: Wadsworth, 1985), p. 32. Used by permission.

†Adapted from Charles Hoffer, *The Understanding of Music*, 5th ed. (Belmont, Calif.: Wadsworth, 1985), pp. 22–24. Used by permission.

Directions: Match a letter from column B with the appropriate number in column A. Place all answers in the answer box.

1. _____

2. _____

3. _____

4. _____

5. _____

_____
80%

(score = # correct × 20)
Find answers on p. 354.

Column A

1. octave
2. pitch
3. melody
4. interval
5. music

Column B

a. a combination of pitches forming a pleasing unit
b. a combination of organized sounds that happen in time and usually have pitch
c. the distance between two pitches
d. the highness or lowness of a sound
e. the most fundamental interval

16 Strategies for Essay Tests and Math or Science Tests

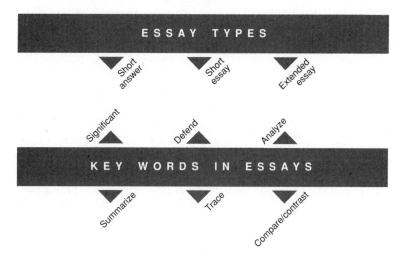

Essay exams are different in many ways from objective tests. Unlike objective tests, which ask you to remember many details, essay exams make you choose main ideas and major details from a large body of material and then form an organized response. When you are writing an essay exam, you need to recall main ideas and major details quickly. Problem-solving questions in math and the sciences are similar to essay questions. The major difference is that instead of using words, you are using numbers and symbols. In both an essay exam and a math or science problem, you need to use skills in logic and organization. Unlike objective exams, the best essay and math or science exams ask you to generate important information yourself.

How to Prepare for an Essay Exam

When preparing for an essay exam, you again need to review your textbook underlinings, textbook comments, study reading notes, lecture notes, and study maps. (See the section in Chapter 15 titled "How to Prepare for Objective Tests.") Instead of trying to remember many details, as you would in preparing for an objective test, for an essay exam you need to concentrate on significant main ideas and details of support.

Your job is to reduce much information into its significant points. This may not be easy for you at first.

If your instructor has provided you in advance with several possible essay topics, find information in your study material to answer them. If your instructor does not provide you with questions, check to see whether there are discussion questions at the end of your textbook chapters. Find the ones that you think are most important, then locate information that would best treat each question. As you study, you should formulate your own essay questions from topics that you think are important. You can often design your own essay questions from the divisions and subdivisions of your textbook chapters or from the lecture titles in your syllabus or lecture notes.

After you have reviewed your notes and underlinings, write the three or four most likely essay topics on a separate sheet of paper or on the blank side of 5 × 8 note cards. These sheets and cards are similar to those mentioned in Chapter 15 for preparing for an objective exam. On the back side of the paper or the lined side of the card, answer the question, giving pertinent main ideas and major details. Use a numeral-letter or indenting format. Don't write this information in paragraph form at this time. Save your more thorough sentence writing for the essay exam itself. The cards or sheets of paper should look something like what is shown in Figures 16-1 and 16-2.

Once you have completed the study sheets or cards, turn each over to the question side to see if you can orally respond to the question. See if you can quickly remember the main idea and the necessary supporting details. If it is hard for you to remember the supporting details, use a memory aid. "RWD" is an abbreviation that you could design to remember "rereading," "writing," and "discussion"—the details for the essay question in Figure 16-1. Review these cards or sheets until your

Question: Define the learning process of rehearsal, and given specific examples of this learning technique.

Front Side

Figure 16-1 *Front of study card, with essay question.*

Rehearsal

Def: the active use of the senses to place information
        into long-term memory

Specific expls:

        rereading—of sig info in your text (seeing)
        writing—making study sheets or maps in the forms of
                summaries (touching)
        discussion—verbal exchange w yourself or in a disc
                    grp to put info into your own wds (hearing)

Back Side

Figure 16-2   *Back of study card, answering the question.*

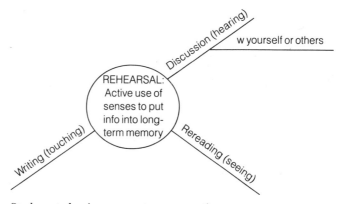

Figure 16-3   *Study map showing answer to essay question.*

response to each question is fast. A key to doing well on an essay exam
is your being able to recall main ideas and accurate details with ease.

Study maps are also good tools to use when you study for essay tests.
Figure 16-3 shows how the information on rehearsal can be neatly arranged into a study map.

***How to Read an
Essay Question***

Having studied well for your essay test, you are now ready for the questions. Understanding the intent of the question is as important as being
prepared for the exam. Study the following key terms, which are commonly used in essay questions, and learn how they are used.

Words That Ask for Retelling of Material

summarize, survey, list, outline

If these words appear in your question, you are being asked to give only the important points. You should not concentrate on many details or on analyzing any one point in depth.

Sample question: List the major stages in the development of the human fetus.

To answer this question well, you should list each step in the fetal development of the child. You should then briefly comment on each stage, but you do not need to discuss the relationship of one stage to another or the importance of any of these stages.

Words That Ask You to Make Inferences

discuss, explain

These are two of the most frequently used words in essay questions. They ask you to give the "why" of an argument. You must carefully choose those details that clarify your main idea.

Sample question: Discuss four reasons for the entry of the United States into World War II.

In this question, you need to choose those examples that account for the United States's entry into World War II. These reasons are often your own, so be sure to include terms of qualification when you are presenting opinions—words like "may," "might," "likely," "it is suggested," and so on. See pp. 126–127 for a more thorough list of qualifiers.

A Word That Asks You to Define

define

Define usually asks you for a short answer, no more than three or four sentences. You are not asked to analyze, just to give the term's major characteristics. Just as a dictionary definition is concise, so should your response be concise.

Sample question: Define prejudice as used in sociology.

Here you are being asked to explain prejudice from a sociological perspective. You are not being asked to list its various meanings or to explain its history. Your focus should be on how prejudice relates to sociology.

Words Showing Similarities and Differences

compare, contrast

"Compare" means to show both similarities and differences. To avoid confusion, some instructors use the phrase "compare and contrast." "Contrast" used singly means to show differences. With contrast questions, you are treating opposite sets of information, so use transitions of contrast: "similarly," "oppositely," "conversely," and so on. With strict comparison questions, you are treating similar sets of information; here, use transitions of similarity, such as "likewise," "similarly," and so on. See p. 78 for a more thorough list of transitions of comparison and contrast.

Sample question: Compare and contrast the attitudes of Presidents Reagan and Carter regarding social welfare programs.

In this question, you need to cite programs and legislation from both administrations that show similarities and differences.

Words That Ask You to Critique

analyze, examine, evaluate

Questions using these words are asking you to express a point of view. When you evaluate, you must even judge the merit of your topic. The details you choose are important because they present the bulk of your argument. Critique words are often used in essay questions in the humanities — literature, art, music, film — where you are asked to judge the value of a poem, a painting, or a film. These questions can be difficult because you are being asked to do more than summarize.

Sample question: Analyze the major characters in Dickens's *Great Expectations*. Are these characters successful?

This question is asking you to choose characters in the novel whose actions and traits make them believable. Ultimately, you are judging the success of Dickens's characters. So you need to choose carefully those details that demonstrate Dickens's success or failure in rendering character.

A Word That Asks You to Take a Stand

defend

"Defend" is often used in speech topics or in essay questions in political science or history. With defend questions, you take a definite stand, only presenting evidence that supports this position. In this sense, defend questions ask you to ignore evidence that goes against your position.

Sample question: Defend the premise that nuclear arms will one day lead to nuclear holocaust.

In answering this question, you should discuss only how nuclear arms are a threat to peace. If you suggested that nuclear arms are a deterrent to war, you would weaken your argument.

A Word That Shows Connections

trace

"Trace" is mainly used in history essay questions where you are asked to discuss a series of events and show their relationship to one other. Again, you need to be selective in choosing details that support the connections you see.

Sample question: Trace the development of labor unions in the United States from 1900 to the present.

In this question, you need to choose the important figures and events that led to the formation of unions in the United States; you also need to show how events or individuals influenced other events or individuals.

Words That Ask for Important Information

significant, critical, key, important, major

In most subjects, instructors use these words to guide you in presenting only meaningful evidence. These terms subtly ask you to distinguish the significant from the insignificant. An instructor using these words will often criticize your essay if you fail to choose the important evidence.

Sample question: Discuss three key factors that led to the Great Depression in the United States.

Your instructor may have discussed ten factors, but you are asked to discuss only three. Here, you need to review the ten factors to determine which three have priority. This is difficult to do because you are both summarizing and evaluating information.

Kinds of Essay Questions

There are three basic types of essay questions used on exams: those that ask for the short answer, the short essay, or the extended essay. Each type requires a different strategy.

The Short-Answer Question. In the short-answer question, you are asked to respond in a phrase, a sentence, or several sentences. In a one-hour exam, you can expect to answer up to twenty short-answer questions. The key to doing well is to be as concise and specific as you can. In biology and geology courses using short-answer questions, instructors are often looking for the breadth and accuracy of your knowledge, not your writing style. Ask your instructor whether you need to answer the short-answer questions in sentences. If the answer is no, answer in phrases; you will be able to write more during the hour. In contrast, in an English course your instructor will likely want you to answer the short-answer questions in complete sentences that are correctly punctuated.

Look at the following short-answer question and study the response that received full credit.

Question: Name and identify the three branches of the federal government.
Answer:

1. legislative: makes laws; made up of House and Senate
2. executive: sees that laws are carried out; President
3. judicial: sees that laws are enforced; Supreme Court and other federal courts

This student has presented accurate information in an organized way. Beside each government branch, the student describes the activity, then names the person or agency responsible.

Now see how this same question is answered poorly.

Question: Name and identify the three branches of the federal government.
Answer:

1. legislative: works on laws; made up of two houses
2. executive: the President
3. judicial: courts

This student has not presented the information in an organized way or with enough detail. Although the student names the legislative branch, "works on laws" is vague. With the executive branch, the student names the President but does not describe the function. With the judicial branch, the Supreme Court is not specifically named, nor does the student mention the Court's function.

The Short-Essay Question.   The short-essay question asks you to write an organized paragraph of several sentences. In an hour, you should be able to answer up to five such questions. Your strategy when writing the short-essay answer is to present your main idea or thesis right away, then present accurate details of support. These details must follow logically from your main idea. If you have completed the writing assignments in this book, you are familiar with how a convincing paragraph is put together.

Read the following short-essay question and the response that received full credit.

> *Question:* Discuss the three major characteristics of human language.
> *Answer:*
>
> Human language has three qualities that distinguish it from animal communication. First, human language uses a limited number of sounds that produce thousands of utterances. Second, human speech is not imitative. The human being can generate a sentence never heard before. Finally, human language can discuss what is not there. Human beings can discuss the past and future as well as the present.

Do you see how the student directly addresses the question? The main-idea sentence comes first, stating that there are three characteristics of human language. Then the sentences of support discuss these characteristics. The student has used the transitions "first, second, and finally" to direct the reader to these three characteristics.

Now consider this second response, which is both poorly organized and less detailed.

> *Question:* Discuss the three major characteristics of human language.
> *Answer:*
>
> Human language has three qualities. Human language uses few sounds. Also, human language uses sentences. Humans can also discuss what is not there. Philosophers have spent centuries discussing what language is all about.

Note how the main-idea sentence is too general, so the student makes no attempt to distinguish human language from animal language. Note how the second detail sentence, "Also, human language uses sentences," does not discuss how the human being can generate sentences that have never before been uttered. This supporting detail does not directly address the uniqueness of human language. Note how the last sentence, "Philosophers have spent centuries discussing what language is all about," introduces an entirely new topic, so the paragraph loses its focus.

The Extended Essay Question.   You will often be asked to write on only one topic during a one-hour exam. Obviously, your instructor is expecting you to write more than one paragraph during this hour. In an hour, you should be able to write several organized paragraphs. This type of essay response is known as the extended essay.

In structure, the extended essay resembles the short essay. The main idea of the paragraph becomes the first paragraph, or introduction, of the extended essay. The detail sentences of the paragraph then each become separate paragraphs. Together, these paragraphs are referred to as the body. Unlike the short essay, the extended essay has a concluding paragraph, called the conclusion, which often summarizes the key points of the essay. Look at Figure 16-4, which shows the structure of the extended essay and states the purpose of its three parts.

The extended essay is difficult to write well at first because you must successfully use several organizational skills. Start by committing the information in Figure 16-4 to memory, so that each essay you write has a recognizable introduction, body, and conclusion. Also, begin using transitions to join sentences and to hook one paragraph to another. By using such transitions as "for example" or "to conclude," you will give additional order to your essay. In Chapter 5, on organizational patterns, there are lists of several transitions that you may want to review and use in your extended essays.

Read the following extended essay question and response. See if you can locate the introduction, the body, and the conclusion, and note how transitions are used.

Question: Discuss the three major functions of religion.
Answer:

(1) Every society has a religion of some sort. Although the beliefs and expressions of religion vary from one culture to another, three basic functions emerge when you study all religions. For one, religion helps

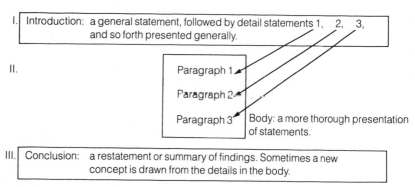

Figure 16-4   *Diagram of an extended essay.*

clarify the unexplained. Second, religion helps reduce anxiety among its followers. Third, religion helps give order to society.

(2) Every culture has tried through religion to answer such questions as where the universe came from and where we go after death. Western religions explain their origin in the Book of Genesis. In this book, we learn that one God created parts of the universe and the world on separate days. Eastern religions see many gods as creating the universe. Western religions believe that human souls live after death, whereas Eastern religions such as Hinduism believe that human beings are reincarnated into other beings after death.

(3) Prayer seems to be part of all religions. In each culture, prayer seems to relieve anxiety. In many African cultures, tribesmen perform rituals to help crops grow or to cure the sick. Prayer in Western cultures works similarly. Western priests often ask their parishioners to pray for the health of their sick loved ones. In each case, prayer becomes an outlet to relieve anxiety.

(4) Finally, religion has an important ordering effect on society. Religious services almost always accompany births, baptisms, marriages, and deaths. And the faithful are invited to witness these events. Such group activities give to the members of the religion a sense of community. Just think of how many wars have been fought over religious beliefs, and you will realize how closely tied religion is to social structure.

(5) In conclusion, it is clear that religion still plays an important role in human life. Religion has through the ages helped explain the mysteries of the universe, comforted people in their grief, and given to each culture a set of social rules.

Note how paragraph 1 presents the three issues that the essay intends to discuss. Paragraphs 2, 3, and 4 give the necessary support for the main idea that religion is found in every society. Each paragraph in the body centers its discussion on a separate function of religion. Nowhere in these paragraphs does the discussion lose its focus.

Note also the transitions that signal different sections of the essay: "for one," "second," and "third" in paragraph 1, and "in conclusion" in paragraph 5. Finally, note that the conclusion summarizes the major points made in the essay.

If you want to study other acceptable models of the extended essay, read some of the longer passages that come at the end of most exercise sections in this book. These longer passages are often modeled after the extended essay.

Now consider how this same question is answered in a disorganized way. Look at this essay to see what is lacking in the introduction, the body, and the conclusion.

Question: Discuss the three major functions of religion.
Answer:

(1) Religion has been used to explain the unexplainable. Each culture has certain creation myths and beliefs about an afterlife. There are many similar creation myths in Western and Eastern religions.

(2) All cultures seem to pray. Prayers help people's problems. People pray in various ways throughout the world. The end is always the same.

(3) Religion has a purpose in society. Many social functions are somehow related to religion. People get together and feel a bond. That is another important function of religion.

Did you note that this essay has no introduction? If you did not have the question before you, you would not know what question this essay was trying to answer. Furthermore, the evidence is vague. In the body, creation myths are mentioned, but no specific creation myths of East and West are discussed. Similarly, the relationship between social functions and religion is presented, but no rituals such as marriage and funerals are introduced. An instructor evaluating this essay would mark it down for its lack of direction and relevant details.

In the next section of this chapter, which analyzes math and science problems and tests, you will see parallels to what you have just learned about essay tests.

How to Prepare for a Math or Science Test

As in preparing for exams in other courses, for a math or science test you will be studying lecture notes, textbook underlinings and comments, and study notes. The study notes are usually solutions to problems. Before you begin studying for your math or science test, see if your instructor has provided you with some sample problems. Also, be sure you know whether you will be allowed to look at your textbook or notes during the test.

You should spend a week reviewing all important material. Because the last class session before an exam in math and science courses is usually a review, it would be helpful if you had done most of your studying before this session. In this review session, you will have the opportunity to ask questions that may have come up during your studying.

When you study, spend most of your time reviewing the problems and solutions shown in your textbook, completed in lecture and study notes, and done as homework. Trace the logic used to solve each problem. While you are reviewing, use note cards to write down important theorems, laws, formulas, and equations. Know these cards well, because you will probably need to recall this information quickly on the exam.

Look at the sample study card in Figure 16-5, from a chemistry study review. Note that the name of the formula is listed on the blank side, and the formula itself and a sample solution using the formula is on the lined side. Using the blank side of the card, you can test yourself to see whether you can recall the variables of the formula.

When it is possible to design a study map of math and science information, do so. Since math and science courses build from one lecture to another, seeing connections among units is most helpful; study maps often help you see these connections more easily. Figure 16-6 shows how the metric system is presented via a study map. In this map,

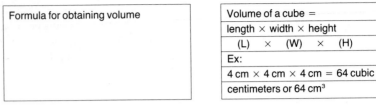

Formula for obtaining volume

Volume of a cube =
length × width × height
(L) × (W) × (H)
Ex:
4 cm × 4 cm × 4 cm = 64 cubic
centimeters or 64 cm³

Blank Side   Lined Side

Figure 16-5   *Study card from a chemistry study review.*

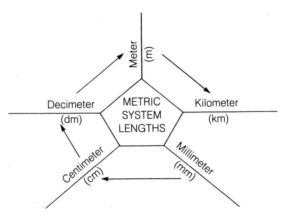

Figure 16-6   *Study map of the metric system.*

the units of measure become progressively larger as your eyes move clockwise.

Once you have made these study cards and study maps, choose three to five problems that you have never done and that will likely be on your test. Complete each problem, and time yourself. If you have difficulty moving from one step to another, try to figure out your confusion. Go back to your notes and textbook.

If your instructor allows crib notes, or notes that list certain formulas and rules, write these out neatly. But do not use these notes as a crutch. Crib notes should be used when you need to use a formula or theorem that is hard to remember.

The night before the exam, do not cram. Just go over your study cards and maps.

How to Take a Math or Science Test

Instructors in math or science generally score an exam by looking at the steps that you used to arrive at a solution. They are often more interested in the way you solved the problem than in the correct answer.

Before you start solving a problem on your test, be sure you know what is being asked of you. The two most commonly used words on math and science tests are "solve" and "prove." Both words ask you to present the logic of your solution, not just give an answer. Look at the following question on the metric system and its solution.

Question: How many kilograms are there in 2543 grams?

Detailed Solution	*Vague Solution*

1. 1 kg = 1000 grams

$$\frac{2543}{1000} = 2.543$$

2. $kg = \dfrac{g}{1000}$

3. $kg = \dfrac{2543}{1000}$

4. kg = 2.543

5. 2.543 kg

Do you see how you can easily follow the pattern of thought in the first solution? Step 1 shows the conversion, step 2 the formula, and steps 3 and 4 the procedures used to solve the equation. The second answer does not present any of these steps and so does not explain why 1000 is to be divided into 2543.

Hints to Use in Solving Math or Science Problems

Use these steps to solve math or science problems on homework or on exams.

1. Read the question carefully. Determine the unknown. If you have to, write out the unknown in the margin. In the previous solution, kg is the unknown.

2. Reread the question to determine the known quantities. In the previous solution, 2543 grams is the known. You may want to write out the known in the margin as well.

3. Then figure out what the problem is asking you to do.

4. Write out the formulas or equations you need to solve the problem. In the example, the needed formula is 1000 g = 1 kg. Then plug your knowns into the formula, and solve for the unknown.

5. When you get an answer, check it by rereading the question. Is it reasonable? In the example, 254,300 kg would be illogical, because you know that kilograms are heavier than grams. You can often spot a simple computational error, such as multiplying when you should have divided, by rereading the question with your answer in mind.

6. If you cannot solve the problem, list the formulas that you know can be used to solve it. Most instructors give partial credit.

Hints for Taking Math, Science, or Essay Tests

Here are some tips for taking all the kinds of examinations discussed in this chapter:

1. Read the directions carefully. Know how many questions you have to answer and the point value assigned to each question.

2. Read through each question, underlining such key words as "analyze," "solve," or "major."

3. Answer the easiest questions first.

4. Jot down a brief outline of what you intend to say for each question or a list of equations you need to use in solving each problem. With these phrases and formulas, you will be able to structure your answers. They will also help you if during the exam you draw a momentary blank.

5. Plan your time wisely. If you are to answer two essay questions or two problems during the hour, be sure to start the second question or problem halfway through the hour.

6. When writing the essay or solving the problem, use only one side of the paper and leave margins. If you want to add information, you can put it either in the margins or on the back side of the paper.

7. If you are pressed for time, list the equations that you intended to use or an outline of the rest of your answer. You will likely get partial credit by including these abbreviated responses.

8. Save at least five minutes at the end of the exam time to review for errors in computation or in spelling, punctuation, and diction.

9. With essay exams, do not expect to write the perfect essay. Your goal is to present accurate information in an organized way.

Summary

Different from objective tests, essay tests ask you to present the important points of what you have studied in an organized way. Unlike objective exams, which ask you to remember many details, essay tests ask you to reduce what you have learned to its essentials. This process of evaluating all that you have studied to find the significant points may be difficult at first. The three most commonly used essay exams are the short-answer exam, the short-essay exam, and the extended essay exam.

Math and science questions are like essay questions; for both, you must present information in a logical way. In place of words, math and science tests use numbers and symbols. Instructors are often looking not just for the correct answer but for how you arrived at your answer.

Effective writing skills and the ability to solve math and science problems are skills that employers are coming to value more and more. Two of your more important goals in college should therefore be to develop efficient writing and problem-solving skills.

Summary Box *Essay Exams and Math or Science Exams*

What are they?	*How do you do well on them?*
Essay exams: ask for organized responses on material that you have studied; can be short answer, short essay, or extended essay	By reducing information to its essentials By presenting accurate information in an organized way
Math or science exams: ask you to use numbers and symbols to solve a problem in a logical way	By determining known and unknown quantities By choosing correct formulas By showing the steps that you used to arrive at your answer

Skills Practice

Exercise 16.1
Answering Short-
Essay Questions

Read the following excerpt on China from an economics textbook. Underline the important points, and make marginal comments. After reading, recite what you have learned either by taking notes or by creating a study map. When you think that you know the information well, answer the essay question that follows. You may want to reread p. 276, on the short essay.

The People's Republic of China

On October 1, 1949, *Mao Tse-tung** (1884–1976) announced to the Chinese people that Chiang Kai-shek's armies were defeated. The Chinese people call this day a day of liberation, and today when they talk of history they speak of "before liberation" and "after liberation." They have good reason.

Before and After Liberation

Before liberation, people died in the streets on cold nights. An American newspaper in Shaghai ran an article in early 1949 stating that eighty

---

*The spelling of Mao Tse-tung is from the Wade-Giles system. At the start of 1979, the Chinese officially adopted a new system called the "Pinyin" (phonetic) system, which more closely approximates Chinese pronunciation. Under the Pinyin system, Mao Tse-tung becomes Mao Zedong; Peking becomes Beijing; Teng Hsaio-ping becomes Deng Xiaoping, and so forth. We'll stick with the older, Wade-Giles system on the theory that it is still more familiar to most readers.

corpses had been found in the morning after a cold wind the night before. Young girls were forced to become prostitutes. Drug addiction from opium was widespread. Rich peasants charged 100 percent interest every six months on loans to tenant farmers. Taxes were repeatedly collected by warlords until the people were paying taxes a year in advance. Large cities like Canton, Nanking, Peking, and Shanghai were divided up into walled "concessions" owned by foreign companies or governments. In one such concession in Shanghai there was a park with a sign that read NO CHINESE OR DOGS ALLOWED.

People were often treated like beasts of burden, forced to work in the factories and fields from the age of seven. Work was long, averaging twelve hours a day, and wages were barely sufficient to maintain life. Workers and peasants were so poor they could not maintain their families and often sold their babies into slavery for a few pennies. No wonder the Chinese were ready to overthrow their economic system.

Today, the Chinese economy is growing rapidly. Despite the fact that there are tremendous masses of people — more than four times the number in the United States in a country only 2.5 percent larger geographically — all receive, at minimum, a subsistence diet; all have a place to live, adequate clothing, medical care, and free education. Illiteracy, starvation, prostitution, sexually transmitted disease, and drug addiction have, with some exceptions, been reduced or eliminated. Cities are clean. Flies, mosquitoes, and other common pests have almost disappeared. A near-miracle seems to have occurred. How has this come about?*

Essay question: The author asserts that China today is a much better place than it was in 1949 under Chiang Kai-shek. To support this point of view, describe China "before liberation" and China "after liberation." Cite at least three details portraying China before liberation and at least three details of China after liberation.

80%

(score = # correct × 10)
Find sample answer on
p. 354

---

*Philip C. Starr, *Economics: Principles in Action*, 4th ed. (Belmont, Calif.: Wadsworth, 1984), p. 48. Used by permission.

Table 2-2 *Commonly Used Prefixes and Multiplier Factors for the Metric System*

Prefix	Abbreviation	Multiply Base Unit By
kilo	k	10^3 or 1,000
deci	d	10^{-1} or 0.1
centi	c	10^{-2} or 0.01
milli	m	10^{-3} or 0.001
micro	μ	10^{-6} or 0.000001

Exercise 16.2
Answering Problem-
Solving Questions

Read the following excerpt on the metric system. Underline the important points, and make marginal comments. After reading, recite what you have learned either by taking notes or by creating a study map. When you think that you know the information well, solve the following problem. You may want to refer to p. 281, which discusses strategies to use in solving math or science problems.

Metric (SI) Prefixes

Values of measurements can be expressed in the fundamental metric or SI units such as meters, kilograms, and seconds. They can also be expressed in larger or smaller units by multiplying the fundamental unit by 10 or some multiple of 10, such as 1,000 (or 10^3) or 0.001 (10^{-3}) (see Table 2-2). Note that any multiple of 10 can be expressed as a positive power of 10 such as 10^3 and 10^6 or a negative power of 10 such as 10^{-3} and 10^{-6}. The power to which 10 is raised is called an *exponent*, and numbers such as 10^3, 10^{-6}, and 8.2×10^4 are called *exponential numbers*.

In the metric or SI system, prefixes are used to indicate how many times the base unit is to be multiplied or divided by 10 to form larger or smaller units. The SI prefixes most commonly used in introductory chemistry are given in Table 2-2.

In the metric or SI system, units are based on 10, and prefixes are used to indicate how many times a base unit is to be multipled or divided by 10 to form larger or smaller units.

Table 2-3   *Metric Prefixes and Units for Length and Mass*

Length	Mass
1 km (kilometer) = 1,000 m (meters)	1 kg (kilogram) = 1,000 g (grams)
1 dm (decimeter) = 0.1 m (meter)	1 dg (decigram) = 0.1 g (gram)
1 cm (centimeter) = 0.01 m (meter)	1 cg (centigram) = 0.01 g (gram)
1 mm (millimeter) = 0.001 m (meter)	1 mg (milligram) = 0.001 g (gram)
1 μm (micrometer) = 0.000001 m (meter)	1 μg (microgram) = 0.000001 g (gram)

Table 2-3 summarizes the use of these prefixes for units of length and mass. The values in metric units for some common objects are

Width of home movie film = 8 mm

Average ski length = 1.60 m to 1.80 m, or 160 cm to 180 cm

Mass of a new nickel = 5 g

Mass of a 150-lb human = 68.2 kg*

75%

Ask instructor for sample answer.

Problem: How many millimeters are there in 27.5 kilometers? In arriving at a solution, show all of your work. List the known quantity, the unknown quantity, and the conversion formulas.

---

*G. Tyler Miller, Jr., Chemistry: A Basic Introduction, 4th ed. (Belmont, Calif.: Wadsworth, 1987), pp. 35–36. Used by permission.

Practice in Applying SQ3R

The following four reading selections are all excerpts from college textbooks. In each selection, you will be applying all of the skills that you have studied in previous parts. If you do well on the examinations that accompany these four selections, you should be adequately prepared to do well in most college courses.

Study Reading 1

Climate

This excerpt from an environmental science textbook discusses weather and those variables in nature that influence it. This excerpt relies on three basic organizational patterns: definition, cause-effect, and spatial-geographic. Read over the following strategies; they should help you learn this information more easily.

1. Read over the definitions carefully. Mark the key words and phrases that explain these terms. Since there are many definitions in this excerpt and since they are critical to understanding the physical laws related to weather and climate, concentrate on learning these words and on seeing how the various terms relate to one another.

2. Study the cause-effect statements carefully. Many of them relate to the effect of warm and cold winds or fronts on the weather. Be sure you can identify both cause and effect. If you do not remember the characteristics of the cause-effect pattern, refer to pp. 73–74.

3. Much of what is said in this excerpt can be visualized. Study the two illustrations carefully; also, when wind and precipitation movements are described, use your spatial-geographic abilities to visualize these processes. If you do not remember the spatial-geographic pattern, refer to p. 76.

4. Because of this excerpt's reliance on the cause-effect and spatial-geographic structures, you can best remember much of this information by designing study maps that illustrate various natural processes of weather and climate. When you are reviewing the material, you may want to design a few study maps.

5. Before you take the quiz on this excerpt, you should not only know the meanings of the key terms but also be able to explain the important cause-effect patterns that underlie the physical processes involved in weather and climate.

A. Survey

Take three minutes to survey this chapter excerpt. Read the title of the excerpt, the titles of the various sections, and any terms that are highlighted. Also, study the two illustrations to see how they relate to the excerpt. Finally, if time permits, read through the first and last paragraphs of the excerpt to get a sense of its style and level of difficulty.

Before you read, you should know the meaning of one word that is not defined in this excerpt: *Topography* refers to the surface features of a region, including the hills, valleys, lakes, rivers, canals, bridges, and roads.

When you have finished with your survey, answer the questions that follow without looking back at the excerpt. Place all of your answers in the answer box.

Global Patterns of Climate

G. Tyler Miller, Jr.

Weather and Climate

(1) **Weather** is the day-to-day variation in atmospheric conditions, such as temperature, moisture (including precipitation and humidity), sunshine (solar electromagnetic radiation), and wind. When the atmosphere thins to nothing, as on the moon or in space, there is no weather. **Climate** is the generalized weather at a given place on Earth over a fairly long period of time such as a season, 1 year, or 30 years. Climate involves seasonal and annual averages, totals, and occasional extremes of the day-to-day weather pattern for an area. Climate is the weather you expect to occur at a particular time of the year in your hometown, whereas weather is the actual atmospheric conditions in your hometown on a particular day.

Global Air Circulation Patterns

(2) Heat from the sun and evaporated moisture are distributed over the Earth as a result of global circulation patterns of atmospheric air masses. Three major factors affecting the pattern of this global air circulation are (1) the uneven heating of the equatorial and polar regions of the Earth, which creates the driving force for atmospheric circulation; (2) the rotation of the Earth around its axis, which causes deflection of air masses moving from the equator to the poles and from the poles back to the equator; and (3) unequal distribution of land masses, oceans, ocean currents, mountains, and other geological features over the Earth's surface.

(3) An *air mass* is a vast body of air in which the conditions of temperature and moisture are much the same at all points in a horizontal direction. A warm air mass tends to rise, and a cold air mass tends to sink. Air in the Earth's atmosphere is heated more at the equator, where the

G. Tyler Miller, Jr., Living in the Environment, *4th ed. (Belmont, Calif.: Wadsworth, 1985), pp. 41–43. Used by permission.*

sun is almost directly overhead, than at the poles, where the sun is lower in the sky and strikes the Earth at an angle. Because of this unequal heating, warm equatorial air tends to rise and spread northward and southward toward the Earth's poles as more hot air rises underneath, carrying heat from the equator toward the poles. At the poles the warm air cools, sinks downward, and moves back toward the equator. In addition, because of the Earth's annual rotation around the sun, the sun is higher in the sky in summer (July for the northern hemisphere and January for the southern hemisphere) than in winter (January for the northern hemisphere and July for the southern hemisphere). Such annual variations in the duration and intensity of sunlight lead to seasonal variations in the different hemispheres and at the poles (Figure 3-8).

(4) The Earth's daily rotation on its axis (Figure 3-8) not only results in night and day; it also produces the major wind belts of the Earth. The general tendency for large air masses to move from the equator to the poles and back is modified by the twisting force associated with the Earth's rotation on its axis. This force deflects air flow in the northern hemisphere to the right and in the southern hemisphere to the left (Figure 3-9). This distortion of the Earth's general air circulation causes the single air movement pattern that would exist in each hemisphere on a nonrotating Earth to break up into three separate belts of moving air or *prevailing ground winds:* the polar easterlies, the westerlies, and the tradewinds (Figure 3-9). The equatorial calm is known as the doldrums (Figure 3-9). These three major belts of prevailing winds in each hemisphere contribute to the distribution of heat and moisture around the planet that leads to differences in climate in different parts of the world.

(5) A *front* is the boundary between two colliding air masses. When a warm air mass and a cold air mass collide, the warm air flows up the front slope of the cold air as if it were a mountain slope, and the cold air forms a wedge near the

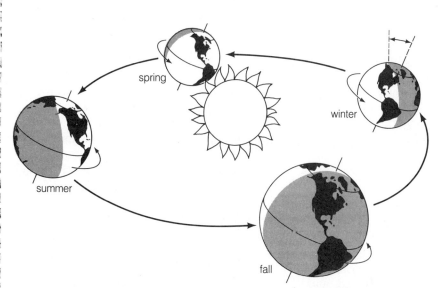

Figure 3-8 *The seasons in the northern hemisphere are caused by variations in the amount of incoming solar radiation as the Earth makes its annual rotation around the sun. Note that the northern end of the Earth's axis tilts toward the sun in summer, making the northern hemisphere warmer, and away from it in winter, making the northern hemisphere cooler.*

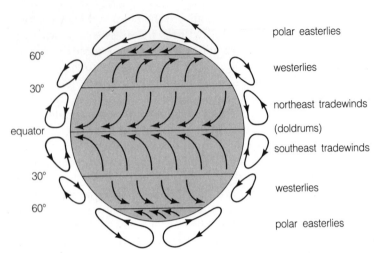

Figure 3-9   *The Earth's daily rotation on its axis deflects the general movement of warm air from the equator to the poles and back to the right in the northern hemisphere and to the left in the southern hemisphere. This twisting motion causes the air flow in each hemisphere to break up into three separate belts of prevailing winds.*

ground. If prevailing winds cause the cold air mass to push the warm air mass back, we have an advancing *cold front*. If the reverse happens, we have an advancing *warm front*, and when no motion of the air masses takes place, we have a *stationary front*. An advancing cold or warm front usually brings bad weather because of the rain, snow, and strong winds that are found in the vicinity of its moving air masses.

(6) The boundary where the warm tropical air masses pushed from the south by the prevailing westerlies collide with the cold polar air masses pushed from the north by the polar easterlies (Figure 3-9) is known as the *polar front*. This front is of major importance in determining the weather and climate of the North American continent. Depending on the relative strength of the polar easterlies and the westerlies, the polar front swings northward and southward in a rather unpredictable way. In general, it moves toward the equator during the winter and recedes to the poles during the summer.

(7) The general global circulation pattern of air masses (Figure 3-9) also influences the distribution of precipitation over the Earth's surface. A great deal of the sun's heat goes not just into warming the Earth's surface but also into evaporating water from the oceans and other bodies of water that cover about three-fourths of the Earth's surface. Evaporation of water from the land and transpiration of moisture from the leaves of plants also contribute water vapor to the atmosphere. A single apple tree, for example, may transpire 6,790 liters (1,800 gallons) of water vapor into the atmosphere during its six-month growing season. The amount of water vapor in the air is called its *humidity*. The amount of water vapor the air is holding at a particular temperature expressed as a percentage of the amount it could hold at that temperature is known as its *relative humidity*. When air with a given amount of water vapor cools, its relative humidity rises; when this same air is warmed, its relative humidity drops. Thus, warm air can hold more water vapor than cold

air, explaining why the humidity tends to rise in warmer summer months.

(8) When an air mass rises it cools, which causes its relative humidity to increase. Once the relative humidity of the rising air mass reaches 100 percent, any further decrease in temperature causes tiny water droplets or ice crystals to condense on particles of dust in the atmosphere to form *clouds*. As these droplets and ice crystals in clouds are moved about in turbulent air, they collide and coalesce to form larger droplets and crystals. Eventually they can become big enough to be pulled downward by gravitational attraction toward the Earth's surface in the form of *precipitation* such as rain, sleet, snow, or hail. Thus, almost all clouds and forms of precipitation are caused by the cooling of an air mass as it rises. Conversely, when an air mass sinks, its temperature rises and its relative humidity can decrease to the point where it can't release its moisture as rain or snow.

(9) Air rising in the tropics is both hot and moist. As this air rises and cools, some of its water vapor is converted to water droplets, giving up some heat in the process. These droplets form the clouds from which tropical rains fall, helping explain why the tropics are wet and thus covered with lush vegetation. Conversely, areas north and south of the equator where the airflow is mainly downward—such as the deserts of the U.S. Southwest and the Sahara—tend to be dry because sinking air can hold more moisture.

(10) An air mass tends to take on the temperature and moisture characteristics of the surface over which it moves. Thus, the climate and weather of a particular area are also affected by the distribution of land and water over the Earth's surface because these surfaces react differently to the incoming rays of the sun. In general, land surfaces are heated rapidly by the sun. Because this heat does not penetrate deeply, land surfaces also cool rapidly. This means that interior land areas not near a large body of water usually have great differences between daily high and low temperatures. Water, however, warms up slowly, holds a much larger quantity of heat than the same volume of land surface,

and cools slowly. As a result, the surface layer of air over the oceans is cooler in summer and warmer in winter than that over the continents. Because warm air rises, a net inflow of cool ocean air moves onto the continents in summer, and in winter there is a net outflow of cool air from the continents onto the oceans. Land and sea breezes result from the land being colder than the water at night and early morning but warmer later in the day.

(11) The Earth's rotation, prevailing winds, and variations in water temperature give rise to ocean currents such as the Gulf Stream, which carries warm waters from the Florida Straits northward along the Atlantic Coast and on to the British Isles. Such currents affect the climate of coastal areas near their flow. For example, air moving across the warm Gulf Stream acquires heat and moisture and influences the climate and weather along the East Coast. The climate of the East Coast is also affected by the cold Labrador Current, which flows southward as far as Norfolk, Virginia. The cool Japan Current has a major effect on the climate and weather of the West Coast of the United States.

Effects of Topography on Local Climate and Weather

(12) Topographical factors can often make local climatic conditions different from the general climate of a region. Such local climatic patterns are called *microclimates*. For example, forests have lower wind speeds and higher relative humidity than open land. Buildings in cities also disrupt wind-flow patterns and heat absorption patterns and cause cities to have different microclimates than surrounding nonurban areas.

(13) Climate is also modified locally by the presence of mountains. An increase in altitude results in a decrease in the density (mass per unit of volume) of the atmosphere, which in turn leads to a decrease in the temperature of the atmosphere. Thus, because of their higher altitudes, mountains tend to be cooler and windier than adjacent valleys. They also act as barriers to interrupt the flow of prevailing winds and the

movement of storms. For example, because most U.S. mountain ranges run north and south, they disrupt the flow of the prevailing westerlies.

(14) Mountain ranges also affect precipitation patterns. When prevailing winds reach a mountain range, the air rises and may decrease in temperature to the condensation level (100 percent humidity). When this occurs, precipitation may occur on the windward side of the range as the air flows upward. After flowing over the mountain crests, the air flows down the lee side of the range. As this happens, it becomes warmer and its relative humidity can decrease to the point where it can't release its moisture as air or snow. Thus, slopes on the lee side of the mountain range and the land beyond these slopes generally lack abundant precipitation. This *rain shadow effect* is the main reason that arid and semiarid deserts lie to the east of the Coast Ranges and the Cascade and Sierra Nevada ranges of California.

1. _____

2. _____

3. _____

4. _____

5. _____

80%

(score = # correct × 20)
Ask instructor for answers.

1. This chapter excerpt makes use of

   a. boldface print
   b. italics
   c. underlining
   d. both a and b

2. The two illustrations relate weather to the Earth's

   a. annual rotation
   b. daily rotation
   c. annual and daily rotation
   d. mountain ranges

3. A topic that will not be covered in this excerpt is

   a. air circulation
   b. weather and climate
   c. topography and weather
   d. the greenhouse effect

4. This excerpt makes no use of mathematical equations.

   a. true
   b. false

5. The title of this excerpt suggests that climate will be analyzed in relation to

   a. all the continents of the Earth
   b. North America
   c. the North and South Poles
   d. the mountainous areas of the Earth

B. Question

Having surveyed this excerpt, make up five questions that you will answer as you study read. Use the chapter title, subdivision titles, and boldface and italicized terms to help you to make up these questions. Answer these questions as you read the chapter.

Ask instructor for sample questions.

1.

2.

3.

4.

5.

C. Read and Recite

1. Having written these five questions, you can begin study reading. Underline important points and make marginal comments. Remember, do not underline too much. Read paragraphs 1–7. Afterward, on a separate sheet of paper, recite what you have read, using the Cornell note-taking system. When you have finished, go back to these seven paragraphs to see if your summary is complete and accurate.

2. Now read paragraphs 8–14. Follow the same procedures as you did for paragraphs 1–7: Recite on a separate sheet of paper, then return to these paragraphs to see if your summary is complete and accurate. Make any necessary additions to your summary.

D. Review

Now you are ready to review all of your material. Read over text underlinings, marginal comments, and your two summaries. You may also want to make study maps from some of this material. Finally, go back to your original five questions to see if you can answer them without any help.

Examination: Global Patterns of Climate

Directions: Give yourself fifty minutes to complete the following questions. Be sure to budget your time to answer all three parts: matching, multiple choice, and short essay.

I. Matching: Match up the following terms with the appropriate definitions. Each term should be matched up to only one definition. Place the letter of the correct definition in the answer box next to the appropriate number. (24 points)

1. _____	
2. _____	
3. _____	
4. _____	
5. _____	
6. _____	
7. _____	
8. _____	

1. microclimate
2. climate
3. weather
4. front
5. air mass
6. precipitation
7. humidity
8. relative humidity

a. amount of water vapor in the air at a specific temperature in comparison to what it could be at that temperature
b. rain, sleet, snow, or hail
c. the boundary between two colliding air masses
d. general weather at a specific place on Earth over a long period of time
e. local patterns of climate
f. day-to-day change in atmospheric conditions
g. a body of air with similar temperature and moisture
h. amount of water vapor in the air

II. Multiple Choice: Choose the letter that correctly completes each question or statement. Place all answers in the answer box. (36 points)

9. Warm air masses are

   a. below cold air masses
   b. above cold air masses
   c. mixed in with cold air masses
   d. only found at the equator

10. The Earth's wind belts are caused by

    a. the Earth's annual rotation
    b. the Earth's daily rotation
    c. ocean currents
    d. land masses

11. The belt of moving air at the equator is known as the

    a. westerlies
    b. easterlies
    c. tradewinds
    d. doldrums

12. Bad weather is usually caused by the movement of a

    a. cold front
    b. warm front
    c. stationary front
    d. both a and b

13. An important force determining weather conditions in North America is the

    a. polar front
    b. westerlies

c. doldrums

d. tradewinds

14. Humidity in the air increases when

    a. an air mass heats up

    b. an air mass cools

    c. a cold front meets a stationary front

    d. it is midday

15. Land tends to be heated

    a. rapidly by the sun

    b. slowly by the sun

    c. as fast as water

    d. as slow as water

16. An important factor affecting the weather of the British Isles is the

    a. Arctic snow

    b. doldrums

    c. westerlies

    d. Gulf Stream

17. Weather and climate seem to be influenced by

    a. unknown variables

    b. few variables

    c. several variables

    d. the Earth's rotation only

III. Short Essay: In a paragraph, discuss how mountains affect weather patterns. In your paragraph, mention (1) mountain altitude and air density, (2) how U.S. mountains affect the westerly winds, and (3) precipitation differences between windward and leeward sides of mountains. (40 points)

9. _____

10. _____

11. _____

12. _____

13. _____

14. _____

15. _____

16. _____

17. _____

_____
70%
Ask instructor for answers

Study Reading 2

Classical Music

This excerpt on Classicism and Mozart, filling in the details on Mozart's music and life that you read about in Exercise 7.3, is from a music history textbook. It is essentially divided into two parts. The first describes the characteristics of the Rococo style and Classicism, and the second section gives a quick biography of Mozart, the great classical composer. The excerpt is structured around two organizational patterns: description and sequence of events.

Use the following strategies to master the important material in this excerpt:

1. Determine the significant characteristics of the Rococo style and Classicism. You may want to write these characteristics down in the margins as you read. You will be reading many details about the Rococo style and Classicism; concentrate only on the important characteristics of each style. If you do not remember what kinds of details characteristics are, reread p. 53.

2. When you begin reading about Mozart's life, you need to put the information about him into its proper sequence. In this section, you will read several details about his life, and sequencing the material should help you remember more of the facts. Refer to pp. 75–76, on sequence of events, to determine the important aspects of this organizational pattern.

3. One part of the test will include true-false questions on Mozart. So commit to memory many of the details of his life.

A. Survey

Take two minutes to survey this excerpt. Read the chapter title, the section titles, and any terms that are highlighted. If time permits, read the first few and last few paragraphs to get a sense of the style and difficulty level of the excerpt.

When you have finished surveying, answer the questions that follow without looking back at the excerpt. Place all of your answers in the answer box.

Classicism, Classical Music, and Mozart

Charles R. Hoffer

(1) By the time of Bach's death in 1750, the Baroque style had faded in popularity. In fact, Bach's own sons thought of their father as something of an out-of-date old man, a not unknown attitude of sons toward their fathers. But the world *was* changing. Passing was the intensity of religious feeling. Gone was the love of the dramatic and grandiose. A new age had arrived, one that would see significant changes in the style of art and music.

Rococo Style

(2) Like all stylistic periods in music, the Classical period did not have a clearly marked beginning. An early instance of the gradual transition from the heavy, complex Baroque style was the **Rococo**, or *galant*, style, which began early in the eighteenth century in the courts of Europe, especially France. It was the art of the aristocracy, of the people at the lavish courts of Versailles and similar places. Like the aristocracy, Rococo music and art were light, elegant, and frivolous. In painting, the Rococo was represented by Fragonard, Watteau, and Boucher. Their subject matter was often fanciful love, and their pictures were laced with figures of cupids and thinly clad nymphs. Rococo furniture and clothing were highly decorated. The lace cuff and the powdered wig were in vogue, and elegant manners were cultivated.

Charles R. Hoffer, The Understanding of Music, *5th ed. (Belmont, Calif.: Wadsworth, 1985), pp. 200–205. Used by permission.*

(3) François Couperin (1668–1733) is probably most representative of Rococo composers. He wrote a large amount of music, mostly suites, for the clavecin, the French version of the harpsichord. Couperin's music was highly embellished, with many ornaments added to the happy, short melodies.

(4) Although music and art in the Rococo style were not profound, they were pleasant diversions for the aristocracy during much of the eighteenth century. More important, the Rococo represented a break from the complex counterpoint of the Baroque, and it ushered in a new type of music.

Patronage

(5) The patronage system existed for several centuries. However, it is especially associated with the eighteenth century because of the experiences of Haydn and Mozart under it. The system was one in which a composer accepted exclusive employment under the auspices of a patron. Patrons were either the wealthy (and sometimes decadent) aristocracy or the Church. When a composer found a good patron, as Haydn did, a secure position and an audience for his compositions were assured. The writing of new works was expected. At its best, patronage was a good incubator for creative talent.

(6) There were liabilities, as shown by Mozart's experiences with patronage. Most serious among these was the fact that composers had to please their patrons, or else they found themselves helping in the stables or looking for a new

patron. The result was much trivial music written according to standard formulas. Too, the patronage system regarded composers not as unique creative artists but as the source of a product for the privileged classes to use and enjoy.

(7) Since the relationship between composers and their work was taken lightly, it was common practice for composers to borrow themes and ideas from one another. In fact, plagiarism was understood to be a form of flattery and commendation. Legal niceties such as copyrights and royalties were unheard of. Not until the advent of the Romantic philosophy of the nineteenth century did composers feel compelled to create in a way that was uniquely individual.

The Classical Attitude

(8) During the Classical period, which scholars consider to stretch roughly from 1750 to 1825, several conditions in society influenced artists and composers. The first of these was a new intellectual outlook of such scope that the period came to be called the Age of Enlightenment or the Age of Reason. The trend was strongly influenced by Descartes, Diderot, Moses Mendelssohn (grandfather of Felix Mendelssohn, an important composer of the Romantic period), Spinoza, and others who revived and added to the idealistic, idea-centered philosophy of ancient Greece. In fact, the word *classical* traditionally refers to the reason and restraint found in the life of the ancient Athenians.

(9) Briefly, the philosophy of eighteenth-century thinkers was this: First, truth can be realized only by the process of reason, so an emphasis must be placed on learning and intellectual pursuits. Second, the universe is a machine governed by inflexible laws that human beings cannot override. Therefore, what is true is true throughout the world; it is universal. Third, emotions as a guide to truth are false, so rational intellect should control human behavior. The intellectuals of the Classical period were not impressed by the unknown, since they believed that in time they would come to know it

through thought and knowledge. They rejected the past, especially the Middle Ages, because they felt mysticism had stifled natural human capacities. Reason, not faith, was to be humanity's beacon.

(10) The American Declaration of Independence written in 1776 is a thoroughly Classical document. It is difficult for us, who tend to think of revolutionaries as bomb-throwing zealots, to consider Jefferson, Washington, Adams, and the others as revolutionaries. But revolutionaries they were, even though their demands and statements of purpose were shaped in the language of reason and Classical thought. These individuals were cultured, intelligent, reasonable men, and their Declaration shows it. Although at its conclusion they pledge "our Lives, our Fortunes, and our Sacred Honor," the Declaration is essentially a legal brief, a list of the colonists' grievances against the King of England. Instead of screaming "Death to the tyrant!" Jefferson begins "When in the course of human events, it becomes necessary for one people to dissolve the political bands which have connected them with another. . . ." At a moment that would seem to require a display of emotion—the declaring of national independence and the pledging of one's life to a cause—these intellectual and political leaders were dispassionate, restrained, sensible, logical.

Wolfgang Amadeus Mozart

(11) Wolfgang Amadeus Mozart stands out among composers. His music has about it a clearness, delicacy, and simplicity that seem to defy analysis. His music is so—musical!

(12) Mozart was born in 1756 in Salzburg, Austria. His father, Leopold, was a recognized violinist and composer in the court of the archbishop. The elder Mozart was quick to realize and capitalize on his son's extraordinary talents. Under his father's teaching, young Mozart showed remarkable mastery of the piano and to a lesser extent the violin. By the time he was five he had composed his first pieces, and at six he performed at the court of the Empress Maria Theresa. When he was seven, Mozart and his

sister, who was four years his elder, went on a tour that included Paris, London, and Munich. By the age of thirteen he had written concertos, symphonies, and a comic opera; at fourteen he was knighted by the Pope.

(13) The most phenomenal aspect of Mozart's musical talent was his memory for music and his ability to work out whole pieces in his mind. He once wrote, "Though it be long, the work is complete and finished in my mind. I take out of the bag of my memory what has previously been collected into it. For this reason the committing to paper is done quickly enough. For everything is already finished, and it rarely differs on paper from what it was in my imagination."

(14) Mozart never enjoyed the stability of a good appointment as a composer to a patron. For a while he worked for the prince-archbishop of Salzburg. The archbishop was a difficult man, and the high-spirited Mozart resented the restrictions of the patronage system. (He wrote his father, "The two valets sit at the head of the table. I at least have the honor of sitting above the cooks.") He quarreled with the archbishop and was dismissed. At the age of twenty-five he left Salzburg to pursue his career in Vienna.

(15) Since Mozart did not fare well under the patronage system, he spent some of the last ten years of his life, as he put it, "hovering between hope and anxiety." Due in part to his impractical and overgenerous nature in financial affairs, he had to eke out an existence by teaching, giving concerts, composing, and borrowing from friends.

(16) In 1791, at the age of thirty-five, Mozart died of uremic poisoning. Because he was so deeply in debt, he was given the cheapest funeral and buried in a pauper's grave.

(17) Despite his short life and its disappointments, Mozart composed over 600 works, many of them sizable compositions such as operas, symphonies, concertos, and string quartets. He never used opus numbers, although some were added later by publishers. His works were catalogued by a Viennese botanist and amateur musician named Köchel.

1. The excerpt makes use of

   a. boldface print
   b. italics
   c. underlining
   d. both a and b

2. One topic *not* covered in this excerpt is

   a. the Rococo style
   b. patronage
   c. the Classical attitude
   d. the sonata form

3. It seems that the Rococo style came

   a. before the Classical
   b. after the Classical
   c. before the Baroque
   d. to be only in France

4. It seems that the section on Mozart discusses only his sonatas.

   a. true
   b. false

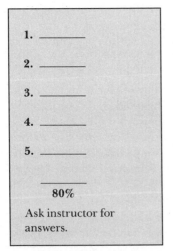

1. _____

2. _____

3. _____

4. _____

5. _____

80%

Ask instructor for answers.

5. This excerpt presents several dates to situate the various stages in the Classical period.

    a. true
    b. false

B. Question

Having surveyed this excerpt, write five questions that you intend to answer when you study read. Use the chapter title and section titles to help you write these questions. You may also want to read the first sentence of several of the paragraphs to formulate some of your questions. Answer these questions as you read the chapter.

1.

2.

3.

4.

Ask instructor for sample questions.

5.

C. Read and Recite

Having written your questions, you are now ready to begin study reading paragraphs 1–7, underlining important passages and making marginal comments about the Rococo style and the Classical attitude. When you have finished reciting (using the Cornell note-taking system), go back to these seven paragraphs to be sure that your summary is both accurate and complete.

Now read paragraphs 8–17. Then recite this material on a separate sheet of paper. In this section, include a definition and list of characteristics for the Classical attitude as well as a list of the important events in Mozart's life. Again, go back to these pages to check for the completeness and accuracy of your summary.

D. Review

Now you are ready to review your underlinings, marginal comments, and two summaries. You may want to design study maps for the Rococo style and Classical attitude as well as the significant events in Mozart's life. Finally, go back to the five questions you made up to see if you can now answer them without any help.

Examination: Classicism, Classical Music, and Mozart

Directions: Give yourself fifty minutes to complete the following questions. Be sure to budget your time.

I. Multiple Choice: Choose the letter that correctly completes each question. Place all answers in the answer box. (30 points)

1. How can you best describe the Rococo style?

    a. light
    b. elegant
    c. frivolous
    d. all of these

2. Rococo music is usually

    a. serious
    b. simple
    c. ornate
    d. all of these

3. A patron is one who

    a. tutors young musicians
    b. supports young composers
    c. writes biographies of great composers
    d. attends concerts

4. The Classical attitude emphasized

    a. reason
    b. emotion
    c. a study of the Middle Ages
    d. a study of mysticism

5. Which characteristic does *not* describe the Classical attitude?

    a. emphasis on learning
    b. emphasis on universal truths
    c. fascination with the unknown
    d. view that universe runs much like a large machine

6. According to this excerpt, the Declaration of Independence is

    a. a reasoned document
    b. a revolutionary document
    c. not Classical in attitude
    d. both a and b

7. The Classical period has also been called the

    a. Age of Enlightenment
    b. Age of Pessimism

1. _____
2. _____
3. _____
4. _____
5. _____
6. _____
7. _____
8. _____
9. _____
10. _____
11. _____
12. _____
13. _____
14. _____
15. _____
16. _____
17. _____
18. _____
19. _____
20. _____

c. New Renaissance
d. Noble Age

8. What the Classical period admired most in the ancient Greeks was

   a. their mythology
   b. their intellectual restraint
   c. Homer
   d. their drama, especially their comedies

9. The Classical mind believed that the unknown was

   a. God's world
   b. unattainable
   c. attainable through faith
   d. attainable through knowledge

10. What do you think was the attitude of the Classical mind toward the human being's potential?

   a. pessimistic
   b. neutral
   c. optimistic
   d. none of these

II. True-False: Write *T* for true, *F* for false. Write all answers in the answer box. (30 points)

11. Mozart's music is often described as complicated.
12. Mozart knew how to play only the piano.
13. At the age of five, Mozart was already composing.
14. As a composer, Mozart had an average memory for musical pieces.
15. Mozart seemingly revised his pieces very little.
16. Mozart spent some of his time composing in Vienna.
17. The prince-archbishop of France was Mozart's patron early in Mozart's career.
18. In his personal life, Mozart was often in debt because his wife was extravagant.
19. Mozart died of uremic poisoning at the age of thirty-six.
20. To Mozart's credit are over 600 musical works.

III. Short Essay: In an organized paragraph, discuss the major characteristics of the Rococo style and the Classical attitude. Show how and where these two schools of thought are similar and different. (40 points)

_____
75%
Ask instructor for answers.

Study Reading 3

Physical Measurement

This excerpt is from a chapter in a college chemistry textbook. The style is straightforward, but this simplicity is deceiving. You may need to reread many of the sections in order to master them and to use this knowledge in solving specific problems. Use the following strategies to master the material in this excerpt:

1. Read the definitions carefully, underlining or circling important parts. You need to know what each term in this excerpt means, so read to understand every part of each definition.

2. Read for cause-effect patterns. You may want to reread the section on cause and effect on pp. 73–74. The cause-effect statements in this excerpt are direct, so don't look for terms of qualification.

3. Read the sample problems and solutions carefully. Follow the solution to each problem step by step. Be sure that you understand each step before you go on to the next.

4. Memorize the formulas regarding temperature conversion. Learn what each abbreviation means and how each term relates to the others.

5. After you finish reading the excerpt, complete the exercises. These problems will give you needed practice in converting the temperatures from one scale to another.

6. By the time you have finished the excerpt, you should be able to recall without help the meanings of the terms. You should also be able to write out the conversion formulas and correctly use each one.

A. Survey

Take three minutes to survey the chapter excerpt. Read the title, the titles of each section, the terms and statements that are highlighted, and the summary and exercises at the end of the excerpt. If time permits, begin reading the first several paragraphs.

Before you read, you should know the meaning of two terms that are not defined in this excerpt. *Kinetic energy* is the energy that matter possesses because of its motion; *SI* (for Système International) is an updated form of the metric system used in the sciences.

When you have finished, answer the questions that follow without looking back at the excerpt. Place all of your answers in the answer box.

Measurement and Units

G. Tyler Miller, Jr.

2.5   Heat and Temperature

Heat Units and Measurement

(1) The official SI unit for heat or any other form of energy is the **joule (J)** (pronounced jool). Many chemists, however, still use an older heat unit known as the calorie (cal). Although the calorie unit is gradually being phased out, it is still widely used so that we need to be able to convert between joules and calories. A **calorie (cal)** is defined as the amount of heat energy required to raise the temperature of 1 g of water from 14.5° to 15.5°C. One calorie is equal to 4.184 joules.

$$1 \, cal = 4.184 \, J \quad or \quad \frac{4.184 \, J}{1 \, cal}$$

(2) Since both the joule and the calorie represent relatively small quantities of heat energy, the larger quantities of heat usually encountered in physical and chemical changes are often expressed in kilojoules (kJ) and kilocalories (kcal or Cal). Respectively, these units are equal to

1,000 J and 1,000 cal. Since 1 cal equals 4.184 J, 1 kcal (kilocalorie) equals 4.184 kJ (kilojoules).

(3) The kilocalorie (also abbreviated Cal with a capital C) is the unit used in dietary tables to show the energy content of various types of food. Thus, a piece of pie containing 500 Cal (or 500 kcal) contains 500,000 or 5×10^5 cal. Individual energy requirements for the human body depend on a number of factors, including body weight and the amount of physical activity. A person weighing 68.2 kg (150 lb) and carrying out moderate physical activity typically needs about 8.4×10^3 kJ or 2.0×10^3 kcal of food energy a day.

Heat and Temperature

(4) It is important to distinguish between heat and temperature. **Heat** or thermal energy can be roughly described as a measure of the total kinetic energy of all the particles in a sample of matter.[1] The relative "hotness" or "cold-

---

G. *Tyler Miller, Jr.*, Chemistry: A Basic Introduction, *2nd ed. (Belmont, Calif.: Wadsworth, 1981), pp. 51–55; p. 59; p. 61. Used by permission.*

---

[1]Heat or thermal energy also includes the rotational and vibrational energy of the particles along with the potential energy of attractions between particles. Since these energies are normally small (except at high temperatures), heat or thermal energy is primarily a measure of the total energy of motion (kinetic energy) of the particles.

ness" of a sample of matter is described by measuring its temperature. **Temperature** is a measure of the average (not the total) kinetic energy of the particles in a sample of matter.

(5) The heat (total kinetic energy) and temperature (average kinetic energy) of a given sample of matter are quite different quantities, just as the total mass of the members of a chemistry class is quite different from the average mass of the class. The heat in a given sample of matter depends on the amount of matter present in the sample. In contrast, the temperature of an object does not depend on the amount of matter in the sample. A cup of hot coffee contains a larger quantity of heat than a drop of the same coffee, but the temperatures of the liquid in the cup and the drop are the same.

(6) When one object has a higher temperature than another object, we know from experience that some of the energy from the hotter object will flow in the form of heat to the cooler object. You discovered this the first time you touched a hot stove or other hot object. In more formal language, then, temperature determines the direction in which heat energy flows when two samples of matter are brought into contact with one another.

Heat is a measure of the total kinetic energy of all the particles in a sample of matter.

Temperature is a measure of the average kinetic energy of the particles in a sample of matter.

Temperature Measurement

(7) A **thermometer** is a device used to measure the temperature of a sample of matter. The most commonly used thermometer is the mercury thermometer. To measure and compare temperatures throughout the world, scientists have established several standard temperature scales. The three major temperature scales are the *Fahrenheit (F) scale*, the *Celsius (C) scale* (formerly known as the centigrade scale), and the *Kelvin (K) scale* (Figure 2-7). A unit of tempera-

ture on each scale is called a **degree**. A superscript, °, is used before the C abbreviation for Celsius and before the F abbreviation for Fahrenheit to indicate a degree. This superscript is not used for Kelvin temperature, since the Kelvin is defined as a unit of temperature. Thus, 100°C is read *100 degrees Celius* and 273 K is read *273 Kelvin*. The term °*K* or *degrees Kelvin*, however, is still a widely used relic of an earlier version of the metric system. Most everyday measurements of temperature in the United States are reported in Fahrenheit temperature, although this scale is being phased out as the United States converts to the metric system. Scientists use both the Celsius and the Kelvin scales. The official SI temperature scale, however, is the Kelvin (K) scale.

(8) As shown in Figure 2-7, the **Fahrenheit temperature scale** is defined by assigning to the normal boiling point of water a temperature of 212°F and to the freezing point of water the temperature of 32°F. Since the difference between 212 and 32 is 180, the glass length between the two reference points is divided into 180 equal segments, each denoting a Fahrenheit degree. For the **Celsius temperature scale** the boiling point of water is assigned a value of 100°C and the freezing point of water is assigned the value of 0°C. This allows the distance between these two reference points to be divided into 100 equal units, each representing a Celsius degree. On the **Kelvin temperature scale**, the normal boiling point of water is 373.15 K (approximately 373 K) and the freezing point of water is 273.15 K (approximately 273 K). The value of 0 K is the absolute zero of temperature on the Kelvin scale. This value is equal to $-273.15°C$ or $-459.75°F$ (Figure 2-7).

Temperature Conversions

(9) Conversions between Fahrenheit and Celsius temperatures can be made using two simple formulas. Since 100 degrees on the Celsius scale is the same as 180 degrees on the Fahrenheit scale (Figure 2-7), then 1°C = 1.8°F. Thus, the unit conversion factor between Celsius and

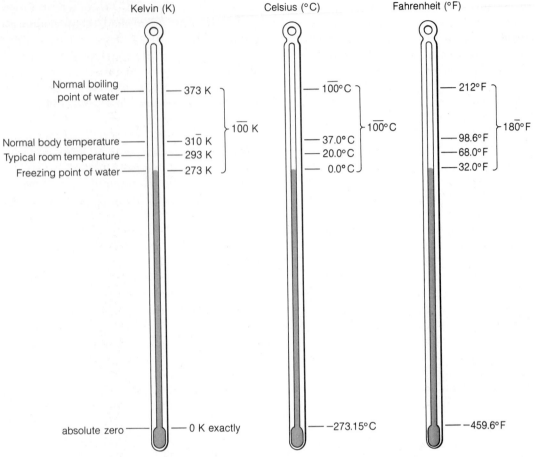

Figure 2-7 *Comparison of the Kelvin (K), Celsius (°C), and Fahrenheit (°F) temperature scales.*

Fahrenheit is 1.8°F/1°C (or 9°F/5°C). The zero point on the Fahrenheit scale is 32°F compared to 0°C for the Celsius scale. Thus, to convert any temperature on the Fahrenheit scale to the Celsius scale, we first subtract 32°F from the Fahrenheit temperature and then multiply by the appropriate conversion factor.

$$°C = \frac{1.0°C}{1.8°F} \times (°F - 32°F)$$

To convert from Celsius to Fahrenheit we multiply the Celsius temperature by the appropriate conversion factor and then add 32°F to the result.[2]

$$°F = \left(°C \times \frac{1.8°F}{1.0°C}\right) + 32°F$$

---

[2]Another set of formulas relating to Fahrenheit and Celsius scales is

$$°C = \frac{1.0°C}{1.8°F}(°F - 40°F) - 40°C$$

$$°F = \frac{1.8°F}{1.0°C}(°C + 40°C) - 40°F$$

The following examples illustrate the use of these conversions.

(10) **Example 2.12.** To help save energy, Americans have been asked to lower their thermostats to 65°F in cold weather. What is this temperature on the Celsius scale?

Solution

Unknown: °C

Known: 65°F

Plan: $°C = \dfrac{1.0°C}{1.8°F}(°F - 32°F)$

Result: $C = \dfrac{1.0°C}{1.8°F} \times (65°F - 32°F)$

$= \dfrac{1.0°C}{1.8°F}(33°F) = 18°C$

(11) **Example 2.13.** On a cold day in Alaska the temperature is $-25°C$. What is the equivalent Fahrenheit temperature?

Solution

Unknown: °F

Known: $-25°C$

Plan: $°F = \left(°C \times \dfrac{1.8°F}{1.0°C}\right) + 32°F$

Result: $°F = \left[(-25°C) \times \dfrac{1.8°F}{1.0°C}\right] + 32°F$

$= -45°F + 32°F = -13°F$

(12) Conversions between the Celsius and Kelvin scales are very easy. From Figure 2.7 we can see that $0 K = -273°C$. Thus, $°C = K -$ 273° and $K = °C + 273°$. In other words, to convert °C to K we merely add 273 to the Celsius temperature. . . .

Accomplishments and Review

(13) After completing this chapter you should be able to do the following:

2.5   Heat and Temperature:

12. Distinguish between heat and temperature and give the units used for heat and temperature measurements.

13. Make conversions between the Fahrenheit (F), Celsius (C), and Kelvin (K) temperature scales.

Exercises

(14) *2.5   Heat and Temperature:*

26. Which of the following is the highest temperature: 250 K, 230°F, 120°C?

27. Make the following temperature conversions:
  a. Room temperature frequently averages 20.0°C. What is this on the Fahrenheit and Kelvin scales?
  b. Milk is pasteurized at 145°F. What is this on the Celsius and Kelvin scales?
  c. What is the normal body temperature of 98.6°F on the Celsius and Kelvin scales?
  d. The normal boiling point of ethyl alcohol is 79.0°C. What is its boiling point on the Kelvin scale?
  e. At normal atmospheric pressure the boiling point of liquid nitrogen is 77 K. What is the boiling point in degrees Celsius? Would nitrogen be a liquid or a gas at $-100°C$?

1. This excerpt makes use of

  a. boldface print
  b. italics
  c. illustrations
  d. all of these

2. The boldface statements on heat and temperature

    a. define both terms
    b. show the difference in the Fahrenheit, Celsius, and Kelvin temperature scales
    c. show the difference between heat and temperature
    d. both a and c

3. The problems that are presented in this excerpt are solved

    a. step by step
    b. by presenting the formulas
    c. by presenting the known and unknown quantities
    d. all of these

4. It appears that in this excerpt you will learn something about

    a. the Fahrenheit scale
    b. the Celsius scale
    c. the Kelvin scale
    d. all of these

5. Which topic will not be covered in this excerpt?

    a. heat units
    b. temperature measurement
    c. temperature conversions
    d. specific heat

1. _____

2. _____

3. _____

4. _____

5. _____

_____
80%

Ask instructor for answers.

B. Question

Having surveyed the chapter excerpt, write five questions that you intend to answer when you study read. Use the chapter title, section titles, and boldface print to formulate your questions. Answer these questions as you read the chapter.

1.

2.

3.

4.

5.

Ask instructor for sample questions.

C. Read and Recite

With these questions, you are ready to begin study reading. Use your best underlining and commenting skills, being sparing with what you underline and making marginal notes on important terms and formulas. Read the entire excerpt. Then, on a separate sheet of paper, use the Cornell note-taking system to recite what you have read. When you have completed your summary, go back to the excerpt to be sure that your summary is both accurate and complete. Make any additions to your summary at this time.

D. Review   Now you are ready to review your underlinings, your marginal comments, and your summary. Before you take the exam, you should solve Exercises 26 and 27 on p. 311. There will be a problem-solving section to the exam, and these problems will serve as review.

Examination: Measurement and Units

Directions: Give yourself fifty minutes to complete the following questions. Be sure to budget your time.

I. Matching: Match up the following terms with the appropriate definitions. Each term should be matched up to only one definition. Place all answers in the answer box. (18 points)

1. joule	a. amount of heat required to raise the temperature of one gram of water from 14.5°C to 15.5°C
2. calorie	
3. heat	
4. temperature	b. measure of the average kinetic energy in a sample of matter
5. Celsius temperature scale	
6. Kelvin temperature scale	c. official SI unit for heat or any other form of energy
	d. boiling point of water about 373°; freezing point of water about 273°
	e. boiling point of water 100°; freezing point of water 0°
	f. measure of the total kinetic energy of all particles in a sample of matter

II. Multiple Choice: Choose the letter that correctly completes each question or statement. Place all answers in the answer box. (27 points)

7. How many joules are in a calorie?

   a. 4184 J
   b. 418.4 J
   c. 41.84 J
   d. 4.184 J

8. The correct abbreviation for kilocalorie is

   a. cal
   b. Cal
   c. KC
   d. kc

9. The heat in a given sample of matter depends on the

    a. average energy of the particles in the sample
    b. amount of matter present in the sample
    c. average kinetic energy of the particles in the sample
    d. none of these

10. Heat tends to flow from a

    a. cooler object to a warmer object
    b. warmer object to a cooler object
    c. gas to a liquid
    d. liquid to a solid

11. On which temperature scale is the superscript ° not used?

    a. Fahrenheit
    b. Celsius
    c. Kelvin
    d. metric

12. On the Celsius scale, what is the boiling point of water?

    a. 0°
    b. 212°
    c. 373°
    d. 100°

13. On which scale is the difference between the boiling point of water and the freezing point of water 180?

    a. Fahrenheit
    b. Celsius
    c. Kelvin
    d. metric

14. In which scale is the difference between the boiling point of water and the freezing point of water 100?

    a. Fahrenheit
    b. Celsius
    c. Kelvin
    d. both b and c

15. 0 K is designated as

    a. absolute zero
    b. the freezing point of water
    c. the boiling point of water
    d. none of these

1. _____

2. _____

3. _____

4. _____

5. _____

6. _____

7. _____

8. _____

9. _____

10. _____

11. _____

12. _____

13. _____

14. _____

15. _____

III. Problem Solving: Complete the following two problems. You will get credit for determining the unknown quantity, the known quantity, the correct formula, and the correct answer. Show all your work.

1. In the desert areas of Southern California the temperature often goes as high as 44°C. What temperature is this on the Fahrenheit scale? (25 points)

    a. unknown: (5 points)

    b. known: (5 points)

    c. formula: (5 points)

    d. work: (5 points)

    e. answer: (5 points)

2. For experimental purposes Dr. Burns placed a virus at 120°F. What is the equivalent Kelvin temperature? (30 points)

    a. unknown: (5 points)

    b. known: (5 points)

    c. formulas: (10 points)

    d. work: (5 points)

    e. answer: (5 points)

70%

Ask instructor for answers.

Study Reading 4

Social Power

Unlike the previous three textbook excerpts that you have read, this one is an entire chapter, the first chapter in a sociology textbook. Study reading it will closely resemble the activities you will engage in when you read textbooks in college. Also, instead of answering objective questions about the chapter, you will be answering essay questions.

This selection introduces and defines the key concepts examined in the textbook. Thus it relies heavily on two organizational patterns: definition and comparison-contrast. You may want to reread the sections in Chapter 5 on these two organizational patterns (pp. 74–75 and 78–79) before you start your study reading of this chapter. And you may want to review how to answer extended essay and short-answer questions.

Use the following strategies to master this chapter's material:

1. Read carefully for definitions. See how the definitions of terms interrelate. Identify and mark the key terms.

2. Look for comparisons and contrasts in the definitions and issues that the author presents. Make marginal comments about these comparisons.

3. Read the case study carefully, as well as the summary of the chapter and the discussion questions.

4. As you study read, see how your previous reading of sociology material in Chapter 5 and your reading of economics material in Chapter 4 help you understand this chapter. You may want to review the exercises in Chapters 4 and 5 after you complete the study reading of this chapter to clarify any questions about sociology or economics that you may have had.

5. As you read the last section of the chapter — on ideology, race, and poverty — see whether you can apply any of your own experiences to the sociological issues that are explained.

A. Survey

Take four minutes to survey this chapter. Read the titles, subtitles, and terms in boldface and italics. Notice the chapter's special features: how the definitions are highlighted, the purpose of the case study, and the kinds of discussion questions at the end.

When you have finished, answer the questions that follow without looking back at the excerpt.

The Nature of Power

Thomas R. Dye

(1) Ordinary men and women are driven by forces in society that they neither understand nor control. These forces are embodied in governmental authorities, economic organizations and markets, social values and ideologies, accepted ways of life, and learned patterns of behavior. However diverse the nature of these forces, they have in common the ability to modify the conduct of individuals, to control their behavior, to shape their lives.

(2) *Power is the capacity to affect the conduct of individuals through the real or threatened use of rewards and punishments.* Power is exercised over individuals or groups by offering them some things they value or by threatening to deprive them of those things. These values are the *power base*, and they can include physical safety, health, and well-being; wealth and material possessions; jobs and means to a livelihood; knowledge and skills; social recognition, status, and prestige; love, affection, and acceptance by others; a satisfactory self-image and self-respect. To exercise power, then, control must be exercised over the things that are valued in society.

(3) *Power is a special form of influence.* Broadly speaking, influence is the production of intended effects. People who can produce intended effects by any means are said to be influential. People who can produce intended effects by the real or threatened use of rewards and punishments are said to be powerful.

(4) *Power can rest on various resources.* The exercise of power assumes many different forms — the giving or withholding of many different values. Yet power bases are usually *interdependent* — individuals who control certain resources are likely to control other resources as well. Wealth,

power
the capacity to affect the conduct of others through the real or threatened use of rewards and punishments

power
based on control of valued resources
unequally distributed
exercised in interpersonal relations
exercised through large institutions

Thomas R. Dye, Power and Society, *5th ed. (Belmont, Calif.: Wadsworth, 1990), pp. 4–14.*

economic power, prestige, recognition, political influence, education, respect, and so on, all tend to "go together" in society.

(5) *Power is never equally distributed.* "There is no power where power is equal." For power to be exercised, the "powerholder" must control some base values. By *control* we mean that the powerholder is in a position to offer these values as rewards to others or to threaten to deprive others of these values.

(6) *Power is a relationship* among individuals, groups, and institutions in society. Power is not really a "thing" that an individual possesses. Instead, power is a relationship in which some individuals or groups have control over certain resources.

(7) The *elite* are the few who have power; the *masses* are the many who do not. The elite are the few who control what is valued in society and use that control to shape the lives of all of us. The masses are the many whose lives are shaped by institutions, events, and leaders over which they have little control. Political scientist Harold Lasswell writes, "The division of society into elites and masses is universal," and even in a democracy, "a few exercise a relatively great weight of power, and the many exercise comparatively little."[1]

elite and masses
the few who have power and the many who do not

(8) *Power is exercised in interpersonal relations.* Psychologist Rollo May writes that "power means the ability to affect, to influence, and to change other persons."[2] He argues that power is essential to one's "sense of significance" — one's conviction that one counts for something in the world, that one has an effect on others, and that one can get recognition of one's existence from others. Power is essential to the development of personality. An infant who is denied the experience of influencing others or of drawing their attention to its existence withdraws to a corner of its bed, does not talk or develop in any way, and withers away physiologically and psychologically. Thus power is essential to *being*. Political scientist Robert Dahl also defines power in terms of *individual interaction*: "A has power over B to the extent that he can get B to do something he would not otherwise do." He argues that every exercise of power depends on interpersonal relations between the powerholder and the responder.

(9) *Power is exercised in large institutions* — governments, corporations, schools, the military, churches, newspapers, television networks, law firms, and so on. Power that stems from high positions in the social structures of society is stable and far-reaching. Sociologist C. Wright Mills observes: "No one can be truly powerful unless he has access to the command of major institutions, for it is over these institutional means of power that the truly powerful are, in the first instance, powerful."[3] Not all power, it is true, is anchored in or exercised through institutions. But institutional positions in society provide a continuous and important base of power. As Mills explains:

> If we took the one hundred most powerful men in America, the one hundred wealthiest, and the one hundred most celebrated away from the institutional

positions they now occupy, away from their resources of men and women and money, away from the media of mass communication that are now focused upon them — then they would be powerless and poor and uncelebrated. For power is not of a man. Wealth does not center in the person of the wealthy. . . . To have power requires access to major institutions, for the institutional positions men occupy determine in large part their chances to have and to hold these valued experiences.[4]

Power and the Social Sciences

social science
the study of human behavior

(10) *Social science* is the study of human behavior. Actually, there are several social sciences, each specializing in a particular aspect of human behavior and each using different concepts, methods, and data in its studies. Anthropology, sociology, economics, psychology, political science, and history have developed into separate "disciplines," but all share an interest in human behavior.

(11) Power is *not* the central concern of the social sciences, yet all the social sciences deal with power in one form or another. Each of the social sciences contributes to an understanding of the forces that modify the conduct of individuals, control their behavior, and shape their lives. Thus, to fully understand power in society, we must approach this topic in an *interdisciplinary* fashion — using ideas, methods, data, and findings from all the social sciences.

Anthropology

anthropology
the study of people and their ways of life

(12) *Anthropology* is the study of people and their ways of life. It is the most comprehensive of the social sciences. Some anthropologists are concerned primarily with people's biological and physical characteristics; this field is called *physical anthropology*. Other anthropologists are interested primarily in the ways of life of both ancient and modern peoples; this field is called *cultural anthropology*.

culture
all the common patterns and ways of living that characterize society

(13) *Culture* is all the common patterns and ways of living that characterize society. The anthropologist tries to describe and explain a great many things: child rearing and education; family arrangements; language and communication; technology; ways of making a living; the distribution of work; religious beliefs and values; social life; leadership patterns; and power structures.

(14) Power is part of the culture or the way of life of a people. Power is exercised in all societies, because all societies have systems of rewards and sanctions designed to control the behavior of their members. Perhaps the most enduring structure of power in society is the family: power is exercised within the family when patterns of dominance and submission are established between male and female and parents and children. Societies also develop structures of power outside the family to maintain peace and order among their members; to organize individuals to accomplish large-scale tasks; to defend themselves against attack; and even to wage war and exploit other peoples.

(15) In our study of power and culture, we shall examine how cultural patterns determine power relationships. We shall examine patterns of authority in traditional and modern families and the changing power role of women in society. We shall examine the origins and development of power relationships, illustrating them with examples of societies in which power is organized by family and kinship group (polar Eskimos), by tribe (Crow Indians), and by the state (the Aztec empire). Finally, as a case study, we shall look at the controversy over "sociobiology" — that is, the extent to which genetics or culture determines behaviors.

Sociology

(16) *Sociology* is the study of relationships among individuals and groups. Sociologists describe the structure of formal and informal groups, their functions and purposes, and how they change over time. They study social institutions (such as families, schools, churches), social processes (for example, conflict, competition, assimilation, change), and social problems (crime, race relations, poverty, and so forth). Sociologists also study social classes.

sociology
the study of relationships among individuals and groups

(17) All societies have some system of classifying and ranking their members — a system of *stratification*. In modern industrial societies, social status is associated with the various roles that individuals play in the economic system. Individuals are ranked according to how they make their living and the control they exercise over the living of others. Stratification into social classes is determined largely on the basis of occupation and control of economic resources.

social stratification
classifying and ranking members of society

(18) Power derives from social status, prestige, and respect, as well as from control of economic resources. Thus, the stratification system involves the unequal distribution of power.

(19) In our study of power and social class, we shall describe the stratification system in America and explore popular beliefs about "getting ahead." We shall discuss the differing lifestyles of upper, middle, and lower classes in America and the extent of class conflict. We shall examine the ideas of Karl Marx about the struggle for power among social classes. We shall describe the differential in political power among social classes in America. Finally, we shall explore the ideas of sociologist C. Wright Mills about a top "power elite" in America that occupies powerful positions in the governmental, corporate, and military bureaucracies of the nation.

Psychology

(20) *Psychology* may be defined as the study of the behavior of people and animals. Behavior, we know, is the product of both "nature and nurture" — that is, a product of both our biological makeup and our environmental conditioning. We shall examine the continuing controversy over *how much* of our behavior is a product of our genes versus our

psychology
the study of the behavior of people and animals

environment. We shall learn that there is great richness and diversity in psychological inquiry. For example, *behavioral psychologists* study the learning process — the way in which people and animals learn to respond to stimuli. They frequently study in experimental laboratory situations, with the hope that the knowledge gained can be useful in understanding more complex human behavior outside the laboratory. *Social psychologists*, on the other hand, study interpersonal behavior — the way in which social interactions shape an individual's beliefs, perceptions, motivations, attitudes, and behavior. They generally study the whole person in relation to the total environment. *Freudian psychologists* study the impact of subconscious feelings and emotions and of early childhood experiences on the behavior of adults. *Humanistic psychologists* are concerned with the human being's innate potential for growth and development. Many other psychologists combine theories and methods in different ways in their attempts to achieve a better understanding of behavior.

personality
all the enduring, organized ways of behavior that characterize an individual

(21) *Personality* is all the enduring, organized ways of behavior that characterize an individual. Psychologists differ over how personality characteristics are determined — whether they are learned habits acquired through the process of reinforcement and conditioning (behavioral psychology), or products of the individual's interaction with the significant people and groups in his or her life (social psychology), or manifestations of the continuous process of positive growth toward "self-actualization" (humanistic psychology), or the results of subconscious drives and long-repressed emotions stemming from early childhood experiences (Freudian psychology), or some combination of all these.

(22) The study of personality is essential in understanding how individuals react toward power and authority. Power is a personal experience. Everyone is subject to one form of power or another during all the waking hours of life. And everyone has exercised some power, if only in microscopic degree, at some time. Individuals react toward these experiences with power in different and characteristic ways. Some individuals seek power for personal fulfillment. Philosopher Bertrand Russel writes, "Of the infinite desires of man, the chief are the desires for power and glory." Other individuals are submissive to authority, while still others are habitually rebellious. It is said that "power tends to corrupt, and absolute power corrupts absolutely." However, there is ample psychological evidence that lack of power also corrupts. The feelings that one cannot influence anyone else, that one counts for little, and that one has no control over one's own life all contribute to a loss of personal identity.

(23) In our study of power and personality, we will examine various theories of personality determination — specifically, those of behavioral psychology, social psychology, humanistic psychology, and Freudian psychology — in an effort to understand the forces shaping the individual's reaction to power. Using a Freudian perspective, we shall study the "authoritarian personality" — the individual who is habitually dominant

and aggressive toward others over whom he or she exercises power, yet submissive and weak toward others who have more power; the individual who is extremely prejudiced, rigid, intolerant, cynical, and power-oriented. We shall explore the power implications of B. F. Skinner's ideas of behavioral conditioning for the control of human behavior. To gain an understanding of humanistic psychology's approach to power relationships, we shall examine Rollo May's formulation of the functions of power for the individual and Abraham Maslow's theory of a "hierarchy of needs." Finally, in our case study, we shall describe the startling results of an experiment designed to test the relationship between authority and obedience.

Economics

(24) *Economics* is the study of the production and distribution of scarce goods and services. There are never enough goods and services to satisfy everyone's demands, and because of this, choices must be made. Economists study how individuals, firms, and nations make these choices about goods and services.

economics
the study of the production and distribution of scarce goods and services

Economic power is the power to decide what will be produced, how much it will cost, how many people will be employed, what their wages will be, what the price of goods and services will be, what profits will be made, how these profits will be distributed, and how fast the economy will grow. Control over these decisions is a major source of power in society.

(25) Capitalist societies rely heavily on the market mechanism to determine who gets what—what is to be produced, how much it will cost, and who will be able to buy it. In our study of economic power, we shall explore both the strengths and weaknesses of this market system, as well as the ideas of economic philosophers Adam Smith and John M. Keynes. In addition, we shall consider the role of government in the economy, which has increased over the years. We shall examine "supply side" economics of the 1980s and describe the results of "Reaganomics." We shall then turn to an examination of America's vast wealth—how it is measured, where it comes from, and where it goes. We shall examine the relationship between wealth and the quality of life, which are not always equivalent things. We shall also examine the concentration of private wealth and corporate power in America. Finally, in our case study, we shall discuss the politics and economics of tax reform.

Political Science

(26) *Political science* is the study of government and politics. Governments possess *authority*, a particular form of power; that is, the legitimate use of physical force. By *legitimate*, we mean that people generally consent to the government's use of this power. Of course, other individuals and organizations in society—muggers, street gangs, the Mafia, violent revolutionaries—use force. But only government can legitimately threaten people with the loss of freedom and well-being to mod-

political science
the study of government and politics

authority
the legitimate use of physical force

ify their behavior. Moreover, governments exercise power over all individuals and institutions in society — corporations, families, schools, and so forth. Obviously the power of government in modern society is very great, extending to nearly every aspect of modern life — "from womb to tomb."

(27) Political scientists from Aristotle to the present have been concerned with the dangers of unlimited and unchecked governmental power. We shall examine the American experience with limited, constitutional government; the philosophical legacy of English political thought; and the meaning of democracy in modern society. We shall observe how the U.S. Constitution divides power, first between states and the national government, and second among the legislative, executive, and judicial branches of government. We shall examine the growth of power in Washington, D.C., and the struggle for power among the different branches. We shall also explore competition between political parties and interest groups and popular participation in decision making through elections. Finally, in our case study "Political Power and the Mass Media," we shall examine the growing power of television in American politics.

History

history
the recording, narrating, and interpreting of human experience

(28) *History* is the recording, narrating, and interpreting of human experience. The historian recreates the past by collecting recorded facts, organizing them into a narrative, and interpreting their meaning. History is also concerned with change over time. It provides a perspective on the present by informing us of the way people lived in the past. History helps us to understand how society developed into what it is today.

(29) The foundations of power vary from age to age. As power bases shift, new groups and individuals acquire control over them. Thus, power relationships are continuously developing and changing. An understanding of power in society requires an understanding of the historical development of power relationships.

(30) In our consideration of the historical development of power relationships, we shall look at the changing sources of power in American history and the characteristics of the individuals and groups who have acquired power. We shall describe the men of power in the early days of the republic and their shaping of the Constitution and the government that it established. We shall discuss Charles Beard's interpretation of the Constitution as a document designed to protect the economic interests of those early powerholders. We shall also discuss historian Frederick Jackson Turner's ideas about how westward expansion and settlement created new bases of power and new powerholders. We shall explore the power struggle between northern commercial and industrial interests and southern planters and slave owners for control of western land, and the Civil War that resulted from that struggle. In

Notes

1. Harold Lasswell and Abraham Kaplan, *Power and Society* (New Haven, Conn.: Yale University Press, 1950), p. 219.

2. Rollo May, *Power and Innocence* (New York: Norton, 1977), p. 20.

3. C. Wright Mills, *The Power Elite* (New York: Oxford University Press, 1956), p. 9.

4. Ibid., p. 10.

About This Chapter

Power in society is not just an abstract concept or a convenient focus for academic exercise. Nor is power something that is located exclusively in the nation's capitals. Power is very much a real factor that affects the lives of each of us. We experience it in some form in our families, in school, and at work; we feel its effects in the grocery store and on the highway. And we each react to it in characteristic ways. Our aim in this chapter was to understand just what power *is*. We also saw why it provides us with a useful perspective from which to gain a unified view of the social sciences and the social problems that concern us all.

Now that you have read this chapter, you should be able to

- define power in society and describe its characteristics,

- define the area of study of each of the social sciences, as well as their common focus, and discuss how each relates to power in society,

- identify the major social problems that the social sciences study and explain why they are interdisciplinary in nature and how they relate to power.

Discussion Questions

1. How would you define power? What characteristics of power deserve to be discussed in any definition of power?

2. Consider the power relationships that directly and indirectly affect your life. On the basis of your experiences and observations, assess the validity of these statements by Bertrand Russell: "The fundamental concept in the social sciences is power, in the same sense in which energy is the fundamental concept in physics. . . . When a moderate degree of comfort is assured, both individuals and communities will pursue power rather than wealth. . . . Love of power is the chief motive producing the changes which social science has to study."

3. Identify and briefly define the area of study of each of the social sciences. Discuss how you would study power from the perspective of each of these disciplines.

4. What is meant by the *interdisciplinary* study of social problems?

5. Choose two of the following social problems and briefly explain how they involve power: (a) racial and sexual inequality, (b) poverty, (c) crime and violence, (d) international conflict.

---

1. How are boldface print and italics used?

2. What is the case study generally about?

3. What types of questions are asked in the "Discussion Questions" section?

4. What are the three basic parts of this chapter?

5. Why do you think the various disciplines that you have studied in this textbook—economics, sociology, anthropology—are introduced in this chapter?

80%

Ask instructor for answers.

B. Question

Having surveyed the chapter excerpt, write five questions that you intend to answer as you study read. Use the chapter title, section titles, italicized words and phrases, or any other feature of this chapter to formulate your questions. Answer these questions as you read the chapter.

1.

2.

3.

Ask instructor for sample questions.

4.

5.

C. Read and Recite

With these questions, you are ready to begin study reading. Use your best underlining and commenting skills, making marginal notes on important terms and comparisons. Then on a separate sheet of paper, recite what you have read, and apply the Cornell note-taking system. When you have completed your summary, go back to the excerpt to be sure that your summary is both accurate and complete. Make changes to your summary and to the main points you highlighted by using the Cornell note-taking system.

Read and summarize paragraphs 1–30 first. Then read and summarize paragraphs 31–46.

D. Review

Now you are ready to review your underlinings, your marginal comments, and your summaries. You may want to make study maps that organize this material even more clearly.

Examination: Social Power

Directions: Give yourself two class sessions (100 minutes) to complete the following essay questions. Be sure to budget your time. Write all of your answers on separate sheets of paper or in a blue book.

I. Definitions: In a few sentences, define the following sociological terms. (25 points)

1. power

2. elite

3. social stratification

4. authority

5. sovereignty

II. *Short Essay:* Answer each question in an organized paragraph. (25 points)

6. Discuss the specific ways that the study of sociology differs from the study of psychology. (13 points)

7. Discuss the specific ways that the study of sociology differs from the study of political science. (12 points)

III. *Extended Essay:* In an essay of at least five paragraphs, define *ideology* and *ideological conflict*. Then explain two conflicts in ideology — for example, Marxism versus fascism and conservatism versus liberalism. Finally, choose *one* of the following three social issues and show how it has been treated differently by different ideologies: (1) women, (2) African Americans, or (3) the American poor. For example, discuss how the American poor are understood differently by a conservative ideology and by a liberal ideology. Your response may incorporate your own experiences or what you have previously studied about this issue. (50 points)

70%

Ask instructor for answers.

Answer Key

Answers have been provided for most odd-numbered exercises. Ask your instructor for the answers to all even-numbered exercises, the essay questions and several short-answer questions, and the study reading selections in Part Five.

Chapter 3
Locating Main Ideas

Exercise 3.1

1. a **2.** d **3.** imp **4.** imp **5.** a **6.** a **7.** a **8.** a **9.** d **10.** imp

Exercise 3.3

Your wording may differ, but your answers should be essentially the same as these:

1. the Industrial Revolution
2. the effects of the Industrial Revolution on the farms
3. how the new inventions were run
4. the results of the new inventions on the farmer
5. machines in the early 1900s
6. how the machines of industrialization affected human life
7. industrialization's effect on the environment
8. the negative effect of industrialization on the environment
9. how industrialization affected society
10. the negative effects of industrialization on society
11. the city's effect on the environment
12. the city's negative effect on the environment
13. the Industrial Revolution's effect on the economy
14. the increased costs caused by the Industrial Revolution
15. the overall effects of the Industrial Revolution
16. the positive and negative effects of the Industrial Revolution
17. the Industrial Revolution and nature
18. the Industrial Revolution making human beings superior to nature
19. the superior attitude toward nature
20. questioning what this superior attitude means for human beings and nature

Chapter 4
Locating Major and
Minor Details

Exercise 4.1

1. a, b, e   **5.** a, c, d   **8.** a, b, d
2. a, b, d   **6.** a, b, c   **9.** a, c, d
3. a, b, c   **7.** a, d, e   **10.** b, c, d
4. a, c, e

Exercise 4.3

1. MN	11. MA	21. MN	31. MA
2. MA	12. MI	22. MA	32. MA
3. MI	13. MN	23. MI	33. MN
4. MA	14. MA	24. MI	34. MA
5. MN	15. MA	25. MN	35. MI
6. MA	16. MI	26. MA	36. MA
7. MA	17. MA	27. MA	37. MN
8. MA	18. MA	28. MI	38. MA
9. MN	19. MA	29. MN	39. MA
10. MA	20. MN	30. MA	40. MI

Exercise 4.5

1. d 2. b 3. a 4. d 5. b
6. Socialism is a form of government controlling all the major industries.
7. Communism is an extreme form of socialism.
8. In theory, people own property under capitalism or choose their own jobs or make the salary they desire.
9. No capitalistic society follows all its stated beliefs.
10. In real capitalistic societies, either government does control some industry or competition is not always encouraged.

**Chapter 5
Identifying
Organizational
Patterns**

Exercise 5.1

1. fact	5. fact	9. thesis	13. a
2. thesis	6. fact	10. fact	14. d
3. fact	7. thesis	11. a	15. d
4. thesis	8. fact	12. d	

Exercise 5.3

Your answers should be essentially the same as these, although your wording may differ. Each definition has two parts, each counting 5 points.

	Term	General Category	Examples
1.	conflict theory	studies why people disagree	crime
2.	deduction	logical process moving from general to specific	women's discrimination
3.	demography	study of population	movement of Mexicans to California in the nineties

4. empirical study	observer gathers data	how American men greet
5. field research	observing in natural setting	political rallies
6. hypothesis	conclusion drawn from intuition or observation	criminals as society's victims
7. induction	conclusion reached by studying data	New Yorkers' attitudes toward taxes
8. population	group meriting study	students in community colleges
9. random selection	selecting data by chance	random numbering
10. social interaction	how a person directs social responses	conversation

Exercise 5.5

1. DEF or C-C	**6.** DEF
2. C-E	**7.** C-E
3. SEQ	**8.** DEF
4. C-C	**9.** C-E
5. SEQ	**10.** C-C

Exercise 5.7

1. d
2. d
3. d
4. c
5. c

6. Factors other than money are involved in determining social status.
7. Some prestigious jobs are doctor, scientist, and Supreme Court justice — none of which makes a huge salary.
8. thesis-support
9. Spiritual and intellectual possessions are also valued by society.
10. thesis-support

**Chapter 6
Summarizing and
Paraphrasing**

Although your response to the excerpt on pp. 105–106 may differ, they should be similar to these:

Philosophy as the Love of Wisdom

(1) If we took the time to trace the history of the physical, natural, and social sciences, we'd find their roots in philosophy as it was practiced about 2,700 years ago in Greece. In those times, people of infinite curiosity puzzled over certain aspects of the world and their experience of them. We saw that one of the questions that they asked concerned reality. But these profoundly curious people wondered about other things as well: Why does anything exist? Why is there something rather than nothing? How can things change? How do we come to know things? What's the nature of knowledge? What's the difference between right and wrong? What's goodness? How can we best achieve happiness?

What's justice? What is the just state? On what basis, if any, can society compel us to obey its rules if we don't wish to obey them? Those who asked these questions clearly showed a marked curiosity in the things of experience, a curiosity that could be described as a vital concern for becoming wise about the phenomena of the world and the human experience. For this reason, such people were termed *philosophers* and their study *philosophy*, which literally means "the love of wisdom." Philosophers were originally lovers or seekers of wisdom; they still are.

(2) Wisdom, then, is not the expertise or technical skills of professional people. Indeed, as Socrates points out, such knowledge may impede the quest for wisdom by deluding people into thinking that they know what they don't. In contrast, the wisdom of Socrates consists of a critical habit, an eternal vigilance about all things and a reverence for truth, whatever its forms, wherever its place. His is a perspective that allows him to transcend the narrowness, the smugness, the arrogance, and the pettiness of mundane ego fulfillment.

(3) Others have viewed wisdom, and thus philosophy, differently. Some, like Aristotle (384–322 BC), have tried to gain an organized knowledge of the world and an understanding of the nature of things and the relationships among them. Part of this is an understanding of how we ought to live. By exposing all stated and implied assumptions, theories, and methods of all beliefs, philosophy seeks the wisdom that comes from systematically organizing, structuring, and relating all available data and experiences. Thus, the love of wisdom is all-encompassing; it is not bounded by the limitations of this subject or that discipline.

(4) Others view wisdom more actively. For them, philosophy consists of participation in life — to change things, to solve human problems, or to discover the meaning of existence. Still others feel that the wisdom of philosophy is in helping us to think more clearly and precisely.

(5) No philosopher has a monopoly on wisdom or its meaning. For us Socrates' critical perspective will do, for it suggests an attitude, a temperament, that underlies other views. But the other perspectives have merit. On wisdom, as on other subjects, our knowledge is a drop, our ignorance an ocean.

I. Philosophy as the Love of Wisdom

    A. Socrates: critically study experience to go beyond everyday concerns

    B. Aristotle: organize understanding of the world

    C. Other philosophies: participate in life

    D. Still others: allow one to think more clearly

    E. No philosophy has all the answers

Exercise 6.1

Score your answers to the five questions, not the underlinings, which will likely differ from this sample underlining. Just check to see that the main ideas have been correctly underlined.

Traditional Concerns of Philosophy

(1) Traditionally, philosophy has sought an organized knowledge of the world and our place in it and knowledge about how we ought to live, including the bases for beliefs and interactions with others. Of course, philosophers have approached these general concerns in diverse ways, each emphasizing different aspects. But, in general, philosophy has dealt with such basic questions as: What is knowledge? What is real? What is good? While none of these questions can be considered in isolation, all philosophical questions fall under one or more of these foundational inquiries, which represent the traditional interests of philosophers. Numerous nonphilosophers have also stressed the importance of investigating these subjects.

(2) These traditional concerns suggest the three categories under which all other philosophical problems fall: knowledge, reality, and value. The fields of philosophy that explore these themes are generally termed *epistemology, metaphysics,* and *axiology.*

(3) Epistemology literally means the study of knowledge. A variety of problems are usually discussed as part of epistemology: the structure, reliability, extent, and kinds of knowledge; truth (including definitions of truth and validity); logic and a variety of strictly linguistic concerns; and the foundations of all knowledge (including the conditions under which an assertion is warranted and numerous concerns dealing directly with science and scientific knowledge).

(4) Metaphysics is the study of the most general or ultimate characteristics of reality or existence. Some of the problems that fall under it are the structure and development of the universe; the meaning and nature of being; and the nature of mind, self, and consciousness. Also, the nature of religion can be considered to fall under metaphysics, which includes the existence of God, the destiny of the universe, and the immortality of the soul.

(5) Axiology refers to the study of values. Specifically, axiological problems often involve values in human conduct; the nature and justification of social structures and political systems; the nature of art; and the meaning of art in human experience.

(6) In approaching these areas, philosophy asks critical questions about the obvious and taken-for-granted. This is an important characteristic of the philosophical enterprise, but there are others.

1. c **2.** b **3.** a **4.** b **5.** b

Exercise 6.3

Here is one correct way to underline this excerpt:

Worth and Meaning in Philosophy

(1) Some modern psychologists, Abraham Maslow among them, point out that humans have needs other than maintenance ones, which they term *actualizing needs*. While more difficult to describe than maintenance needs, actualizing needs appear to be associated with self-

fulfillment, creativity, self-expression, realization of your potential, and, in a word, being everything you can be. Why mention these? Because evaluating the worth of courses and disciplines in terms of their job preparation value is to take a narrow view of what human beings need. It completely overlooks higher-level needs. This doesn't mean, of course, that studying philosophy will necessarily lead to self-actualization. But philosophy assists by promoting the ideal of self-actualization, or what psychotherapist Carl Rogers terms the "fully functioning person."

(2) Consider some characteristics of the self-actualized or fully functioning person. One is the ability to form one's own opinions and beliefs. Self-actualized people don't automatically go along with what's "in" or what's expected of them. Not that they are necessarily rebels; they just make up their own minds. They think, evaluate, and decide for themselves. What could better capture the spirit of philosophy than such intellectual and behavioral independence?

(3) A second characteristic is profound self-awareness. Self-actualized people harbor few illusions about themselves and rarely resort to easy rationalizations to justify their beliefs and actions. If anything, philosophy is geared to deepen self-awareness by inviting us to examine the basic intellectual foundations of our lives.

(4) A third characteristic is flexibility. Change and uncertainty don't level self-actualized people. Indeed, they exhibit resilience in the face of disorder, doubt, uncertainty, indefiniteness, even chaos. But they are not indifferent or uncaring. Quite the opposite. They are much involved in their experiences. Because of their resilience, they not only recognize the essential ambiguity of human affairs but also develop a high ambiguity tolerance. They are not upended by a lack of definite answers or of concrete solutions. When seriously undertaken, the study of philosophy often promotes what some have termed a philosophical calm, the capacity to persevere in the face of upheaval. This stems in part from an ability to put things in perspective, to see the "big picture," to make neither too much nor too little of events.

(5) A fourth characteristic of self-actualized or fully functioning people is that they are generally creative. They are not necessarily writers, painters, or musicians, for creativity can function in many ways and at various levels. Rather, such people exhibit creativity in all they do. Whether spending leisure time or conversing, they seem to leave their own distinctive mark. Philosophy can help in this process by getting us to develop a philosophical perspective on issues, problems, and events. This means, in part, that we no longer see or experience life on the surface. We engage it on deeper levels, and we interact with it so that we help to fashion our world. In another way, because philosophy exercises our imaginations, it invites a personal expression that is unique and distinctive.

(6) <u>Finally</u>, self-actualized or fully functioning people have clearly conceptualized, <u>well-thought-out value systems in morality, the arts, politics</u>, and so on. Since a fundamental concern of philosophy is values and since philosophy often deals directly with morals, art, politics, and other value areas, it offers an opportunity to <u>formulate viable assessments of worth</u> and find meaning in our lives. For some psychologists, the search for meaning and values constitutes the human's primary interest.

Although your wording will likely differ, most of the information in your outline should be essentially like this one:

I. Philosophy and Your Self-Understanding

   A. Helps you realize your potential, making you self-actualized
   B. Deepens self-awareness
   C. Allows you flexibility in dealing with life's uncertainties
   D. Allows you to experience life creatively
   E. Gives you a value system in interpreting ethics, politics, and the arts

Exercise 6.5

Wording may vary, but paraphrases should be essentially the same as these. Take partial credit where you think it is appropriate.

  7. We want to understand our questions and work at understanding ourselves.
  9. When no one can criticize our speech, then we are on our way to becoming enlightened.
 11. The way we act, like our way of talking, shows how sincere we are.
 18. With right effort, you do not allow any of your feelings or wants to take over.
 24. By practicing deep thought and looking into ourselves, we can become enlightened.

**Chapter 7
Reading and
Listening for
Inferences**

Exercise 7.1

You may want to go back to the paragraphs marked *V* to see how they could be made more credible.

1. D **2.** V **3.** D **4.** V **5.** V **6.** D **7.** V **8.** D **9.** D **10.** V

Exercise 7.3

Wording may vary, but the information should be essentially the same as in the following answers. You may take partial credit where you think it is appropriate.

1. A "miracle" is an event that goes beyond human abilities. The author is suggesting that Mozart's accomplishments were almost unbelievable in their quality and genius.
2. To "astonish" is to shock. The author is expressing extreme surprise at Mozart's ability to compose at the age of five.
3. "Phenomenal" suggests exceptional abilities. Again, this word suggests that Mozart's musical abilities were superior.
4. "Impossible" suggests that something cannot be done. In regard to Mozart, this word again suggests his surprising greatness.
5. "Unfathomable" suggests that one cannot fully grasp something; in regard to Mozart, this word suggests the complexity of his musical abilities.
6. "Disastrous" suggests great hardship and suffering. This word shows how destructive Mozart's personal life was to his career.
7. A "giant" is someone who is extremely large; this word shows how important Mozart was as a musician in relationship to others.
8. To "explore" is to travel and study carefully; this word suggests how carefully Mozart examined and used various types of classical music.
9. "Indelible" means that something cannot be erased or destroyed. It suggests that Mozart's music will endure.
10. A "genius" is one with exceptional talents, and the word aptly describes Mozart's musical abilities.

Answers to the question about the tone of this excerpt on Mozart will vary but should approximate this one:

The tone suggests the writer's great respect for Mozart as a musician. All the words about Mozart's musical talent are strongly positive. The one word about his personal life is strongly negative, showing how different Mozart's life was from his musical contributions.

Chapter 8
Reading Graphs
and Tables

Exercise 8.1

1. d **2.** c **3.** b **4.** b **5.** d **6.** b **7.** c **8.** b **9.** b **10.** c

Chapter 10
Traditional Note-
taking Techniques

Exercise 10.1

Your wording may differ, but the condensed information should be essentially the same as shown here. You may take partial credit.

1. Def.: what people do when they buy, sell, or produce a product
2. Consumer behavior interdisciplinary, relying on sociology, anthropology, and psychology

3. Consumer behavior related to sociology in its focus on group behavior
4. Psychology shows how a person acts when purchasing a product — ex: motivation
5. Anthropology shows how culture determines buying — ex: ethnic preference
6. Def. consumer: anyone purchasing or using a product
7. Def. purchasing: getting an item from a seller
8. Later in course focus on where people buy and how they use products
9. Relationship between psychology and economics: how often people buy a product and why
10. Seeing yourself as consumer helps you understand yourself anthropologically, sociologically, and psychologically

Exercise 10.3

Your phrasing may differ from what is shown here, but the information should be essentially the same. Be sure that main ideas are separated from major details. Take 2 points for each correct entry and partial credit where you think it is appropriate.

1. I. How American culture affects purchasing

    A. Interest in buying material items
    B. Belief in self
    C. Optimism
    D. Order

2. I. Is there an American culture?

    A. Movement away from material wealth
    B. Is it still optimistic?
    C. Self-reliance makes some afraid of being alone
    D. Is order valuable?

3. I. Ethnic groups questioning American culture

    A. African-Americans and Latinos huge marketing challenge
    B. Some fit into American mold
    C. Some of their buying interests different

4. I. How class influences purchasing

    A. How do lower, middle, and upper classes shape buying?
    B. Is class question difficult, like culture question?
    C. Does income influence buying?
    D. Does income influence beliefs?

5. I. Relationship of family and purchasing

    A. Family seems to have much to say

B. Family gives certain values
C. Which family member will product serve?
D. Who is more powerful: father, mother, children?
E. Purchasing decisions change as family gets older

6. Individual's influence on consumer behavior

People learn — are not born to buy in certain way
Consider past experience
Def. brand loyalty: consistent buying of a product

7. How perception affects purchasing

Each of us perceives products differently
For some, price important
For others, look or image important

8. Determining purchasing choice has no definite answers

Personality has effect on purchasing
Ex: sports car versus station wagon buyer, shade of lipstick person buys

9. Attitude and buying

Sports figures or actors help sell product
Stars provide positive and negative images
Attitudes help sell product

10. Attitudes difficult to change

A marketing challenge
Can marketing campaign change attitudes?
Can changed attitudes change buying patterns?
Researchers still unclear

Exercise 10.5

1. =	**11.** without
2. >	**12.** compare
3. + or &	**13.** versus
4. ⊃	**14.** incomplete
5. re	**15.** important
6. nec	**16.** principal
7. pos	**17.** continued
8. incr	**18.** number
9. lg	**19.** therefore
10. max	**20.** is both cause and effect

Exercise 10.7

You may take partial credit for your answers to 1–10. Answers will vary for 11–20.

1. Marketing is becoming an international activity.
2. It's easy to make large mistakes in this international market.
3. Many marketers do not understand cultural setting.
4. Anthropology helps consumer behavior to understand cultures.
5. Anthropologists use a study called cross-cultural research.
6. Cross-cultural research shows how cultures are the same and different.
7. Cross-cultural research studies attitudes regarding love in cultures.
8. Cross-cultural research also works with political power in each culture.
9. Cross-cultural research studies the cultural meaning of color.
10. In some cultures black and gray are good.
11. CCR resrch shows yllow, whte, gry, weak evrywhre
12. Red & blk strng clrs in ev country
13. Some mrktrs see ea cltr unque
14. ⊃ focus on local mrktng techs
15. othrs believe in stndrdzd mrktng plans
16. These mrktrs believe in cltrl uniformty in wrld
17. Sev cntrys as 1 mrkt
18. Toursm and mass media → sim mrktg needs
19. Mrktrs see Europe as 1 cntry
20. Answrs have pos or neg impct on ad campgn

Exercise 10.9

Below are sample responses. Your approach may differ.

Consumer Behavior and Ethics (Consumer Behavior = CB)

How is CB rel to ethics? Consider:
   Trth in mrktng
   Prdct quality
   Prdct safety

Mrktrs obliged to be hnst
   Fdrl Trade Comms monitors ads (FTC = Federal Trade Commission)
   Mny mail order frauds FTC has uncovrd
   Pckgng and labeling impt concern
      Ex: what is fat-free prdct?
         FDC has made spec rqrmts

Prdct reliability
   What can consmr do if prdct a hazard?
      Read warranty (W = warranty)
      Exchange prdct or get rfnd
   W/expnsve prdct, see what W promises

What if W is bad?
   Consmr can go to court
      expensive and lngthy

Respndg to complaints in pos way
    Being honest, cmpnys incr profits
    Pays to be hnst
    Some compnys ask cstmrs to be frank re prdct

How can cmplnts be effctv?
    Provide useful info
    Cmpnys can rewrite Ws
    Fmlys and frnds oftn go to honest cmpny

Ethics wrks 2 ways
    Both unethical cstmrs and unethical cmpnys
    Cstmrs and cmpnys need to wrk togethr
    Hnsty goes a long way
    Pays to be honest → profits for cmpny and satisfctn for cstmr

Chapter 11
Mapping and the Cornell Note-taking System

Exercise 11.1

Answers will vary. Take credit if you think your study maps clearly show the relationship between main idea and major details.

1.

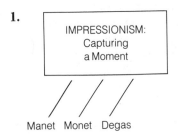

2.

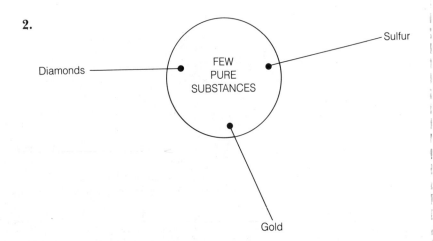

3.   British Literature to 1800

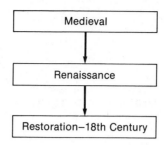

4.

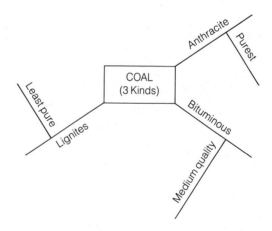

5.

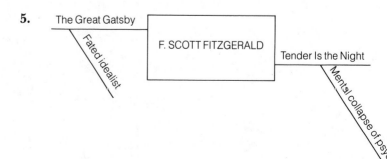

6.   Great American Depression—1929

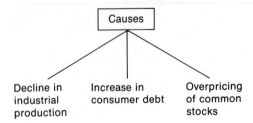

7.

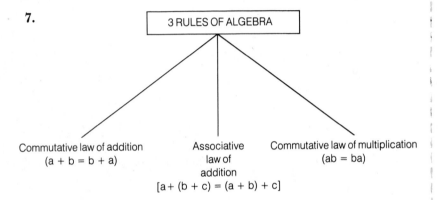

8.   Both breast-feed young

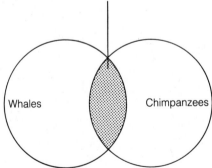

9.   Stages of language development

1) understanding ⟶ 2) speaking ⟶ 3) reading ⟶ 4) writing

10.

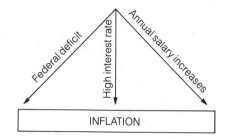

Federal deficit   High interest rate   Annual salary increases

INFLATION

Exercise 11.3

Your wording will vary from that shown here, but your answers should be essentially the same. Be sure that main ideas are clearly separated from major details. The study map that accompanies this outline is only an example. Only score your outline, not the study map.

	Nuclear Energy: Facts Pro and Con

two important facts	Facts about
	    Produces 8% electricity in U.S.
	    1990 — may be slightly more expensive than coal

two safety reasons	Safety
	    Less radiation emitted from coal plants of same size
	    Does not let out carbon monoxide

4 steps in meltdown	Nuclear accidents: meltdown steps
	    1. Fuel overheats
	    2. Turns water to steam
	    3. Steam makes plant expode
	    4. Radiation sent to environment

how wastes are cared for	Nuclear wastes
	    Must be removed to central locations
	    Decay slowly
	    Put in steel cylinders in salt deposits
	    Salt areas not prone to earthquakes
	    No guarantee

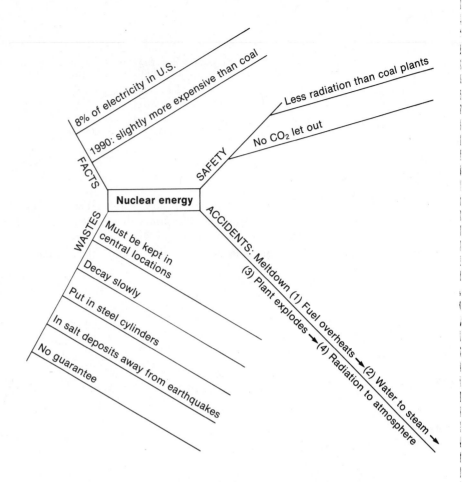

The concept map shows "Nuclear energy" at the center with the following branches:

- **FACTS**
  - 8% of electricity in U.S.
  - 1990: slightly more expensive than coal
- **SAFETY**
  - Less radiation than coal plants
  - No CO₂ let out
- **WASTES**
  - Must be kept in central locations
  - Decay slowly
  - Put in steel cylinders
  - In salt deposits away from earthquakes
  - No guarantee
- **ACCIDENTS:** Meltdown (1) Fuel overheats → (2) Water to steam → (3) Plant explodes → (4) Radiation to atmosphere →

**Chapter 13
The SQ3R Study
System**

Exercise 13.1

The following are examples of correctly underlined and marked passages. Your underlinings may differ.

1. Catching More Fish and Fish Farming

Fish are the major source of animal protein for more than one-half of the world's people, especially in Asia and Africa. Fish supply about 55 percent of the animal protein in Southeast Asia, 35 percent in Asia as a whole, 19 percent in Africa, about 25 percent worldwide—twice as much as eggs and three times as much as poultry—and 6 percent of all human protein consumption. Two-thirds of the annual fish catch is consumed by humans and one-third is processed into fish meal to be fed to livestock.

　　Between 1950 and 1970, the marine fish catch more than tripled—an increase greater than that occurring in any other human food source during the same period. To achieve large catches, modern fishing fleets use sonar, helicopters, aerial photography, and temperature measurement to locate schools of fish and lights and electrodes to attract them. Large, floating factory ships follow the fleets to process the catch.

Despite this technological sophistication, the steady rise in the marine fish catch halted abruptly in 1971. Between 1971 and 1976 the annual catch leveled off and rose only slightly between 1976 and 1983. A major factor in this leveling off was the sharp decline of the Peruvian anchovy catch, which once made up 20 percent of the global ocean harvest. A combination of overfishing and a shift in the cool, nutrient-rich currents off the coast of Peru were apparently the major factors causing this decline, which also threw tens of thousands of Peruvians out of work. Meanwhile, world population continued to grow, so between 1970 and 1983 the average fish catch per person declined and is projected to decline even further back to the 1960 level by the year 2000.

2. Types of Jazz

The 1920s saw the real emergence of jazz, which was given impetus in 1918 by Joe "King" Oliver's famous Creole Jazz Band in Chicago. Other musicians soon became prominent: Bix Beiderbecke, who started "white" jazz with his cornet and a band called the "Wolverines"; Paul Whiteman, whose band presented the first jazz concert in 1924, featuring the premiere of George Gershwin's *Rhapsody in Blue*; Bessie Smith, the famous blues singer; Fletcher Henderson and his band; and the notable Louis Armstrong. Through his trumpet playing and vocal renditions, Armstrong had much influence on the basic sound and style of jazz.

Dixieland

The prevailing style in the 1920s was *dixieland*. It is characterized by a strong upbeat, a meter of two beats to the measure, and certain tonal and stylistic qualities that are impossible to notate. It has a "busy" sound because there is simultaneous improvisation by perhaps four to seven players. The result is a type of "accidental" counterpoint that is held together only by the song's basic harmony and the musical instincts of the players. The presence of simultaneous improvisation in both African music and jazz can hardly be a coincidence. Dixieland style is often described as "hot"; it is rather fast and usually loud.

Boogie-Woogie

During the depression of the 1930s the hiring of bands became prohibitively expensive. So pianists enjoyed increasing popularity, especially as they developed a jazz piano style called *boogie-woogie*. It features a persistently repeated melodic figure — an ostinato — in the bass. Usually the boogie-woogie ostinato consists of eight notes per measure, which explains why this type of music is sometimes called "eight to the bar." Over the continuous bass the pianist plays trills, octave tremolos (the rapid alternation of pitches an octave apart), and other melodic figures.

3. Matter: Types, States, Properties, and Changes

A lump of coal, an ice cube, a puddle of water, air — all are samples of matter. Matter is anything that occupies space and has mass. *Mass* is the quantity of matter in substance.

A substance or pure substance is one of millions of different types of matter found in the world. Any substance can be classified as either an element or a compound. An element is one of the 108 basic building blocks of all matter. Examples include iron, sodium, carbon, oxygen, and chlorine. Scientists have discovered 90 naturally occurring elements on Earth and have made small quantities of 18 others in the laboratory.

A compound is a form of matter in which two or more elements are held together in a fixed ratio by chemical bonds. Water, for example, is a combination of the elements hydrogen and oxygen, and sodium chloride (the major ingredient in table salt) is a combination of the elements sodium and chlorine. About 5 million compounds of the 108 known elements have been identified, and about 6,000 new compounds are added to the list each week. With proper guidance, you could make a new compound yourself. At least 63,000 compounds are combined in the food we eat, the air we breathe, the water we drink, and the countless products we use.

Exercise 13.3

A. Survey

1. a **2.** b **3.** a **4.** b **5.** c

B. Question (answers will vary)

1. What is absolute poverty?
2. What is the definition of "less developed countries"?
3. How does GNP relate to understanding less developed countries?
4. What is the Physical Quality of Life Index?

C. Read and Recite *(answers will vary)*

	Poverty in the Developing Countries
def.: absolute poverty	Absolute poverty — people so poor their life is threatened
	1 billion people in absolute poverty
	Difficult to identify what a less developed country is
2 categories of countries	Two categories: less developed and more developed
	GNP imperfect measure
why GNP inefficient	Often understates income of poor in LDCs
	Ex: Tanzania people do not always use money in buying and selling
what PQLI measures	Physical Quality of Life Index (PQLI): considers infant mortality, life expectancy, and literacy abilities
	Another way to study LDCs
	Shows differences that GNP does not show
	Ex: Saudi Arabia with low PQLI and high GNP

D. Review

1. d **2.** c **3.** a **4.** b **5.** d **6.** b **7.** c **8.** b **9.** b **10.** a

Compare the following sample study map and marked-up excerpt with yours.

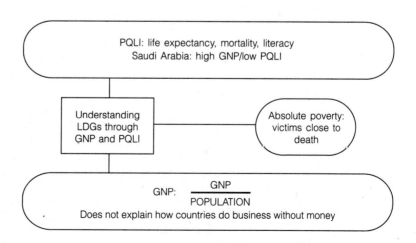

Poverty in the Developing Countries

(1) This section is about poverty among nations. Poverty is, of course, a relative matter. Whenever there is any inequality in the distribution of income, some people will always be poor relative to others. But much of the world is so abjectly poor that some observers speak of *absolute* poverty, a condition of life so destitute that its victims are chronically on the verge of death.

def:
absolute
poverty

(2) Almost 1 billion people—one-quarter of the world's population—are in this category. A quarter of a million people in Calcutta are homeless. They eat, live, and die in the streets. Three million people in Bolivia (out of a total population of five million) have a life expectancy of thirty years. The average Bolivian eats less than half an ounce of meat per year; in effect, the peasant population is too poor to eat any meat at all.

imp't
detail

What Is a "Less Developed" Country?

(3) Several phrases are used to describe countries that are poorer than others: underdeveloped countries, third world countries, sometimes even fourth or fifth world countries. Economists have no specific criteria or explicit definitions of such terms. A nation's position is usually determined by dividing its GNP by population (per capita GNP) so that there is a ladder of countries from rich to poor—from $21,920 per person per year in the United Arab Emirates to $110 per person per year in Ethiopia in 1984.

hard to define
LDCs

formu

(4) Usually, all countries are classified as either "more developed" or "less developed." The World Bank in its *Development Report for 1986* uses six subcategories of less developed countries, which we will overlook for the sake of brevity. Instead, we will use just the two categories "more developed" and "less developed" and set the dividing line at $1,000 per person per year, although such a division is arbitrary and often unrevealing. We know that GNP says little about the quality of life. Moreover, a per capita GNP figure conceals the distribution of income within a nation. For example, per capita GNP in Brazil was about $2,000 a year in 1984, but 30 million of Brazil's 133 million people had average annual incomes of only $77. Because this section is about the less developed countries, we will use a common abbreviation, LDCs, to indicate that group of about 90 of the 170-odd countries of the world.

The Trouble with Comparing Per Capita GNPs

(5) When we use per capita GNPs to compare countries, we find ourselves trapped by numbers that offer little help in describing real differences in standards of living. Not only is GNP an imperfect measure of welfare or progress *within* a country, it has even less meaning when used for comparisons among countries. Two examples will clarify this point.

ex #1

(6) In a poor, less developed country (LDC) like Tanzania, with a per capita GNP of $210 per year, the $210 figure is imperfect because it is based primarily on cash transactions. But much of Tanzania's production and consumption typically involves little or no cash. The people in

Tanzania's villages feed themselves out of their own production. Therefore, in most cases, per capita GNP figures in poor countries understate their true incomes. Of course, that doesn't mean such people are rich. We could double the numbers, and these people would still be abjectly poor by any standard.

ex #2

(7) In another example, let's look at the comparative lifestyles of Americans and New Zealanders. In the fall of 1978, New Zealand's per capita GNP was about half that of the United States. But it would be very foolish to conclude that New Zealanders' standard of living was half that of the average American. Fresh food prices were generally half of U.S. prices, so that with much lower wages, the New Zealanders ate just as well as or better than Americans. Housing costs (rents and home purchase prices) were also about half of ours. Education, medical care, and retirement pensions were all provided from a highly progressive schedule of income taxes. In one specific case, a highly skilled New Zealander construction worker retired from his job at age 60. At the time of retirement, he earned $3.80 per hour—by our standards an abysmally low wage after a lifetime of work. Nevertheless, he owned a home and automobile free and clear, had $50,000 in the bank, and began receiving a pension of 80 percent of his highest earnings. He and his wife were comfortable and content, traveled overseas occasionally, and had no financial worries. However, New Zealanders also have to contend with the high prices of imported products like automobiles.

key question

(8) So how does one evaluate these differences in lifestyles? Can one say that Americans are better off than New Zealanders or vice versa? The question is impossible to answer. Nevertheless, the GNP per capita method of comparison among different countries is the method most commonly used.

def.: PQLI

(9) In one attempt to improve on the GNP per capita measure, economists devised an index called the **Physical Quality of Life Index (PQLI)**. The PQLI is a composite of a nation's life expectancy, infant mortality, and literacy. The index is 97 for Sweden, 94 for the United States, 35 for Bangladesh. The index reveals the weaknesses of looking only at GNP per capita: GNP per capita in Saudi Arabia is a healthy $10,530 (1984), but its PQLI is only 28.

(10) In this section we review the plight of the LDCs, including the distribution of the world's income, the reasons why the more developed countries (particularly the United States) should be concerned about world poverty, the two major problems of population increase and lack of capital, and some conclusions.

Chapter 14
Mnemonic Strategies

Exercise 14.1

Here are possible answers:

1. Station<u>ary</u> refers to cold and warm air fronts. "Air" rhymes with "ary."
2. People who have <u>ill</u>usions may be psychologically <u>ill</u>.
3. <u>Between</u> means that no more than two items are compared, and b is the second letter of the alphabet.
4. Capit<u>ol</u> buildings are usually <u>old</u>.

5. Hunters carry spears and <u>rods</u>. I see a hunter with a <u>rod</u> in his hand chasing an animal.
6. Roy G. Biv (a name)
7. We Are Just Mighty Mice.
8. MTM
9. ERS
10. zeal, zealously, zealot, zealousness

Chapter 15
Strategies for
Objective Tests

Chapter 16
Strategies for Essay
Tests and Math or
Science Tests

Exercise 15.1

1. c 2. b 3. c 4. b 5. d

Exercise 15.3

1. e 2. d 3. a 4. c 5. b

Exercise 16.1

Your wording will differ, but the information should be essentially the same as shown here. You may want to use the following method for calculating a score.

1. Take 1 point for noting that China after liberation was a better place to live.

2. Take 6 points for mentioning three of the following (2 points each): famine, drug addiction and prostitution, unreasonable taxes, large cities owned by companies, people treated like animals, workers worked long for little salary, babies sold for pennies.

3. Take 3 points for mentioning three of the following: all people eat; all people have housing, clothing, medical care, and free education; no illiteracy, starvation, or prostitution; no sexually transmitted diseases or drug addiction; cities clean without flies, mosquitoes, or other pests.

Here is a sample paragraph receiving all 10 points:

China before liberation was in a dreadful state. It was a country experiencing famine and having a high incidence of opium addiction and prostitution. The workers worked long hours for a meager salary. Today, all Chinese get something to eat. Illiteracy, starvation, and prostitution have also been eliminated. Finally, cities are clean and free of disease-ridden insects.

Index